Achieving

QTS

mee D0531619

Teaching

Humanities

in Primary Schools

Second edition

Pat Hoodless, Elaine McCreery,
Paul Bowen, Sue Bermingham,

⑤SAGE | LearningMatters

Los Angeles | London | New Delhi
apore | Washington DC

First published in 2003 by Learning Matters Ltd
Reprinted in 2003
Second edition published 2009
Reprinted in 2010, 2012

British Library Cataloguing in Publication Data
A CIP record for this book is available from the British Library.

ISBN 978 1 84445 211 8

The right of Pat Hoodless, Sue Bermingham, Elaine McCreery, Paul Bowen to be identified as the Authors of this Work has been asserted by them in accordance with Copyright, Design and Patents Act 1988.

Cover design by Topics – The Creative Partnership
Text design by Code 5 Design Associates
Project management by Deer Park Productions, Tavistock
Typeset by PDQ Typesetting Ltd, Newcastle-under-Lyme
Printed and bound in Great Britain by TJI Digital, Padstow, Cornwall

Learning Matters
An imprint of SAGE Publications Ltd
1 Oliver's Yard
55 City Road
London EC1Y 1SP

SAGE Publications Inc.
2455 Teller Road
Thousand Oaks, California 91320

SAGE Publications India Pvt Ltd
B 1/1 1 Mohan Cooperative Industrial Area
Mathura Road
New Delhi 110 044

SAGE Publications Asia-Pacific Pte Ltd
3 Church Street
#10–04 Samsung Hub
Singapore 049483

MIX
Paper from
responsible sources
FSC
www.fsc.org
FSC® C013056

Contents

Acknowledgements

The authors would especially like to thank Diana Selby and Lyndsay Thomson for their help, advice and provision of resources which have informed many parts of this book, Andrea Kershaw and Linda King for their advice on SEN, and Anna Neave, Sally Shaw and Lisa Gillie for their contributions. We would also like to thank Ben Steel for his illustrations in the planning chapter.

The authors wish to thank all the children and students who have donated examples of work to illustrate the text. We would like to thank teachers in the following schools for their examples of school planning and help with selecting examples of children's work: Button Lane Primary School, Sale, Manchester; Prospect Vale County School, Cheshire; Hilton Lane County Primary School, Manchester; Linden Road County Primary School, Greater Manchester; Frodsham Church of England Primary School, Cheshire; Frodsham Manor House Primary School, Cheshire; The Brow Community Primary School, Cheshire; and Hursthead Primary School, Cheshire.

Every effort has been made to trace the copyright holders and to obtain their permission for the use of copyright material. The publisher and authors will gladly receive any information enabling them to rectify any error or omission in subsequent editions.

Introduction

About this book

This book has been written for primary trainees on all courses of Initial Teacher Training in England and other parts of the UK. By the end of their course, trainees must be prepared to teach the National Curriculum in selected humanities disciplines, either geography or history, and Religious Education (RE). This book focuses on the planning, teaching and assessment methods necessary for successful teaching of children in the Early Years Foundation Stage and at Key Stage 1 and Key Stage 2. The role of citizenship is also discussed as an important element of primary education. The book will be useful for those working towards Qualified Teacher Status (QTS), but will also be useful to Newly Qualified Teachers (NQTs) in their induction year and other teachers and professionals working in education who have identified areas within humanities pedagogy that are in need of further development. It has the Professional Standards for Teachers (TDA, 2007) firmly at its core. Many of the general Standards for the award of QTS within each section apply to the humanities disciplines, and in this book the specific characteristics of each discipline are clearly linked to the relevant Standards. The book sets out the knowledge and processes within each discipline required by trainees to secure children's progress in each of these curriculum areas. Where a thematic or topic-based approach is used, the place within it of each humanities subject is clearly specified.

Features of each chapter of this book include:

- chapter objectives;
- clear links with the Professional Standards for QTS;
- links to the National Curriculum for England in geography, history and citizenship;
- links to the Agreed Syllabuses for RE and QCA Model Syllabuses;
- knowledge and understanding of geography, history, citizenship and RE;
- classroom stories to illustrate important points;
- research summaries;
- practical tasks;
- reflective tasks;
- summary of key points;
- further reading;
- moving on.

Each chapter of this book addresses particular areas of the Professional Standards for Teachers. The book concentrates on issues of pedagogy (how to teach geography, history, RE and citizenship to primary-aged children) and children's development and learning in each of these curriculum areas. The knowledge that teachers need in order to teach these subjects effectively is provided in the form of examples, stories and activities within each chapter. The agendas of the *Primary National Strategy* (DfES, 2003b) and *Every Child Matters* (DfES, 2004) underpin discussion throughout the book.

What are the humanities?

Learning in primary humanities begins with a deepening of children's understanding of themselves, the people around them, their communities and eventually the wider world. This knowledge and understanding enables children to develop an awareness of their identity, their place (both in space and time) and their significance within the social, cultural and religious communities in which they live. They will begin to learn what is special about the human condition.

The teaching and learning of humanities subjects or themes in the primary classroom seeks to make use of, and build on, children's direct experience of the world around them, making use of a range of key concepts and skills. It also aims to inform, interest, enlighten and challenge children. Most significantly, perhaps, teaching in the humanities aims to encourage awareness and questioning of values, attitudes and beliefs and, above all, an informed and critical view of the world. The humanities have a strong political and moral dimension. Therefore, humanities teaching aims to engender a respect not only for the individual in society, but also for different societies and cultures. Children should be empowered by this education, and be able to interpret and respond to events that affect their lives.

The place of geography in children's education

To many people, geography involves learning the names of capital cities and facts about the longest rivers and tallest mountains. However, like other humanities subjects, it involves far more than simply memorising factual information. In common with history, geography requires the development of subject-specific concepts such as a sense of place. As part of this process, children develop an understanding of the relationship between people and their surroundings. Methodological concepts underpin much geographical study; concepts such as change, continuity, causation, and particularly conflict and consensus, for example, when there is a conflict of interests over the building of a new airport runway or motorway.

Above all, geography involves the use of a wide range of skills, which are set out in the documentation outlining statutory requirements for early years and primary education. In the Early Years Foundation Stage (DCSF, 2008a), geographical skills and content may be found throughout the requirements for 'Knowledge and Understanding of the World', and more specifically in the requirements to 'Observe, find out about and identify features in the place they live' and 'Find out about their environment' (DCSF, 2008b, p15).

Throughout both Key Stages 1 and 2 of the National Curriculum for Geography (DfEE/QCA, 1999), children are required to ask questions, identify, describe and explain, gather and record evidence, analyse and communicate findings, use subject-specific language and techniques, use sources, plans and maps, ICT, and a range of decision-making skills to enable them to fully understand how to work as a geographer. The breadth of study requires children to use these skills in looking at local, regional, national and international localities and to study specific themes, such as settlements, and environmental effects on landscapes, leading to change and the management of sustainable development. Geographers investigate areas of major global significance, such as pollution in the environment, climate change and its effects and sustainability.

Cross-curricular work is an important part of geographical learning. Geography has a particularly significant role in providing a context for much work in history, RE and citizenship.

Without a grasp of the environments in which societies have evolved, children's developing understanding of their histories, beliefs and social systems would be incomplete. As part of the process of developing a sense of place, children learn to see themselves as citizens, not just of their own community and nation, but of an increasingly interdependent world. Geographical concerns about the beautiful yet fragile world we live in forges links with science and technology. Geography also provides wide opportunities for the use of core skills in literacy and numeracy, and particularly mathematical, graphical and data-processing skills which can be applied to real-life contexts. Skills and understanding of the application of ICT is also a vitally important link with the real world. As the Geographical Association says in its leaflet for primary school parents and governors, geography is learning:

- from the real world;
- about the real world;
- in the real world.

The place of history in children's education

Learning about the past enables children to begin to build up a 'context' for their understanding of the present. Practically everything that we see or do, or know about, has its roots somewhere in the past. History entails a study of the human condition in past times, and looks at how people learned to live in different circumstances from our own. It provides contextual material for the development and extension of key humanities concepts, such as the methodological concepts of continuity and change, cause and effect, conflict and consensus. It also encompasses key substantive concepts, such as power, communication, war and empire. A distinctive feature of history is the opportunity it provides for children, from the Early Years Foundation Stage to Key Stage 2, to develop an understanding of time and to see where significant events and people fit within the overall chronological framework.

History provides a context for the development of a range of important skills. These include the intellectual skills required in the use of sources, such as inference, analysis, synthesis and hypothesis. Social awareness is developed in history through work on the features of past societies and events, and through study of the experiences of peoples of varying religious, ethnic and cultural traditions. Social skills may be fostered through the teaching of historical methods, which are most effective when they involve collaboration, with discussion, argument and consensus in the analysis and reconstruction of the past. Historical activities in school should provide children with opportunities to critically examine evidence, to research, to ask questions and to put forward their own viewpoints – key skills which are valuable across the whole curriculum and subsequently the world of work.

Perhaps most importantly, history is a vehicle for developing the affective domain in children's education, in that it provides opportunities for empathy with people in other circumstances and times, and an appreciation of how and why life was different from the present. By providing children with the opportunity to explore the history of Britain and the wider world, multicultural understanding can be promoted, which is of benefit in today's culturally diverse society. History is also an important discipline for promoting a variety of values and clearly has much to contribute to the developing area of citizenship within the primary curriculum.

Finally, history provides excellent contextual background and material for developing work in other areas of the curriculum, particularly the core subjects such as literacy and numeracy. The vast range and variety of written sources from the past encompass all the text genres required to teach the literacy hour. Skills and concepts in history contribute to aspects of mathematical knowledge and understanding – for example, those of time and chronology, where a sound grasp of number is fundamental. Above all, the study of geography, RE and citizenship is enriched by an understanding of the historical context of each of these aspects of human experience.

The place of RE in children's education

Despite the fact that RE has been a compulsory part of the curriculum since 1944 (Butler Education Act), for many, the role and purpose of RE in children's education is still not clear. The 1988 Education Reform Act states that RE in community schools is not designed to convert children or promote belief in one religious tradition. Instead the emphasis is on 'education' – children are to be educated about religion. This emphasis recognises that the children we teach come from a range of religious backgrounds, and that for many children, religion is not part of their daily experience. The purpose of RE, then, is to help children explore the notion of religion and the part it plays in human experience. It recognises that religion is a universal human phenomenon that has helped shape the world we know today. Religion has been, and remains, a motivating force in people's lives, providing a way of understanding the world and one's place within it. Religion seeks to answer the perennial questions that humans face – who am I, where do I belong, what kind of life should I live? In this context, RE in school attempts to present to children the range of religious experience by introducing them to the world views shared by their neighbours. It helps them to understand what it is like to live one's life according to a particular set of beliefs. At the same time, RE gives children the opportunity to reflect on their own beliefs and experiences – whether or not these are drawn from religious traditions.

The Professional Standards for Teachers and their application to the humanities

The Professional Standards for Teachers (TDA, 2007) provides the framework of requirements for all classroom teachers. Underpinning these Standards are the five key outcomes identified in *Every Child Matters* (DfES, 2004) and the six areas of the common core of skills and knowledge for the children's workforce. A further requirement is that the work of teachers should be informed by the legislation concerning the development and well-being of children (see www.tda.gov.uk page 1). This book focuses primarily on the Standards for QTS, pointing out opportunities in the teaching of the humanities subjects for meeting the agenda of *Every Child Matters*. There will, where relevant, be reference to the Professional Standards for induction year and main scale teachers seeking further guidance on the teaching of geography, history, RE and citizenship.

The Professional Standards are set out in three sections: professional attributes, professional knowledge and understanding and professional skills. While there are no additional Standards or annexes for geography, history, RE or citizenship, this book refers to those Standards in each section which have direct relevance to teaching in the humanities and discusses how they can be effectively addressed through the humanities disciplines. The Professional Standards are shown at the beginning of each chapter, which then provides ideas and examples of how to meet them.

The organisation and major themes of the humanities subjects

The curriculum requirements as specified in the National Curriculum (DfEE/QCA, 1999) are outlined below. However, should the recommendations of the Rose Review (DCSF, 2009) be implemented, the requirements for teaching each separate humanities subject will be substantially reduced. For example, children will be required to study in depth only two specific periods in history. There will, however, be greater flexibility for schools to decide what to teach in outline or in depth, and for cross-curricular thematic work. For further information on current developments, see www.dcsf.gov.uk/primarycurriculumreview/.

Geography

Geography in the National Curriculum is conceptualised through four aspects of knowledge, skills and understanding:

- *Geographical enquiry and skills*, which require children to:
  - ask geographical questions;
  - observe, collect and record information and evidence;
  - analyse evidence and draw conclusions;
  - express their own views, and identify and explain other people's viewpoints;
  - communicate in a variety of ways;
  - use decision making;
  - use geographical vocabulary;
  - use fieldwork skills;
  - use and make globes, maps and plans;
  - use secondary sources of information;
  - use information and communication technology (ICT).
- *Knowledge and understanding of places*, including the concepts of location, human and physical features, similarities and differences, change and wider geographical contexts. Children should be able to set their investigations about places in the present within a timeframe which draws on the past and predicts the future.
- *Knowledge and understanding of patterns and processes*, i.e. recognising and explaining patterns created by both human and physical features, and how changes to places and environments are brought about by human and physical processes.
- *Knowledge and understanding of environmental change and sustainable development*, i.e. recognising how people have positive and negative impacts on the environment and how those environments may be managed. Children are encouraged to take a participatory view about decision making in the local and wider environment.

In order to develop an integrated understanding of geography, children should use the first of these aspects, geographical enquiry and skills, when developing the other three aspects of geographical knowledge and understanding.

Knowledge, skills and understanding of geography are currently taught through the study of localities at different scales thus ensuring a breadth of study.

- At Key Stage 1 children study at a local scale and focus on the locality of their own school and a contrasting locality (either in the UK or abroad).
- At Key Stage 2 this broadens into the study of a locality in the UK and a locality in an less economically developed country. Additionally, at Key Stage 2, children develop their knowledge skills and understanding

of geography through three themes: water and its effects on landscapes and people, how settlements differ and change, and environmental issues (change and sustainable management).

- At both Key Stages 1 and 2 children are required to carry out fieldwork investigations outside the classroom. This can take the form of work in the school grounds, the immediate vicinity of the school, the local area or a contrasting locality.

History

History in the National Curriculum is currently organised under the same headings of 'Knowledge, skills and understanding' and 'Breadth of study'. The 'Knowledge, skills and understanding', although increasingly detailed and complex, are common across all National Curriculum key stages, and are to be taught through the specified content. These are the key concepts and skills that underpin historical study:

- *Chronological understanding*. This requires children to be taught how to place events, people and changes in chronological order, and to use dates, common phrases and increasingly refined vocabulary relating to the passing of time.
- *Knowledge and understanding of events, people and changes in the past*. This requires children to be taught about: the key features of past societies and their cultural, religious and ethnic diversity; the causes of historical events and changes; how to make links between the main events, situations and changes within and across the different periods and societies studied.
- *Historical interpretation.* This requires children to be taught to recognise how and why the past is represented and interpreted in different ways.
- *Historical enquiry.* This requires children to be taught how to use historical sources, such as artefacts, pictures, music, historic buildings and sites, galleries and museums. They are also required to use ICT-based sources, such as CD-Roms and computerised databases.
- *Organisation and communication.* This requires children to be taught how to recall, select and organise historical information; use dates and historical vocabulary to describe the periods studied; communicate their knowledge and understanding of the past in a variety of ways, such as talking, writing or using ICT.

The 'Breadth of study' outlines the subject content that needs to be used in teaching the 'Knowledge, skills and understanding' in history. The content specified in this section is different at Key Stage 1 and Key Stage 2.

At Key Stage 1, children are required to be taught the 'Knowledge, skills and understanding' through the following areas of study:

- changes in their own lives and the way of life of their family or others around them;
- the way of life of people in the more distant past who lived in the local area or elsewhere in Britain;
- the lives of significant men, women and children drawn from the history of Britain and the wider world;
- past events from the history of Britain and the wider world.

During Key Stage 2, the content to be covered is considerably greater, and gradually attempts to widen the scope of the child's awareness of the past. It includes a local history study, three British history studies, a European history study and a world history study. The British history studies are specified as Romans, Anglo-Saxons and Vikings in Britain; Britain and the wider world in Tudor times; and Victorian Britain or Britain since 1930. The European history study is a study of the way of life, beliefs and achievements of people living in Ancient Greece and the influence of their civilisation on the world today. The world history study similarly looks at the key features of a past society selected from: Ancient Egypt, Ancient Sumer, the Assyrian Empire, the Indus Valley, the Maya, Benin, or the Aztecs.

RE

Under the terms of the 1988 Education Reform Act, schools are required to provide religious education for all their children. However, unlike the other humanities subjects, RE is not part of the National Curriculum. Instead it is part of the 'basic curriculum' which all schools should provide.

This means that the Secretary of State for Education has no power to determine what kind of RE schools provide. Instead, RE is 'locally determined'. Community schools follow an 'Agreed Syllabus' provided by their local education authority. Voluntary schools follow a syllabus in line with their trust deeds. This means that for many religious schools a syllabus will be provided in line with their religious foundation. There are no prescribed national attainment targets or units of work for RE. These are provided through whichever syllabus the school is following. Guidance for the content of RE can be found in DfES and QCA documentation, but again this is not statutory. Local education authority Agreed Syllabuses must 'reflect the fact that the religious traditions in Great Britain are in the main Christian whilst taking into account the teaching and practices of the other principal religions represented in Great Britain' (Education Reform Act 1988, section 8(3)). Many authorities use the QCA's 'Model Syllabuses' (1998) as a guide to their own.

This means that the type of RE provided for children in primary schools varies from school to school and from place to place. However, it is possible to suggest some common features and themes within RE. For example, most syllabuses will include the six major religions represented in the country: Buddhism, Christianity, Hinduism, Judaism, Islam and Sikhism.

Schools may teach a range of topics that include some or all of these six. The model Syllabuses (QCA, 1998) recommend that at Key Stage 1 children should be introduced to Christianity and at least **one** other religion, and that at Key Stage 2 there should be a minimum of Christianity and **two** other religions. RE may be taught in a variety of ways. Each religion can be taught separately as a unit, or within a wider topic, for example, Celebrations. Guidance for which aspects of a religious tradition might be covered can be found in Agreed Syllabuses and in the SCAA's 'Faith Communities Working Group Reports' (SCAA, 1994). Typical primary topics might include: Religious Leaders, Sacred Writings, Worship, Beliefs and Festivals.

When beginning to teach RE in a new school it is important therefore to find out:

- whether the school has its own syllabus for RE identifying which religious topics are to be taught in each term;
- which Agreed Syllabus or other syllabus the school is following.

Further government guidance on how to approach the teaching of RE can be found in the RE 'Scheme of Work for Key Stages 1 and 2' (QCA, 2000) and 'Non-statutory guidance on RE' (QCA, 2000).

Statutory and exemplary documentation

DCSF (2008a) *The Early Years Foundation Stage*. London: DCSF.

DCSF (2008b) *Statutory Framework for the Early Years Foundation Stage*. London: DCSF.

DCSF (2009) *Independent Review of the Primary Curriculum: Final Report (The Rose Review)*. London: DCSF.

DES (1989) *The Education Reform Act 1988: Religious Education and Collective Worship*. (Circular 3/89). London: DES.

DFE (1988) *Education Reform Act 1988*. London: HMSO.

DFE (1994) *Religious Education and Collective Worship*. (Circular I/94). London: DFE.

DfEE/QCA (1998) *Geography: A Scheme of Work for Key Stages 1 and 2*. London: QCA.

DfEE/QCA (1998) *History: A Scheme of Work for Key Stages 1 and 2*. London: QCA.

DfEE/QCA (1999) *Geography: the National Curriculum for England*. London: HMSO.

DfEE/QCA (1999) *History: the National Curriculum for England*. London: HMSO.

DfEE/QCA (1999) *The National Curriculum. Handbook for Primary Teachers in England Key Stages 1 and 2*. London: DfEE/QCA.

DfES/TTA (2002) *Qualifying to Teach: Professional Standards for Qualified Teacher Status and Requirements for Initial Teacher Training* (Circular 2/02). London: TTA.

DfES (2003b) *Excellence and Enjoyment: A Strategy for Primary Schools*. London: DfES.

DfES (2004) *Every Child Matters: Change for Children*. London: DfES.

QCA (1998) *Model Syllabuses for Religious Education (Model 1: Living Faiths Today and Model 2: Questions and Teachings)*. London: QCA.

SCAA (1994) *Faith Communities' Working Group Reports*. London: SCAA.

SCAA (1994) *Model Syllabuses for Religious Education (Models I & 2) (Model 1: Living Faiths Today and Model 2: Questions and Teachings)*. London: SCAA.

TDA (2007) Professional Standards for Teachers. London: TDA.

Useful websites

refit.ucsm.ac.uk

re-xs.ucsm.ac.uk/schools

vtc.ngfl.gov.uk/resource/cits/re/

www.bbc.co.uk/history

www.canteach.gov.uk/community/itt/requirements/qualifying/ standards1

www.dcsf.gov.uk/primarycurriculumreview

www.geoworld.co.uk/pupilresources.htm

www.historyonthenet.co.uk

www.learningcurve.gov.uk

www.nc.uk.net

www.ngfl.gov.uk/ngfl/index/html

www.open.gov.uk/qca/RE

www.qca.org.uk

www.reonline.org.uk/

www.schoolhistory.co.uk

www.schoolshistory.org.uk

www.spartacus.schoolnet.co.uk/britain.html

1
Aims and values in humanities education

By the end of this chapter you will have:

- become aware of the links between the Professional Standards for Teachers and *Every Child Matters*;
- developed an understanding of the importance of building good working relationships with children to enable them to achieve their full potential;
- developed an understanding of ways of demonstrating positive values, attitudes and behaviour.

Professional Standards for QTS

Q1: Have high expectations of children and young people including a commitment to ensuring that they can achieve their full educational potential and to establish fair, respectful, trusting, supportive and constructive relationships with them.

Q2: Demonstrate the positive values, attitudes and behaviour they expect from children and young people.

Professional attributes

The requirements outlined within the 'Professional attributes' section of the Professional Standards for Teachers (TDA, 2007), particularly Q1–Q2, are concerns that have long been fundamental to work in the humanities. R. S. Peters (1966) produced a clearly articulated account of the fundamental principles for educational practice devised by educational philosophers. These included, among others, the notion of respect for persons, regardless of age, race, gender or class, which he argued must underpin all work in education. This work has influenced and informed much educational philosophy over recent decades and its influence is still visible in the principles underpinning the National Curriculum and the Professional Standards for Teachers (TDA, 2007).

The Professional Standards have been heavily influenced by, and have been built upon previous initiatives, such as the NACCCE Report, *All our Futures: Creativity, Culture and Education* (NACCCE/DfEE, 1999), *Excellence and Enjoyment – A Strategy for Primary Schools* (DfES, 2003) and *Every Child Matters: Change for Children* (DfES, 2003). The Children Act, passed in 2004, made the agenda of *Every Child Matters* a legal requirement. Since then, a series of documents have been published which provide guidance under the act to support local authorities and their partners in implementing this agenda of the *Children's Plan* (DCSF, 2007). The agenda central to all these initiatives is to place an emphasis on the child and the personalisation of learning. The centrality of the child as learner, emphasised in *Every Child Matters: Change for Children* (DfES 2004), has led to a return to integrated, cross-curricular approaches, similar to those popular prior to the introduction of the National Curriculum! It is a widely held belief that young children often learn in a holistic way; in other words they learn through topics which are relevant and of interest to them (Jarvis and Parker, 2005). The well-being of the child underpins all learning and is the main focus of an integrated support system for all children.

The wide scope of human interest embodied within the humanities offers endless opportunities for varied topics of work which will enable you to set high expectations and enable children to meet their potential. Children's interests and concerns can guide the choice and course of a humanities topic, thus engaging them and raising their motivation to study. Cross-curricular themes looking at an aspect of their locality, such as shops; the lives of children in different times and places; or features of modern multi-cultural communities, for example, will enable you to combine geography, history and RE in a meaningful way, while providing scope for children's own, open-ended enquiries. Appropriate and strong relationships can be built up in the course of this type of work, where the needs and interests of the child need to be considered at the planning stage, enabling you to build up your knowledge and understanding of each individual in the class.

Knowledge and understanding of different backgrounds and cultures is a prerequisite for building respect for the characteristics of these different cultures. It is through the knowledge acquired in learning humanities subjects that we gain that essential awareness of beliefs, attitudes and traditions that are different from our own. We are then in a better position to understand the motives, views and ideas of people from different backgrounds, and hence to respect them. The notion of 'culture' is complex; it can include local differences within the same country, or national, ethnic or religious differences on a global scale. As we all know, it is ignorance of different cultures that promotes fear, distrust and eventually dislike and disagreement, frequently leading to disputes and wars lasting for many centuries.

Every Child Matters

Respect for children goes beyond being concerned with children from a diversity of backgrounds. We need to have high expectations for *all* children as people, individuals in their own right, in the tradition so well articulated by Peters (1966). Respect for the individual child as a person should underpin all work in education, and although this view was brilliantly articulated so long ago, it is heartening to see it once again at the forefront of the Professional Standards for Teachers and the basis of the *Every Child Matters* (ECM) agenda. Moreover, respect is generally mutual. A respectful teacher is setting a certain kind of role model for the children to emulate and it is usually the case that a caring teacher will receive respect in return and promote an atmosphere of respect among the children in their class.

Taught with sensitivity, teachers have in the humanities an excellent opportunity to 'demonstrate the positive values, attitudes and behaviour' as required in the Professional Standards for Teachers (TDA, 2007). The humanities subjects are best placed to enable you to build this healthy atmosphere of mutual respect in your classroom, and to instil interest, empathy and sensitivity in children towards people from diverse backgrounds. Indeed, this is a major focus of all humanities disciplines. There are, of course, obvious ways of respecting children's contributions, by listening and responding positively to their verbal contributions, marking their work promptly and with care, displaying and valuing work they have produced – the list is endless. However, we now need to focus specifically on the features of the humanities that can engender this respect, which we will argue go far beyond these general points. As trainee teachers you will have a particular responsibility to develop your own knowledge and understanding of those aspects of the primary curriculum which will assist you in meeting these Standards. This is for two major reasons: firstly, to be in a position to set a good example to children in promoting positive values; secondly, so that you will be able to plan appropriately. To achieve these aims you need a good knowledge of the curriculum and also the ability to reflect about it. You need to be able to identify aspects of the curriculum which will particularly lend themselves to teaching and learning aimed at values. An initial introduction to the process and practice of reflective teaching can be found in Pollard (2008). You may then wish to investigate specific curriculum areas, or think about themes or topics that will meet your planning needs.

Dealing with sensitive issues in the humanities

The subject matter of the humanities demands that on occasion personal views and beliefs are brought into the teaching context. This can be daunting for the beginning teacher and it is important that we are prepared to deal with issues when they arise.

There are two areas that give teachers concern. Firstly, there is the issue of their own beliefs and values and how far these have an impact on how and what they teach. The first thing to recognise and accept is that everyone brings their own beliefs and values into the class-room, whether they are religious, political or social. Be suspicious of anyone who says they have no strong beliefs. This may indicate that they have not articulated their beliefs, which can be far more unhelpful in the classroom than where someone clearly states their position on a subject. It is important therefore to recognise your own views in sensitive areas; your next decision is how to deal with these in the classroom. Remember that it is very difficult for us to leave our beliefs outside the classroom door – do we need to?

The second area of concern is how to deal with children's beliefs and commitments. Children will ask some challenging questions – and not always at a time when we are ready for them! Questions of a religious nature can be particularly problematic. How do we respond if a child asks 'Is there really a God?' or 'Do you believe we go to heaven when we die?'

The QCA publication *Religious Education, Non-statutory guidance* (QCA, 2000) gives some useful suggestions on how to deal with these kinds of issues in the classroom. General advice would include the following.

- Be as honest as you can. If children know 'where you are coming from' that can give them permission to be confident in their own viewpoint. For example, if you are a strict vegetarian, and the children know this, they will be able to predict your views on issues such as whaling. They may not be vegetarian, but may still share your views on this issue.
- Be fair to ideas you don't agree with. Remember that you act as a 'model' for the children and so you need to be careful in your language, including body language.
- If you don't know something, admit it and discuss with the children ways of finding out about it. We need to demonstrate to children that we too are in the process of learning. If you make a genuine mistake or misrepresent the views or traditions of a group of people, acknowledge it and apologise. Correct any mistakes that children make and challenge stereotypical or racist views.
- Acknowledge your own biases, explain them, so that the children can judge your contribution to discussion. Teachers are often nervous of sharing their views, partly through fear of influencing the children unduly. It helps here to explain where your views come from and then ask about theirs.
- If pupils reveal some personal information, e.g. a death in the family, make time to follow it up either immediately, by setting the class a 'holding' task or using support staff, or by making time for a one-to-one meeting later. Use your own judgement and knowledge of the child as to which is more appropriate.

Any issues which relate to child protection must obviously be followed up in line with the school's policies.

- Don't dismiss serious questions the children want to ask. If there is no time to do it immediately, build it in later, telling the children that it's what you plan to do. Ask children about the origins of the questions they ask – what they have been thinking about. This often helps in giving the most appropriate answer. Throw the question back to them – what do they think?
- Distinguish between matters of fact and belief. Do not try to give answers to those 'ultimate questions' pondered by humankind. Let the children know that these are questions that people have wrestled with across the generations. In religious matters, use the teachings of the faiths to help, i.e. 'many Christians would say, but many Hindus believe that...' Allow children to share their understandings of their own traditions.
- Allow children not to take part in discussion. In circle time type activities they should be allowed to pass. There should also be rules in place guiding discussion activities to protect individuals and establish the ground rules for such work.
- Keep a sense of humour. Children quickly move on from one thing to another. Consider the story about the boy who asked his dad, 'Where did I come from?' Dad takes a deep breath and begins to explain the facts of life. At the end of his explanation Dad asks, 'Well, son, did that answer your question?' Son replies, 'Sort of, only Billy next door says he comes from Liverpool.'

The contributions of the humanities to professional values and responsibilities

History aims to identify the origins and development of different cultures over time, probing the differences between societies, their politics, religions and ethnic origins. More than this, a key aspect of historical study is the need to empathise with those who have had different experiences from your own. A basic aim of history teaching is to develop in children the ability to see problems, changes, issues and ways of life from the perspective of others, that is, to appreciate and fully understand their point of view. This does not necessarily mean to agree with it, but to know in a deep sense why people hold different views, opinions and attitudes. Hilary Claire has carried out research into issues such as equality and inclusion in history, and books such as *Reclaiming Our Pasts* (Claire, 1996) show clearly how the curriculum need not marginalise women or minority groups. She suggests further reading and a wide range of resources to assist you in planning for an inclusive curriculum. Geography can locate different cultural developments and trace the movements of peoples across the world. Religious education offers deep insights into the values and beliefs that drive different ethnic groups and nations. The following sections in this chapter look at the contributions made by each subject that will assist the trainee teacher to address these Standards in their own teaching placements.

REFLECTIVE TASK

Study the National Curriculum for History at Key Stage 2 and select a period such as 'Victorian Britain'. Consider how you might illustrate the role of girls and women in your teaching of this period of history. For example, how might you adjust your planning or choice of resources?

Geography

One of the major aims in studying geography is to develop understanding and respect for the environment and to foster an interest in environmental issues, such as pollution, global warming and sustainability. You can become an excellent role model to children through the way in which you present and involve children with these issues. The study of geography encourages children to reflect on the importance of decisions they make and the effects of their decisions on their own environment and that of others. A fundamental aim which underpins this concern is to develop children's *spatial awareness and locational understanding* (Scoffham, 2004, p77). According to Morgan (2001) one of the most exciting things about geography is that it *builds upon children's curiosity about places*. Geography also looks at the people who live in those places, making use of skills such as fieldwork and using resources such as artefacts, music, food, or stories, to name just a few. All of these strategies assist the child in building up an increasingly detailed picture of people in their different environments and of how their different cultures have evolved in the wider world. When surveying views of pupils in five primary schools about British cities, Chris Durbin (2001) points out that while children were good at mentioning the weather, landscapes and environments, there was a lack of reference to people. Both Cultural Geography and Citizenship help to highlight the 'people' within geography, and these two subjects combine effectively in a study of local cultures.

CLASSROOM STORY

Studying local cultures

Malcolm's first teaching placement was in a primary school in Oldham in a predominately white area with a 2 per cent ethnic minority including a child with a Caribbean background. This was a contrast to his fellow student, also on teaching practice in Oldham, who was in a school with over 90 per cent children with a Pakistani culture and only 1 per cent white.

The geography unit of work Malcolm was asked to teach was 'Shopping' with Year 1. He thought this was an ideal unit to help children appreciate, tolerate and value the wealth of cultures that live in Oldham. He looked at the Ofsted report for his school to determine the ethnic range – White, Bangladeshi, Black Caribbean, Black African and Indian. Malcolm carried out further research with the Oldham government website for up-to-date census figures. He found that the main ethnic minority group was Pakistani, followed by Bangladeshi, Black Caribbean, Black African, Indian plus a very small minority of Chinese, Ukrainian and Polish.

Malcolm spent a weekend exploring the local shops and markets, taking photographs to use in class and purchasing some food items from these different countries. The local studies centre was a useful resource, plus the Tourist Information Centre. Searching in the local phone book he found a variety of restaurants and take-aways. Malcolm collected menus from a range. He wanted to demonstrate via the unit of work, how fortunate the children were to have such a diversity of cultures on their doorstep. Table 1.1 shows the scheme of work that Malcolm generated.

Table 1.1 A scheme of work

Duration. 10 hours	Age group: Year 1	
Learning objectives	**Teaching and learning activities**	**Assessment criteria**
Children should learn to: • Use geographical terms in exploring their surroundings. • Investigate the physical and human features of their surroundings. • Undertake fieldwork activities in the locality of the school. • Make maps and plans of real and imaginary places using pictures and symbols, e.g. a plan of a supermarket. • Use secondary sources e.g. pictures, menus and photographs to obtain geographical information.	**What food do we like to eat?** • Class survey – describe favourite foods. • Draw or create a collage of food we like. **What food is in my shopping bag?** • Ask children to identify items. • Sort into types of food. **Where do we buy our food?** • Discuss range of local shops and take-aways, markets, restaurants, chip van, etc. • Use of photographs. • Fiction containing a variety of foods, e.g. *The Green Banana Hunt* by Jenny Bent (Leamington Spa: Scholastic 1992). This story is set in a city and the reader is taken on a journey through the streets. Foods including sweet potatoes, bananas and melons are mentioned. As geographers we want to know how the different foods grow, the climates and how the food is transported to our shops. **Let's make our own shop** • Use dough to make items. • Draw around products to make plan views. • Cut out pictures from magazines. **What does the local corner shop sell?** • Visit shop to find out what it sells, where it gets the goods from, the jobs undertaken. • Have a questionnaire ready to interview shopkeeper – tape or video answers. **What is sold in a supermarket?** • Visit local supermarket, e.g. ASDA. Provide children with a simple plan of the supermarket, leaving off a few areas that are easy to recognise, e.g. vegetables, milk, bread. Ask children to mark on missing items. (For less able provide pictures to stick on.) • Note the types of jobs carried out. • In class – sorting/sequencing exercise of the journey of a product, e.g. milk from cow to carton of milk in supermarket to milk on breakfast cereal. **What was sold in the past?** • Children to listen to a tape made from a visit to a nursing home – asking people what shopping was like 10, 20, 50 years ago. • Invite a school governor/grandparent to come and talk to the class.	Most children will understand that there are different places we can buy food. Be able to identify a range of food items. Understand that some of our food comes from other countries. Some children will not have made so much progress and will: • be able to describe their favourite food; • describe some of the items sold in the shops visited; • be aware of a huge variety of food within Oldham. Some children will have progressed further and will also: • understand that what people eat has changed over time; • can name examples of food from different countries.

	What extra foods can you buy today? ● Show children items available today, e.g. prickly pears from the tropics, from the different cultures living in Oldham. ● Add pictures of food items to a class wall map. Discuss how it gets to Oldham. ● Study menus from a range of restaurants/take aways. **Are shops the same around the world?** ● Study photo, travel brochures, fiction, e.g. *Grace & family* by Mary Hoffman and Caroline Binch (London: Frances Lincoln, 1997). ● Discuss advantages and disadvantages. ● Children can design a shop suitable for all kinds of weather.	

Sharing information about our own locality while learning about another locality is exciting. This excitement can be enhanced through the use of the internet to communicate directly with children in other parts of the world. Many schools link their classes to teaching groups in another country through e-mails, video conferencing and chat rooms. By sharing information in this way they are able to learn from each other.

Sponsoring a child is a method some schools adopt to help their children develop an understanding of a less economically developed country (LEDC). By sponsoring, children can learn more about people's lives abroad and develop a sense of global citizenship. A very useful resource for teachers is their nearest Development Education Centre, for example the Development Education Centre (DEC) in Birmingham and the Development Education Project (DEP) in Manchester. These centres help local teachers with resources, ideas and practical training sessions to enhance our teaching about different cultures and cross curricular themes such as environmental awareness, sustainable development and citizenship.

CLASSROOM STORY
Studying cultures abroad
In Darren's school in Salford, children are linked with the city's twin towns. Year 5 classes exchange letters with Lünen in North West Germany and Year 6 classes with Clermont-Ferrand in France. Children write on a termly basis. Some of the teachers have already been to visit the twin towns, to establish a face-to-face contact. Teachers fax each other at the start of the school year for a theme for each letter, such as 'My family', 'Holidays', 'My hobbies'.

The British Council have web pages of possible school links at www.globalgateway.org.uk. Below is an example of a school wishing to link:

Oasis International School, Bangalore, India
Type of school or college: primary
Normal language of instruction: English
Internet facilities: e-mail; www
Existing school or college partnership: no
Oasis International School seeks to develop in each student a positive Indian
identity, preparing him intellectually, socially, emotionally, spiritually and physically
to succeed in tomorrow's world.
Type of project sought: class project
Target groups: ages 7–11; teachers
Project areas: arts; computing (ICT); crafts; geography; health; history; literature;
personal & social education; religious studies; science; sports; technology; Islamic
studies
Preferred partner language: English

PRACTICAL TASK PRACTICAL TASK PRACTICAL TASK PRACTICAL TASK PRACTICAL TASK

Think of ways that a link with the Oasis school could help your children develop an understanding of their
own and another culture. Search the British Council website www.globalgateway.org.uk for potential
partners to support humanities teaching. Contact your local education authority (LEA) – find out the twin
towns for your placement school. Be active – find out about the twinning committee.

History

History offers an extensive range of stories, sources and experiences about both immigration and emigration which can be used to build the self-esteem of children from families
which have arrived in Britain as immigrants themselves in previous generations (Claire,
1996). Topics such as these can be used effectively to promote empathy on the part of
their peers with the backgrounds and family histories of children from minority ethnic
groups.

Other aspects of the history curriculum serve a similar purpose, such as the units which look
at famous or significant people, where careful selection and choice of resources can provide
a rich and rewarding learning experience for all children in a class. Knowing that people of
historical significance and importance are drawn from all backgrounds and communities
fosters a spirit of equality and respect for all children and their different heritages.

CLASSROOM STORY

Ruth noticed one day in her Year 6 class that there were some unpleasant comments
being made among the children. Her class was one of very mixed backgrounds. There
were children from local white indigenous families that had lived in the area for many
generations. There were also a considerable number of children from African-
Caribbean backgrounds, who spoke slightly differently and sometimes had different
views from the others.

The comments she had overheard had clearly not originated from the children. They
were things that the children would have overheard at home or in the street perhaps,

and had repeated in school, thinking that they were appropriate, comments such as: 'Why aren't you like us? We can't understand you sometimes. Why are you like this?' Ruth was naturally very upset at this. She firmly believed that all the children in her class deserved respect, both from herself and from the other children. She decided that she must take positive action to rectify the misunderstandings from outside that were obviously influencing the children in her class. Given the nature of the children who made up the ethnic minority group in her class, Ruth decided to plan and teach a unit of work with a historical focus on the Windrush.

SS *Empire Windrush* was the name of a ship on which hundreds of immigrants travelled to Britain from Jamaica in 1948. It was a controversial event; questions were asked in Parliament and the daily newspapers offered their often somewhat unpleasant views on the occurrence. Would there be enough jobs for British people with all these people competing from outside? What would be the effect of all these strangers coming to our country? In fact the immigrants from Jamaica had simply responded to an advertisement placed in a newspaper in Kingston, Jamaica, for people to come to work in Britain, since there was a shortage in the workforce following the Second World War.

Ruth designed the plan shown in Table 1.2 for her history topic. She researched the subject further and found that there were quite a number of books about it, many of which contained first-hand accounts by the people who travelled from their homeland to settle in Britain (Wambu, 1999; Phillips and Phillips, 1998). She selected some useful accounts and rewrote some to make them more accessible in terms of the reading ability of some children in her class.

Table 1.2 Plan for a unit of work with a history focus on the *Windrush*

Learning objectives	Activities	NC reference	Key vocabulary	Resources	Assessment
Lesson 1 Develop contextual under- standing of the Caribbean	Use maps, look at pictures, listen to descriptions and accounts	Breadth of study: 11b – Britain since 1930 Knowledge, skills and understanding – 2b, 4a, 4b	Jamaica, Caribbean, colony, Empire, mother country, immigrant, immigration	Maps, pictures, photographs, descriptive accounts	Question children at the end of the lesson on their under- standing of the concept of empire and colonies
Lesson 2 Develop a sense of chronology	Place the *Windrush* period on a timeline, sequence the *Windrush* events	Breadth of study: 11b – Britain since 1930 Knowledge, skills and understanding – 1a, 1b	national newspaper, 1948, Second World War, SS *Empire Windrush*	Class timeline of twentieth century simple sequence line for individual children	Observe and record children's comments in discussion and their skill in sequencing events
Lesson 3 Use written sources	Listen to and read oral history accounts of the *Windrush* journey	Breadth of study: 11b – Britain since 1930 Knowledge, skills and understanding – 4a, 4b	apprehen- sive, adventure, adventurer, survivor, comradeship, optimism	Oral history accounts of travellers on the *Windrush*	Check children's under- standing of key vocabulary and of the texts used

Lesson 4 Consider different inter-pretations	Compare different accounts of the journey and arrival in Britain	Breadth of study: 11b – Britain since 1930 Knowledge, skills and understanding – 3, 4a, 4b	destitute, gleaner, passport, booking office, queue, massive journey	Oral history accounts of travellers on the *Windrush*	Check children's use of key vocabulary in the texts used
Lesson 5 Use sources, communicate findings	Look at accounts and different viewpoints about the new immigrants, report to the class on their findings	Breadth of study: 11b – Britain since 1930 Knowledge, skills and understanding – 4a, 5a, 5b, 5c	account, differing, contradictory, reports, Parliament, resistance	Newspaper reports, Parliamentary debates and comments	Observe and mark children's presentations, writing or displays

Ruth then wrote her rationale. She knew that the majority of the children in her class had no knowledge of how the ethnic minority children had come to be in Britain. She believed that more knowledge and understanding of these origins would enable the indigenous population to understand and accept them more readily. She also knew that the first-hand accounts would be so real to the class that they would begin to empathise with the plight of the immigrants, understand their fears and doubts and relate personally to them. Finally, the class would realise that the current generation of children had been born and grown up in Britain in just the same way as they had themselves. They therefore had no reason to see them as outsiders. Moreover, the treatment of the subject as an important one would surely raise the self-esteem of the African-Caribbean children. She also believed that by exploring these issues with her class, she would be setting a good role model, showing interest in and respect for the backgrounds and experiences of this group within the class. She hoped that the experience would be beneficial and positive in its overall effect on the class.

PRACTICAL TASK PRACTICAL TASK PRACTICAL TASK PRACTICAL TASK PRACTICAL TASK

Devise a theme based on history that would achieve the same results for children from Pakistani origins in a class. Write a classroom story about your actions and give an outline rationale for a unit that you might teach. You could make use of the QCA Scheme of Work history unit (DfEE/QCA, 1998) on the Indus Valley for this topic.

History also provides good opportunities for involving other adults in the work of the child. For example, a piece of work such as a simple timeline of the child's life might be sent home for parents or carers to make a contribution and to help the child construct a picture of their own past. Other adults in the school might be invited as 'guest speakers' to talk about their experiences of particular incidents in the past. Such contributions to children's learning experiences can encourage them to learn and motivate them to achieve high levels of attainment.

RE

Any Agreed Syllabus or diocesan syllabus usually begins with a statement of the aims of RE. Many of these will consider what knowledge, understanding, skills, concepts and attitudes the children should be developing in relation to their study of religion. It is not enough to focus just on knowledge and understanding of a religious tradition; more important is the way in which such knowledge helps children to develop positive attitudes towards their own and other people's beliefs and traditions. The model syllabuses for RE (DfEE/QCA, 1998) make these concerns explicit. As well as reference to knowledge and understanding their statement of aims includes helping children to:

- develop an understanding of the influence of beliefs, values and traditions on individuals, communities, societies and cultures;
- develop the ability to make reasoned and informed judgements about religious and moral issues, with reference to the teachings of the principal religions represented in Great Britain;
- reflect on their own beliefs, values and experiences in the light of their study;
- develop a positive attitude towards other people, respecting their right to hold different beliefs from their own, and towards living in a society of diverse religions.

CLASSROOM STORY

Sarah was the teacher of a Year 1 class in a Church of England school on the outskirts of a large city. She had a keen interest in RE but was aware that her knowledge of world religions was limited and was dissatisfied with how she introduced her class to them. She knew that the children had little contact with people of faiths other than Christianity and was afraid that her approach might be rather superficial. More importantly, she was concerned that the work she did with the children might offer stereotypical images and only serve to reinforce a sense of 'us and them' among the children.

She decided on a course of action that involved three strategies:

- Develop her own subject knowledge in a world religion other than Christianity.
- Devise learning opportunities which offered children a realistic picture of another faith community.
- Consider ways to improve her own delivery to ensure that she presented that community in a positive way which did not suggest it was in any way inferior to the Christian community.

One of the religions identified for study within the diocesan syllabus and in the school long-term plan was Sikhism. Sarah decided to focus her development of subject knowledge on Sikhism in relation to the QCA unit of work 'Beliefs and Practice'. She collected reading material from the local library, the teacher's centre and the internet. The advisory teacher for RE from the diocesan education board was also a good source of information and he told Sarah that there was a Sikh gurdwara in the city which welcomed school groups. Sarah made contact with the gurdwara and arranged a visit for herself. The visit was invaluable and she discussed the possibility of bringing her class for a visit during which the children would be able to talk to members of the community. She also established e-mail contact with an inner city school which had a large number of Sikh children.

Table 1.3 Plan for a unit of work on Sikhism for Year 1

	Learning outcomes	Activities
Week 1	Children will reflect upon the things that are important to them.	Circle time – what is important to me?
Week 2	Children will have an initial understanding of the presence of a Sikh community in the city.	Video, pictures, images and artefacts of Sikhism on display. Discussion – what is important to Sikhs?
Week 3	Children will find out about Sikh children's lives, views and beliefs.	List questions to ask the children at Claremont St school. Use e-mail to exchange information.
Week 4	Children will find out more about Sikh beliefs and values.	Visit Gurdwara and talk to members of the community.
Week 5	Children will consider further how beliefs affect daily life.	Construct a display showing Sikh artefacts, drawings, paintings, written work.
Week 6	Children will reflect upon their learning and develop skills of presenting this to others.	Preparation for class assembly. Children choose content.

From this preparation and research Sarah was able to devise a series of lessons which aimed to introduce her class to the Sikh community in the city (see Table 1.3). During all activities Sarah made sure that she presented Sikhism in a positive way, making links between the experiences of her class and those of the other school. She also made clear to the children that she was not an expert in Sikhism, but that she too would be learning as they studied the community. When preparing her lessons Sarah was conscious of her use of language. Rather than tell the children they were going to study Sikhism, she told them that they would be getting to know some children from another school and finding out about their lives. She made sure that when she presented information to the children she used phrases such as 'many Sikhs' or 'for some Sikhs' or she would refer explicitly to the particular community they were studying, for example 'at the gurdwara we will be visiting...'. When children identified similarities between Christianity and Sikhism, Sarah was careful to avoid saying 'we believe this...'; instead she would say 'many Christians believe...'. If children displayed negative attitudes about any aspect, Sarah would challenge it by encouraging the children to unpack their thoughts, consider why it seemed unusual to them and focus on what it means to Sikh children.

PRACTICAL TASK PRACTICAL TASK PRACTICAL TASK PRACTICAL TASK PRACTICAL TASK

Identify a religious tradition that you are not familiar with. Collect a range of resources including books, images and internet material and from reading these make a list of questions you would like to ask about the tradition. Find your nearest contact with the tradition and arrange either a meeting or use other means of communication to explore the questions you have.

A SUMMARY OF **KEY POINTS**

> The humanities subjects are highly suitable for addressing the Standards on 'Professional attributes', and the agenda of ECM.

> Remember to plan in the humanities for the development of children's knowledge and understanding of people from different backgrounds.

> You can focus in geography on the reasons and issues surrounding the movement of peoples to different parts of the world.

> Issues about immigration and emigration relate to many minority ethnic groups in Britain. You can address these through historical topics in particular.

> You can develop positive attitudes and values in relation to other religions through your teaching of RE.

MOVING *ON* > > > > > > MOVING *ON* > > > > > > MOVING *ON*

Standard C1, Standard C2

Familiarise yourself with the documentation relating to *Every Child Matters* (DfES 2003/www.everychild-matters.gov.uk), noting where you will be able to meet aspects of this agenda in your teaching of the humanities.

FURTHER READING FURTHER READING **FURTHER READING** FURTHER READING

Blaylock, L. and Johnson C. (eds) (1997) *A Teacher's Handbook of Religious Education.* Derby: CEM. A detailed guide to many aspects of RE teaching. It outlines the legal framework, offers teaching approaches and considers issues arising from approaching world faiths in the classroom.

Burns, S. and Lamont, G. (1995) *Values and Visions – A Handbook for Spiritual Development and Global Awareness Research.* London: Hodder and Stoughton. This book provides many useful examples of how children's spiritual development can be a focus within a range of activities.

Children's Geographies. Look out for this journal by Taylor & Francis.

Cooper, H. (2007) *History 3–11: A Guide for Teachers.* London: Fulton. A clear introduction and guide to teaching primary history, which makes links with the National Strategies and Frameworks.

Davies, G. (1999) 'Should world religions be taught to primary school children in predominantly white, traditionally Christian areas? A survey of headteacher attitudes in West Wales; *Journal of Beliefs and Values*, vol. 20, no. I. A consideration of how schools with very little contact with faiths other than Christianity approach the teaching of world religions.

DfES (2003) *Every Child Matters.* London: DfES. A document which sets out the government's aims of

Geographer, Oct 2001. An article exploring what children

ligions. Oxford: Heinemann. Contributions from authors ow these might be approached in the classroom. Advice otyping and make world religions meaningful for children. geographies', *Primary Geographer*, October. Morgan's content of geography textbooks is enlightening. Early uperiority of the 'British race'. Fortunately most textbooks ticultural society.

arned: meeting beliefs, values and community through efs and Values, vol. 21, no. 2. Ota uses interviews with explore how children make sense of their experiences.

h: the Irresistible Rise of Multi-racial Britain. London:

[handwritten note: Childrens attitudes toward place — teacher role in planning lessons from classroom]

Primary History. A journal of the Historical Association with guidance, advice and ideas for teachers.

Primary Geographer. A journal of the Geographical Association with guidance, advice and ideas for teachers.

Scoffham, S. (ed) (2004) *Primary Geography Handbook*. London: Geographical Association. A comprehensive guide to primary geography teaching, full of detailed, practical ideas.

Wambu, O. (1999*) Empire Windrush: Fifty Years of Writing about Black Britain*. London: Phoenix Press. Both of these books provide invaluable information about the arrival of immigrants from Jamaica in the 1960s.They also include first-hand accounts of many of the people who travelled across on the ship *SS Windrush*.

Useful websites

www.everychildmatters.gov.uk
   Website for the Every Child Matters documentation.

www.geography.org.uk
   Website of the Geographical Association.

www.geography.org.uk/eyprimary/primaryhandbook/
   Web-based resources for the Primary Geography Handbook.

www.history.org.uk
   Website of the Historical Association.

www.tda.gov.uk/teachers/professionalstandards
   Website with documentation on the Professional Standards for Teachers.

Buddhism

http://theravada.net
www.buddhanet.net/monkey1.htm
www.buddhanet.net/mag_kids.htm

Christianity

www.anglicansonline.org

Hinduism

www.hindu.org
www.hindunet.org/home.shtml

Islam

www.islamworlduk.com
www.ummah.org.uk/sitemap

Judaism

www.shamash.org
www.torahtots.com
www.virtual.co.il

Sikhism

www.oneworld.org.uk
www.sikhnet.com

Other

http://humanism.org.uk
www.livingvalues.net/
vecuk.org.uk/

2
Knowledge and understanding: key concepts, skills and content

By the end of this chapter you will have:

- developed your understanding of the content, concepts and skills that underpin the humanities;
- developed your understanding of the legal requirements for teaching in each subject, as set out in the National Curriculum and in the Agreed Syllabuses for RE;
- begun to build up your understanding of the range of work that is appropriate for each subject;
- begun to develop your awareness of the variety of non-statutory guidance and frameworks which relate to teaching in the humanities.

Professional Standards for QTS

Q14: Have a secure knowledge and understanding of their subjects/curriculum areas and related pedagogy to enable them to teach effectively across the age and ability range for which they are trained.

Q15: Know and understand the relevant statutory and non-statutory curricula and frameworks, ...for their subjects/curriculum areas, ...applicable to the age and ability range for which they are trained.

Note: Standard Q15 is addressed in more detail in further chapters.

Introduction

A thorough knowledge and understanding of the curriculum for each humanities subject is clearly essential in preparing to teach. What is important is to remember that, in the humanities, the 'process' of learning is as important as the factual information that is learned (Bruner, 1977; Blyth et al, 1976). There are a number of concepts and skills which make up a particular process of learning in the humanities. These help to form all humanities subjects into a cognate subject area. Because the humanities all focus, in one way or another, upon the human condition, common approaches underpin each of the disciplines. Common key ideas or concepts tend to arise when studying people in the past, in different places and with different beliefs because of these broadly common approaches to the humanities. These are often enquiry-based approaches which use skills of research and questioning. They involve data collection and analysis, and they require skills in presenting and communicating the results of the enquiries in a variety of ways, which may involve the use of mathematics and ICT.

Concepts

Hilda Taba (1962) identified a set of concepts which she found to be common to all the humanities disciplines. Taba argued that children needed a set of key ideas around which they could build new learning. She referred to them as 'Key Concepts' in her research, which was carried out in the USA. These key concepts have continued to be used as the basis for organising the curricula of the humanities subjects, within a number of Schools Council humanities projects and currently in the National Curriculum for each subject.

Among the 'Key Concepts' identified by Taba are:

- similarity and difference;
- continuity and change;
- cause and effect;
- conflict and consensus.

As you can see, each of these is a very abstract idea. However, further thought will reveal how each one relates particularly to human activity of one kind or another. For example, things that are similar or different easily relate to people, places and human experience, as do continuity and change – what has stayed the same and what has changed. Each of these questions might sensibly be asked of history, geography, citizenship or RE. All the great dilemmas in human affairs have involved causation, conflict and, very often, eventual consensus. Each humanities discipline might equally well determine a curriculum based on these overarching ideas.

The concepts themselves are seen by Taba, and many who have followed her thinking, as 'organisational' or 'methodological' concepts. Nicol and Dean (1977) describe the same concepts in linguistic terms as 'syntactic'. In other words they are ideas which can organise and direct thinking and enquiry into specific incidents or events. For example, when studying the outbreak of the Second World War, thinking is usually guided by a consideration of the reasons for the outbreak of war, the conflict that ensued and the eventual consensus that was achieved in order for normal life to be resumed. The basic underlying concept for this study, therefore, would be cause and effect.

In addition to these organisational or methodological concepts, there are the 'substantive' concepts, those which tell us what the content of a study is, such as 'revolution', 'conquest', 'communication' or 'transport'. These are equally important in planning, since children's thinking, conceptual development and acquisition of skills must take place within a meaningful, subject-related set of content or knowledge.

REFLECTIVE TASK

Think about the broad key concepts listed above, and consider how they might be used in teaching geography, history, RE and citizenship.

Skills

Bruner (1960) developed the early work of Piaget and began to define general 'process skills', that is, those skills which are needed for the process of enquiry. Gagné (1985) created a hierarchy of fundamental intellectual, or thinking skills which involved:

- discriminating;
- categorising;
- forming concrete concepts;
- using rules to make inferences and formulate hypotheses;
- problem solving.

Each of these broad intellectual skills encompasses other sets of skills. For example, 'discriminating' involves the use of observational skills, noting similarities and differences, and recognising change and continuity. Communication, number, ICT and social skills are also vitally important in teaching and learning in the humanities and will be discussed in greater detail in subsequent chapters.

Considerable research has identified common key skills in the humanities (see, for example, the research reported in Cooper, 2006, 2007, Hoodless, 2008, McCreery, Palmer and Voiels, 2008).

However, the above intellectual skills constitute the process by which we study in the humanities and are often referred to in the literature about teaching each subject as 'process skills'. There are accepted methods and modes of enquiry, for example in history and archaeology, which contribute to the credibility and reliability of research undertaken in that area. In other words, the method of working is as important to the discipline as are the findings of the research.

The key concepts and skills which underpin all work on the humanities in schools, therefore, constitute the 'process' whereby the subjects are studied and understood. They are a fundamental part of each curriculum area, since they are seen as a necessary part of the subject knowledge related to that area. For example, in the history curriculum, study units 1–5 all focus upon these skills and concepts at Key Stages 1, 2 and 3.

Content

While the skills and concepts are fundamental, factual content is an equally important element of work in the humanities. The content of these subjects covers the whole range of human experience, both past and recent on a global scale. While they can all contribute to a topic-based thematic approach, each subject has its own specific type of content, and this is where the subjects begin to diverge. However, much closer links may be made between them following the *Independent Review of the Primary Curriculum* led by Sir Jim Rose (DCSF, 2009).

Knowledge, skills and concepts in geography

In geography, the breadth of study in Key Stage 1 focuses on:

- the locality of the school;
- a locality either in the United Kingdom or overseas that has physical and/or human features that contrast with those in the locality of the school.

Within these studies of localities, children should study places at local scale and carry out fieldwork investigations outside the classroom.

At Key Stage 2 geography studies focus on:

- a locality within the United Kingdom;
- a locality within a country that is less economically developed;
- water and its effects on landscapes and people (rivers or coasts);
- how settlements differ and change and an issue arising from the changes, e.g. building new houses or a

leisure complex;
- environmental issues caused by a change in the environment and attempts to manage the environment sustainably.

Within these studies of localities and themes, children should study places at a range of scales, including local, regional and national, and a range of places and environments in different parts of the world, including the UK and the European Union. They should also carry out fieldwork investigations outside the classroom.

Thus geography contains many concepts including:

Place KS 1 & 2	Patterns KS 1 & 2	Processes KS 1 & 2	Conflict KS 2	Relationships KS 1 & 2
Sustainable Development KS 1 & 2	Similarity and Difference KS 1 & 2	Inequality KS 2	Change KS 1 & 2	Interdependence KS 1 & 2
Attitudes & Values KS 1 & 2	Scale KS 1 & 2	Land use KS 2	Location KS 1 & 2	Environment KS 1 & 2

PRACTICAL TASK PRACTICAL TASK PRACTICAL TASK PRACTICAL TASK PRACTICAL TASK

'Odd one out' is a useful thinking skills activity to help develop one's understanding of terms. Which of the following geographical concepts can you make links between, and which is the odd one out?

Example

Processes   Change   Development   Conflict

- Processes – procedures that change something
- Change – alteration from previous state
- Development – a change leading to improvement
- Conflict – difference of opinions, opposing views

The first three are to do *with* changes, but conflicts can arise *from* changes.

Now it's your turn:
- Interdependence   Change   Sustainable   Processes
- Inequality   Conflict   Attitudes and values   Interdependence
- Scale   Patterns   Location   Land use   Environment

Geographical skills

The humanities skills outlined above are essential to be an effective geography teacher. However, a unique skill needed to teach geography is that of spatial awareness and an ability to help children develop their spatial abilities. Studying geography helps to develop a wide range of skills. Maps, globes and atlases are vital tools for a geographer and develop a child's ability to use maps and to draw images (graphicacy), two specific geographical skills.

Geographers are inquisitive and like to ask questions and to carry out enquiries to find answers. Collecting primary data (fieldwork), recording the data (first-hand and secondary), analysing data to discover patterns and drawing justified conclusions are important skills developed within the subject.

Skills must be developed in order to interpret secondary data from a range of resources including aerial photographs and satellite images or written sources. Geography helps to develop decision-making skills and empathy when considering different viewpoints.

PRACTICAL TASK PRACTICAL TASK PRACTICAL TASK PRACTICAL TASK PRACTICAL TASK

A geographical skills checklist

Have a go at auditing your own skills – can you do the following?

Type of Skill	Example	Evidence? I can do?
Basic Skills	• *Annotating diagrams/maps/graphs/sketches* • *Drawing field sketches* • *Use and interpret photographs including aerial/satellite*	
Cartographic Skills	• *Using atlas maps to describe patterns* • *Interpreting sketch maps* • *Interpreting Ordnance Survey maps 1:25 000 and 1:50 000 by using grid references, distances, direction, cross sections, slopes, contour patterns, land use, symbols*	
Graphical Skills	• *Draw line, bar, pie, scatter graphs* • *Draw a variety of maps including choropleth, isoline, and proportional symbols* • *Interpret a variety of graphs and maps, e.g. underground tube/bus routes*	
Enquiry Skills	• *Creating hypotheses to investigate* • *Identifying and collecting primary (first-hand) and secondary evidence* • *Recording and processing data into maps/diagrams/ graphs, etc.* • *Describing and analysing data finding patterns* • *Justifying conclusions* • *Awareness of limitations of methods*	
ICT Skills	• *Using photographs and satellite images* • *Using databases, e.g. census* • *Searching for up-to-date case studies via the internet* • *Extracting information from TV and video* • *Word processing, presenting information* • *Using spreadsheets to manipulate data* • *Collecting data, e.g. recording the weather*	

Adapted from AQA GCSE syllabus checklist of skills

REFLECTIVE TASK

Choose one of the key stages above and consider opportunities for cross-curricular studies in history and geography – for example, how the local settlement has changed in shape and size (geography) and the causes of change (history). Reflect on the potential of the two subjects for linked, creative thematic work.

Knowledge, skills and concepts in history

For history, the National Curriculum outlines specified areas of historical content that must be taught in Key Stages 1 and 2, under the heading 'Breadth of Study'.

At Key Stage 1 children learn about:

- changes in their own lives and the way of life of their family or others around them;
- the way of life of people in the more distant past who lived in the local area or elsewhere in Britain;
- the lives of significant men, women and children drawn from the history of Britain and the wider world;
- past events from the history of Britain and the wider world.

At Key Stage 2 children learn about:

- a local history study;
- Romans, Anglo-Saxons and Vikings in Britain;
- Britain and the wider world in Tudor times;
- Victorian Britain or Britain since 1930;
- a European history study: Ancient Greece;
- a world history study: Ancient Egypt, Ancient Sumer, the Assyrian Empire, the Indus Valley, the Maya, Benin or the Aztecs.

Many of these topics could easily relate to geographical study. With the current relaxation of National Curriculum requirements, therefore, it may be possible to find suitable areas of content that overlap, and thus to develop cross-curricular or linked units of work which use common processes of learning. It is mainly through the process skills and concepts that the common features of the humanities can be addressed and maintained. (See Chapter 6 for further information on cross-curricular work.)

Skills in history

Historical skills appear quite simple and straightforward. However, practice has shown that children do not automatically make use of them when asked to research a given topic or theme. They will often simply resort to copying from a book or printing off swathes of information from the internet. This is not what we mean by using historical skills.

The part of the research that the children are doing here (see Figure 2.1) is simply retrieving information. A key skill that they must acquire, of course, is that of being able to question a source of information to find out historical information from it. This is actually quite a difficult skill, and it needs planning for, demonstrating and extending very carefully. Just as we would not expect children to do complex mathematical calculations without any prior learning in maths, we cannot expect them to make use of difficult skills without teaching them first. For example, skills in chronology are quite complex and need to be developed progressively in much the same way as work in numeracy is taught. There is a vast range of source material to support teaching these skills in a real life context, such as through the use of street directories and the census data (see Figure 2.1). The classroom story on the following pages and the associated practical task give more detail on one way of developing children's enquiry skills.

Alsager – A census from 1871

1. I can tell the Holland family were wealthy because they had three servants.

2. The Holland family lived in Prospect Cottages, in the family it consisted of:...
   James Holland = Head = aged 25
   Mary Holland = Wife – aged 25
   James Holland = Son – aged 5 months

3. Jobs that people had were...

   maids,
   collier agents,
   engine fitters,
   Gardener,
   Carter,
   brick setter

Figure 2.1 Alsager – A census from 1871

CLASSROOM STORY
Developing skills in history

Marcia had come to live in England after growing up in Mexico. She had recently trained to teach and now had a chance to teach some history about her native country, because her new school included the Aztecs as part of their history curriculum. Unfortunately, the school had not been able to resource the topic well and only had a few books in the school library.

Marcia was very excited at the prospect of using all her knowledge about Mexico to get the children involved in the topic. She had an excellent, large map of the world, which she could use to talk about the journeys of the Spanish explorers and invaders who settled in Mexico, and who defeated the Aztec Empire. From her own education, she had a great deal of factual knowledge about life in Mexico before and after the Spanish Conquest, plenty for teaching a Year 4 class about the Aztecs. She also had many pictures and photographs of Mexico, which she knew would be invaluable for starting off the topic and engaging the children's interest.

However, Marcia knew that if she only told the children about her knowledge, she would not be meeting the requirements of the National Curriculum, or of the school. She knew that, somehow, she must engage the children in practical activities and provide sources for them to use in order to develop their historical skills of enquiry, research and questioning as the topic progressed. Giving herself plenty of time to gather resources (she was aware that she would need several months!), Marcia began to make enquiries to find where she might borrow or purchase sources about the Aztecs. She soon found that there is an 'Aztec Gallery' within the British Museum in London, so she contacted the education officer there and was amazed at how much the museum could offer. She could take the class on a visit, and the museum also provided an excellent pack of resources and teacher's notes containing ideas for classroom activities.

Marcia then turned to the publishers' catalogues in the school and found that there were numerous resource and picture packs, as well as a large number of books about the subject. Some companies produced large pictures, posters and charts about the Aztecs. Marcia began to order some of these, and to search in local libraries for others. She found that the Historical Association in London also produced some useful publications about the Aztecs, particularly a pamphlet full of teaching ideas by Angela Horton (1995).

She then realised that many resources would be available on the internet, and was not disappointed when she looked! There was a huge amount of material there, but she realised that some of it was not well written and that some was not suitable for the age group in her class. Marcia set aside some time to look through what was on the internet and to make a selection of what she might want the class to use. She had a word with the ICT coordinator in her school, who offered to put the materials she chose onto the school's intranet, so that the children would only have access to the selected materials.

Once she had gathered all these materials together, Marcia knew that this was really only the beginning. She needed to ensure that the children made the best use of them. Clearly, she wanted the children to make first-hand use of the materials, but she was aware that these were quite young children, and that some of them would struggle with using enquiry skills on their own. From horror stories heard at college, she knew that sometimes, when left to their own devices with history books, children would resort to copying out large chunks of text, because they did not have any historical skills to put into practice. She remembered carrying out small hands-on activities on her teacher training course, and decided to try to implement some of these approaches.

First, she knew that she must model ways of working and ways of carrying out source questioning and analysis to get the children started. So she chose some simple sources for a whole-class lesson, which included pictures of Aztec domestic life. She planned a lesson where she could demonstrate to the whole class how to question these pictures and how to summarise the information gained from them. Her next lesson would provide similar sources which the class were to use on their own while working in pairs. She then planned to divide the class into small groups, each with a different type of source material, and to give them time to work with the sources and then feed back their findings in a plenary at the end of the lesson. Marcia hoped that this approach would provide the children with enough initial support to develop some good historical enquiry skills of their own.

PRACTICAL TASK PRACTICAL TASK PRACTICAL TASK PRACTICAL TASK PRACTICAL TASK

Working with a group of colleagues, choose a history study unit about which members of the group have very little factual knowledge, such as the Aztecs, Maya, Indus Valley or Benin. Divide up the topic into useful teaching components, such as domestic life, children's lives, dress, etc., and allocate one subject for each person to research. Within a set amount of time, carry out enquires as Marcia did, and identify useful places and publishers for resourcing this topic. Choose one source to work with and make notes on how you would demonstrate to children how to question this source in order to extract historical information. Set a date for a second meeting, where you can share the resources you have found and discuss ways of introducing and modelling the questioning of your sources. This will be a way of beginning a useful collection of resource materials for teaching history.

Concepts in history

Concepts in history include time and chronology, change and continuity, cause and effect. Time is a specifically historical notion, but it is a notoriously difficult notion for children to acquire. Research has shown that the most appropriate way of introducing the concept of time to young children is to make it relevant to their own lives and experiences, and to make it as visual as possible through the use of timelines, charts, models and pictures. It is only through a concrete representation that children can begin to understand what is meant by time and chronology. These and other concepts can, however, be very effectively used as 'organisers' in planning. If a concept underpins your thinking at the planning stage then you are more likely to succeed in extending children's understanding of it. The concept should be at the forefront of your thinking when you plan activities for the children, learning objectives and assessments. The following practical task gives an indication of how to put this approach into practice.

PRACTICAL TASK PRACTICAL TASK PRACTICAL TASK PRACTICAL TASK PRACTICAL TASK

Planning with concepts in mind

Working with one other trainee, choose a well-known history unit of work. Using the concept of 'change' draw up a simple outline plan for a lesson, in which you focus closely on developing children's understanding of the concept. Devise activities and assessments based on and using the concept. Keep this in your file as an example of planning using concepts as organisers.

Knowledge, concepts, skills and attitudes in RE

Knowledge

The content for RE is largely determined by whichever syllabus the school is using, either local authority or diocesan, and these will differ across the country. It is usually recognised that there are six major world religions represented in this country: Buddhism, Christianity, Hinduism, Islam, Judaism and Sikhism, and these form the basis of many local authority syllabuses and of the QCA model syllabuses. At Key Stages 1 and 2, the emphasis is on familiarising children with the main features of a religious tradition, for example: main teachings, places of worship, festivals, religious leaders, home life, etc. These will vary according to each tradition and across different syllabuses. However, the main aims remain similar and relate to the concepts, skills and attitudes that it is hoped children might develop through a study of world religions.

Teachers are often concerned about their own subject knowledge in RE. They worry that they may misrepresent traditions or communicate stereotypical images. There are some steps that can be taken to address these concerns. Firstly it is important to recognise that study of each of the major world religions involves a vast wealth of historical and contemporary understanding. There is no way in which all primary teachers can become experts in every religious tradition. We have to be realistic and recognise that such knowledge can only grow with time and experience. Some basic understanding of the tradition we plan to teach would obviously be required. After this, it is possible to research thoroughly those aspects of the tradition which are a focus for teaching. For example, if the unit of work is on Jewish beliefs and practice, some detailed knowledge of Shabbat (Sabbath) would be appropriate.

To avoid misrepresentation or stereotyping a useful strategy is to establish contact with members of that faith tradition. Another idea is to focus on one group within that tradition, e.g. Roman Catholicism within Christianity. An even closer focus is to introduce the children to an imaginary family within a tradition and talk about their beliefs and experiences. Adopting certain phrases can also help, e.g. *'many* Jews celebrate Shabbat in this way' or 'for *some* Roman Catholics, attendance at Mass is the highlight of their week'.

Concepts in RE

These are often related to the specific religious tradition that is being studied; for example, in Christianity the concept of 'salvation' might be explored, or in Hinduism the concept of 'reincarnation'. Such concepts are abstract and teachers need to find ways of presenting them to children in an accessible way, using examples and illustrations from modern living or from children's literature. An example of this would be using the children's book *Dogger* by Shirley Hughes (1993) to explore the notion of 'sacrifice'. In this story a sister gives up her beautiful new teddy to retrieve her brother's beloved toy, Dogger. Another example would be exploring the notion of 'forgiveness' in preparation for further work on 'reconciliation' in Christianity.

Attitudes in RE

Central to the aims of RE is a concern to develop positive attitudes to people who hold beliefs different to our own. This means that any RE work we do should be designed to help children appreciate and respect other people's beliefs and traditions. The accumulation of knowledge alone is not sufficient to develop these attitudes – we can be knowledgeable about something but that might not make us respect it. Children should not go away from an RE lesson thinking that some people are stupid or odd because of the things they do or believe. Examples of positive attitudes in RE will relate not only to the religious traditions but to people in general, to themselves and to the world around them.

Skills in RE

Alongside those skills which are common to all the humanities, there are specific skills in RE which should be part of children's learning and experience (see McCreery, Palmer and Voiels, 2008). They need to be able to handle religious material, process it and come to conclusions about it. Skills in RE include those of asking and responding to questions of identity and experience, meaning and purpose, and values and commitments (QCA, 2000).

CLASSROOM STORY

Julie's Year 2 class were following the topic of 'Myself' as a cross-curricular theme. She wanted to include some RE work and chose the notion of identity, which she called 'Who Am I?' for the children. As part of their first lesson, Julie read the story *Nothing* by Mick Inkpen (1996). The story tells of a creature who has no sense of who he is or where he belongs. He embarks on a personal quest to find out who he is and gradually, through his encounters with others and self-reflection, he arrives home. The children spent some time discussing aspects of the story: How must it feel to not know who you are or where you belong? How does Nothing build a picture of who he is? How does it feel to be lonely?

The children reflected on these questions for themselves – how do I know who I am, where I belong, etc. They talked about what made them 'them', picking up on elements such as their names, their features and their personalities.

The work culminated in the production of booklets using words and pictures to describe 'Who Am I?' and Julie felt that the work had enabled the children to reflect on their own sense of identity and recognise that each of them had their own particular life story and context. She felt that this served to prepare them for future RE work as further up the school, the children would be studying the lives of Christian and Jewish children. The work on identity would help the children to explore 'religious identity' and appreciate the different life contexts and stories of children from other traditions.

Auditing your subject knowledge

As part of specialist subject training, it is often the case that trainees are required to audit their subject knowledge, in other words to review and list how and what subject knowledge they have acquired before and during their course. Clearly, as we have seen above, subject knowledge, for example in history, does not simply refer to the content areas specified in the National Curriculum. Knowledge includes the process skills and concepts by which children acquire knowledge of the content in history. When auditing your knowledge, therefore, you will need to consider what aspects of the history study units you know something about, such as the Tudors or Victorians; however, you will also need to review your knowledge and understanding of time and chronology. How do children acquire concepts like these, and where have you gained your knowledge of this? You therefore need to audit each aspect of the subjects as outlined above. An extract from an audit used by history trainees is included in Table 2.1.

History subject knowledge	Where knowledge gained	Date
Tudor Britain	GCSE course	1999
Significant men, women and children	Year 1 placement in a Key Stage 1 class	2002
Children's awareness of chronology	Year 1 undergraduate course	2002

Table 2.1 Extract from a history audit

Draw up an outline for an audit of your subject knowledge in history based on the example Table 2.1 and complete it to the present date.

Auditing knowledge in RE

You may be concerned that your knowledge of world religions is limited to one or two traditions. This is a valuable starting place and you can begin by jotting down some of the key features you know about those traditions. You may remember some things from school, television and newspapers, for example, and from this you can identify which traditions you are less familiar with and therefore need to study further. Note here that many teachers make the mistake of relying on their own primary school knowledge – particularly of Christianity – for their teaching. This should be avoided and the same kind of research needs to be done even if you *think* you are confident in any area.

There are several ways to start adding to your subject knowledge in RE:

- textbooks on individual religious traditions;
- teachers' handbooks for RE;
- television programmes – not just those focusing on religion, but any programme where people's religious background is identified;
- the internet – there are lots of sites about religion. The most efficient way to locate these is through educational websites, as they tend to be the most reliable sources;
- meeting people from other backgrounds – don't be afraid to ask someone politely about their tradition as many people are delighted to talk about this aspect of their life.

Citizenship

The non-statutory content of the curriculum for citizenship at Key Stage 1 focuses, in much the same way as the history curriculum, on children learning about themselves and their own communities. There is a focus on social and emotional development and the development of affective skills, such as being aware of the feelings and needs of others. There is an emphasis on the social skills involved in learning to live and work as part of their own small community in school. At Key Stage 2, children continue to focus on their own experiences as growing individuals and on themselves as members of a community. They begin to learn more about the wider world and how to participate in wider communities, making informed decisions and taking responsibility for their own actions and learning. In both Key Stages, health and safety are important concerns. Citizenship and Personal, Social and Health Education (PSHE) will be discussed in more detail in Chapter 12.

Non-statutory guidance

There is a considerable amount of non-statutory guidance to give teachers a clearer idea and provide exemplary material for their humanities teaching. The notes that accompany the National Curriculum for Geography, History and Citizenship give guidance on how to interpret the sections on 'Knowledge, skills and understanding'. The notes also indicate suitable cross-curricular links that could be made with other subjects. The QCA Schemes of Work in Geography, History, Religious Education and Citizenship have been of great assistance to primary teachers, providing ideas, examples of planning, resources and references. Their aim was to encourage schools not to lose sight of the importance of a balanced curriculum, and to support them in delivering this. However, to make best use of these schemes, you will need to take account of your teaching context and ensure that your planning meets your children's needs. This may entail revision of the outlines provided in the schemes, the addition of different activities and the omission of others which you feel inappropriate. In other words, you will need to reshape the units to suit your own school and locality.

Other useful non-statutory guidance is available on the internet, for example, in the form of the *'Innovating'* areas of the QCA website (www.qca.org.uk). The website is very clearly set out. Key aspects of planning are explained under the heading 'improving curriculum planning' and case studies from specific localities illustrate the planning process and how this is based on the Schemes of Work. Under the heading 'contributing to the wider curriculum', there is guidance on making links between curriculum areas, including ICT, literacy and creativity. The website National Curriculum in Action (www.ncaction.org.uk/) provides further illustrative examples taken from on-going work in schools. Teachernet (www.teachernet.gov.uk) and Teachers' TV (www.teachers.tv) provide summaries of current developments and ideas for planning, teaching and curriculum development. Both the BBC (bbc.co.uk/schools) and Channel 4 (www.channel4learning.net/) produce schools broadcasts to support the humanities curriculum.

The *Primary Framework for Literacy and Mathematics* (DfES, 2006) is designed to ensure that the principles of *Every Child Matters* and *Excellence and Enjoyment* are put into practice across the curriculum in schools. The learning of literacy and mathematics as part of the whole learning experience, and not in isolation from the rest of the curriculum, is a principle that underlies the renewed framework. Examples of the many, varied links that can be made between the framework and the humanities subjects are indicated and discussed in detail in Chapter 9.

A SUMMARY OF **KEY POINTS**

> **Skills and concepts form an important part of the process of studying and teaching each humanities subject.**

> **These skills and concepts are often referred to as 'process skills and concepts'.**

> **They are thought to be common to all humanities subjects.**

> **There are two types of concept: methodological and substantive.**

> **Factual content differs more than the skills and concepts of each subject, but there are still many common areas of study.**

> **When carrying out audits of your subject knowledge in humanities subjects, you will need to consider the process skills and concepts as well as the factual content that you need to know.**

MOVING *ON* > > > **> > >** MOVING *ON* > > > **> > >** MOVING *ON*

Standard C14, Standard C15

Review your teaching of geography, history, RE and citizenship and consider areas which might be appropriate for cross-curricular work. For example, a study of a society distant in both place and time, which is different from society in Britain and where different major religions are practised, such as in India or Pakistan, might be a valuable opportunity to link work across the humanities.

FURTHER READING FURTHER READING **FURTHER READING** FURTHER READING

Bastide, D. (1999) *Co-ordinating Religious Education across the Primary School*. London: Falmer Press. A detailed consideration of the role of the RE co-ordinator, covering areas such as the legal framework and developing RE across the primary age phase.

Blaylock, L. and Johnson, C. (1997) *A Teacher's Handbook of Religious Education*. Derby: CEM. A detailed guide to many aspects of RE teaching. It outlines the legal framework, offers teaching approaches and considers issues arising from approaching world faiths in the classroom.

Claire, H. (2004) *Teaching Citizenship in Primary Schools*. Exeter: Learning Matters.

Cooper, H. (2004) *Geography 3–11: A Guide for Teachers*. London: Fulton.

Cooper, H. (2007) *History 3–11: A Guide for Teachers*. London: Fulton.

Hoodless, P. (2008) *Teaching History in Primary Schools*. Exeter: Learning Matters.

McCreery, E., Palmer, S., and Voiels, V. (2008) *Teaching Religious Education*. Exeter: Learning Matters.

Rowe, D. (2001) *Introducing Citizenship: A Practical Handbook for Primary Schools*. London: A. & C. Black.

Scoffham, S. (2004) *Primary Geography Handbook*. Sheffield: Geographical Association.

The above books are all useful introductions to teaching the humanities subjects.

Owen, D. and Ryan, A. (2001) *Teaching Geography 3–11: The Essential Guide*. London: Continuum. On pages 15–17 of this book you will find an example of a subject knowledge audit, which may be useful if you want to create your own audit.

QCA (2000) *Religious Education. Non-statutory Guidance for RE*. London: QCA.

QCA (2000) *Schemes of Work for Geography, History and Religious Education at Key Stages 1 and 2*, London: QCA.

Non-statutory guidance for the humanities subjects. Guidance for citizenship can be found in the back of *The National Curriculum: Handbook for Primary Teachers* (DfES/QCA, 1999) pages 136–141.

Walford, R. (2001) *Geography in British Schools, 1850–2000: Making a World of Difference*. London: Woburn Press. Especially relevant is chapter 1.

Useful websites

www.channel4learning.net/
www.ncaction.org.uk/
www.teachernet.gov.uk
www.teachers.tv

All the above are useful websites with examples of children's work, resources, lessons and planning in the humanities.

3
Humanities in the Early Years Foundation Stage

By the end of this chapter you will have:

- recognised the value of the humanities in very young children's education;
- established some of the main links between the Early Years Foundation Stage (EYFS) curriculum and the humanities subjects;
- developed your skills in planning, teaching and evaluating learning in relation to the humanities subjects in the EYFS.

Professional Standards for QTS

This chapter on the Early Years Foundation Stage will touch upon most of the Professional Standards for Teachers. However, those that it will consider in more depth are:

Q10: Have a knowledge and understanding of a range of teaching and learning strategies and know how to use and adapt them, including how to personalise learning and provide opportunities for all learners to achieve their potential.

Q12: Know a range of approaches to assessment, including the importance of formative assessment.

Q15: Know and understand the relevant statutory and non-statutory curricula and frameworks, including those provided through the National Strategies, for all their subjects/curriculum areas, and other relevant initiatives applicable to the age and ability range for which they are trained.

Q18: Understand how children develop and that the progress and well-being of learners are affected by a range of developmental, social, religious, ethnic, cultural and linguistic differences.

Introduction: the value of the humanities for children's learning

For very young children, the humanities subjects of geography, history, RE and citizenship can provide opportunities for them to explore a range of human experiences. They offer principles, language and activities which can help children make sense of the world around them. Through topics which make use of these subjects very young children can begin to understand their own place in the world, develop their sense of identity and begin to consider their relationship to other people and the natural world.

At first glance, however, the humanities subjects may not seem like appropriate subjects for very young children to study; after all, they include some complex language and skills, and very abstract concepts. Geography is wide-ranging, history raises issues that are often abstract and in the past, while RE and citizenship also include discussion of beliefs and lifestyle which many people might consider controversial.

The key to approaching these subjects with young children is to consider where the child is now, in terms of their intellectual, social and emotional development, since all of these are highly influential in learning in the humanities. A guiding principle is to begin with the experiences of the child. We need to ask ourselves what aspects of the subjects they are likely to have encountered and what our role is in helping them to move on from this starting point.

For example, a child may have encountered geography through:

- local travel, e.g. to school, to shops, and further afield, e.g. on holidays and visits;
- experiencing the weather;
- seeing the sky at night;
- experiencing their local environment;
- experiencing a different environment, such as the seaside.

They may have encountered history through:

- family photographs;
- seeing old objects, pictures and books around the house;
- family stories;
- talking to older relatives;
- thinking about past events;
- seeing old buildings.

They may have encountered religion through:

- celebrating festivals;
- attending family celebrations;
- hearing religious stories;
- attending a place of worship.

Our responsibility as teachers is to offer children the opportunity to share these experiences and begin to identify patterns and similarities between different people's experiences.

REFLECTIVE TASK

How do we get to know what experiences children have had so that we can identify a starting point for learning? Consider the following questions in relation to a group of children that you have worked with in school:

- What did you learn about their ethnic, religious, cultural, linguistic, geographical, historical backgrounds?
- How did you gather this information?
- How much did you learn from the children's parents?
- How much did you learn from other adults?
- How much did you learn from the children?
- What use did you make of this information in your planning?
- What other information might you have found out?

List ways in which you might find out more about children's backgrounds in future. Think about the opportunities you could create in order to find out more, for example, meetings with parents and carers and different ways of communicating with parents and carers, such as a 'home diary' for notes to be made at home and then returned to school with the child's story book.

The humanities and the EYFS curriculum

The Early Years Foundation Stage (DCSF, 2008) brought together three main documents: *The Curriculum Guidance for the Foundation Stage* (DfEE/QCA, 2000), *Birth to Three Matters* (DfES/MMU, 2002) and the *National Standards for Under 8s' Daycare and Childminding* (DfES, 2003) into one coherent and flexible approach to care and learning from birth to five. The aim of the EYFS is to enable every child to achieve the government's five outcomes for children: being healthy, staying safe, enjoying and achieving, making a positive contribution and economic well-being.

Four guiding principles underpin the EYFS, all of which are significant in learning related to the humanities:

* Unique child – every child is a unique and competent learner from birth.
* Positive relationships – children learn to be strong and independent from the base of a loving and secure relationship with parents and/or key worker.
* Enabling environment – the environment plays a key role in supporting and extending children's development and learning.
* Learning and development – children develop and learn at different rates and in different ways.

The curriculum for the EYFS is divided into six areas of learning. These are inter-connected and cannot be delivered in isolation. Moreover, the areas of learning must be presented within the context of planned and purposeful play opportunities that develop from the child's interests with the emphasis on child-initiated activities. The six areas of learning are:

* personal, social and emotional development;
* communication, language and literacy;
* problem solving, reasoning and numeracy;
* knowledge and understanding of the world;
* physical development;
* creative development.

(DCSF, 2008)

Aspects of the humanities subjects can be found in all of these areas, offering specific contexts in which children can develop their understanding and skills. However, some areas have explicit links with the humanities subjects. Some examples are set out in Table 3.1 on page 40.

Two areas of learning link directly to the humanities subjects and contain Early Learning Goals (ELGs) which overlap with the aims of the humanities subjects. The two are 'Knowledge and understanding of the world' and 'Personal, social and emotional development'.

Early Learning Goal	Area of learning	Humanities context
'Understand that people have different needs, views, cultures and beliefs, that need to be treated with respect.'	Personal, social and emotional development	RE Citizenship
'Use talk to organise, sequence and clarify thinking, ideas, feelings and events.'	Communication, language and literacy	History Citizenship
'Use everyday words to describe position.'	Problem solving, reasoning and numeracy	Geography
'Find out about past and present events in their own lives, and in those of their families and other people they know.'	Knowledge and understanding of the world	History
'Show awareness of space, of themselves and others.'	Physical development	Geography Citizenship
'Use their imagination in art and design, music, dance, imaginative and role play and stories.'	Creative development	RE

Table 3.1. Examples of links between the humanities and the Early Learning Goals

REFLECTIVE TASK

Consider these Early Learning Goals (ELGs) from the EYFS documentation. To which aspects of history, geography, RE and citizenship do you think they link?

Personal and social development

Self confidence and self esteem

Making relationships

Behaviour and self control

Sense of community

Knowledge and understanding of the world

Exploration and investigation

Time

Place

Cultures and beliefs

Providing geographical experiences as part of 'Knowledge and understanding of the world'

In the early years, children are forming values and attitudes towards the world they see around them, which will influence their motivation to learn about it. Martin and Owens (2004) argue that this is a crucial period in laying the foundations for children's future development. Understanding their place in the world is an important factor in the development of children's identity and sense of well-being and belonging.

While geography is incorporated into 'Knowledge and understanding of the world', experiences which touch on aspects of geography can be found throughout all six areas of learning. For example, space and distance can be explored through 'Physical development' or 'Creative development'. However, a sense of place is a specifically geographical understanding, which is embodied in the following ELGs, which state that children should:

- observe, find out about and identify features in the place they live and the natural world;
- find out about their environment, and talk about those features they like and dislike.

CLASSROOM STORY

Ben decided that he would like to encourage his pre-school nursery group to find out more about their environment, but he wanted the children to engage mostly in self-directed activities while doing so. He wanted the children to express their likes and dislikes about the different areas in the nursery setting, but he did not want to impose his own ideas on the activity.

He realised that the first step was to observe the children and note which areas they chose to play in. He noted children who always played in the same area and those who moved freely among them. In response to this, on some days, he removed the areas where some children always went, leaving them to choose a different one. Eventually, he managed to ensure that all the children had spent time in most of the different areas. After some days, he reinstated all the play areas to their original layout and the children spent one more day in this context.

At the end of the day during a short circle time, Ben asked some open-ended questions, such as: 'Which places in the nursery do you like to play best?', 'Do you like the sand?', 'Why do you like the outdoor toys?' In encouraging the children to express their likes and dislikes, Ben learned a lot about some weaknesses in provision and also found that the children had begun to explore and talk about their learning environment more often. In the following week, Ben took the opportunity to ask the children to choose which area in the nursery they would like their work to be placed or displayed in.

PRACTICAL TASK PRACTICAL TASK PRACTICAL TASK PRACTICAL TASK PRACTICAL TASK

Make a note of the ways in which you could engage the children's interest in the outside environment and motivate them to talk about it. For example, they could explore the grounds of the setting, or you could take them on a short walk to a nearby park, post office or play area.

Providing historical experiences as part of 'Knowledge and understanding of the world'

In the EYFS the key element of historical understanding is identified as a 'Sense of time' and this is one aspect of 'Knowledge and understanding of the world'. In this section you will explore ways of developing children's sense of time within the context and principles of the EYFS document, which has been statutory since September 2008 (DCSF, 2008). There are many activities which use children's own experiences as a starting point, such as daily and weekly routines and how these relate to the passing of time.

Every child learns rapidly from birth. From their home visits and children's visits to the setting, the practitioner will be aware that children already have a growing awareness of a sense of time and the past through their experiences at home with their families or carers. They gradually become aware of daily routines, mealtimes, bedtimes, daytime and night time and can recognise these in picture books and stories. They might have extended this understanding through spending time with grandparents and other family members, and through religious and cultural activities (Thornton & Brunton, 2004). In addition, through the medium of stories, film and television, young children are constantly developing an awareness of time past. Wood (1995) suggests that young children have a natural awareness of time through such experiences.

PRACTICAL TASK PRACTICAL TASK PRACTICAL TASK PRACTICAL TASK PRACTICAL TASK

Find an opportunity to engage with children in conversation in Foundation Stage settings. Try to explore their understanding of time in terms of the experiences they will have had at home, such as those mentioned above. You could also talk about birthdays or holidays to see how the child attempts to place these events in time.

Research has shown that young children become aware of time through their daily routines, or through experiences specific to themselves (Friedman, 1982). It has also been found that children between the age of four and six can begin to sequence events from their daily routines (Thornton and Vukelich, 1988). Children can learn to recall these experiences and routines through talking about them and looking at photographs of them. Their understanding can then be further developed through visual 'timelines' and through discussion about the passing of time in stories and picture books, from the later years of the Foundation Stage into Key Stage 1 (Hoodless 1997, 2002).

CLASSROOM STORY

Ann was interested in developing a sense of time with her group of 3/4 year-olds in her Foundation Stage setting. She knew that this was one of the ELGs of the EYFS and was interested to see what strategies would help children to achieve it. First, she worked out all the key events during the children's day at the setting. She then wrote down a list of the key vocabulary associated with these events.

On the days when she was trying out the strategy, she made a point of referring clearly to each new event in the day, such as 'snack time', and getting the children to repeat her words. She took photographs at each important point and made a collection of these on cards. The next day, in circle time, she talked about the daily routine and played a simple game to encourage children to recall what they did each day. She then set out her new picture cards and asked small groups of children in turn to put them in the right order.

Finally, she made a simple picture timeline on the wall with the photographs, with the name of each activity printed above it. She encouraged the children to talk about the pictures to their parents and carers at home time, and explain what happened at each point in the day.

REFLECTIVE TASK

Consider how these activities could be continued in the next year of the Foundation Stage or Key Stage 1. Make a note of the strategies you might use to carry on this teacher's work. For example, a Year 1 class made a timeline of toys and the teacher helped them to create a display of old and new toys on the wall:

Figure 3.1 Old and new toys

Here, the teacher had used the toys as artefacts as a way of prompting discussion about the past. An emphasis was given to the development of the vocabulary of time and children's ability to use this vocabulary.

PRACTICAL TASK PRACTICAL TASK PRACTICAL TASK PRACTICAL TASK PRACTICAL TASK

Make a list of all the words you know that are to do with time. Decide which ones are most important for children to learn to use in the Foundation Stage.

Providing experiences in RE as part of 'Knowledge and understanding of the world'

As discussed in Chapter 2, guidance for RE will usually be found in a local authority syllabus or, in the case of faith schools, in a syllabus agreed in line with the school's foundation. Further guidance can also be found in the QCA document *Religious Education, the non-statutory framework* (QCA, 2004). These documents recognise that schools are not required to provide RE for children below Key Stage 1. However, they do offer some suggestions of what aspects might be covered during the EYFS. The QCA guidance suggests that during this stage, children might:

- begin to explore the world of religion in terms of special people, books, times, places and objects;
- listen to and talk about stories;
- be introduced to religious words and use their senses in exploring religions and beliefs, practices and forms of expression;
- reflect on their own feelings and experiences;
- use their imagination and curiosity to develop their appreciation and wonder of the world in which they live.

(QCA, 2004, p 21)

Planning for the humanities in the EYFS classroom

Independent activity: 'home corner'

The 'home corner' in the early years classroom offers an ideal opportunity to reflect the various cultural and religious backgrounds of the children in the class, as well as the opportunity to introduce children to other people's homes. People's homes often contain features which are distinctive of particular traditions. Items need to be selected carefully as some objects can be considered precious and it could cause offence to members of communities if their artefacts are not treated with respect. We also need to be sensitive to the fact that where shrines are part of the home, we should not encourage children to use them for worship. It is best that the area that represents the shrine does not contain any specifically religious artefacts. Flowers and incense sticks might suffice.

A Buddhist home might contain:	Shrine with Buddha image, flowers, incense sticks Images of the Buddha Vegetarian food
A Christian home might contain:	Images of Jesus Receptacle for holy water Bible Rosary beads Prayer book Children's versions of Bible stories Palm Cross
A Hindu home might contain:	Shrine with images of deities, flowers, incense sticks Pictures of deities Vegetarian food Traditional Indian costume Bhagavad Gita
A Jewish home might contain:	Mezuzah on doorpost Jewish Bible Prayer book Candlesticks Kosher food Separate utensils for meat and milk Prayer shawl Cappel Phylacteries
A Muslim home might contain:	Qu'ran Prayer mat Topi Halal food Images of Makkah Head scarves Calligraphy containing words from the Qu'ran
A Sikh home might contain:	Turban Selected texts from Guru Granth Sahib Images of the Gurus

Table 3.2 Religious features in homes

CLASSROOM STORY

The home area as a Sukkah

The children at Rosebery Street children's centre had been introduced to Judaism. Although there were no Jewish children in the class, the school was very near to an area which had a large Jewish community. The teachers knew that the community was about to celebrate the festival of Sukkoth and thought it would be a good idea to share this festival with the children. They invited the local Rabbi in to talk about the festival. He told the children that in the Jewish tradition, many families construct a shelter called a Sukkah outside their home during the festival of Sukkoth. It reminds them of a time in the past when they had no fixed home, but travelled around making shelters to sleep in at night. The Rabbi showed the children pictures of these shelters and the children could see that they contained lots of fruit and vegetables as well as a table and chairs.

The children then had a discussion about how they could build their own Sukkah in the home area. The teachers bought reed mats from the local garden centre and these were used to construct the walls and roof. The children made fruit and vegetable pictures out of modelling clay and attached them to the walls. A table and chairs were moved in, as well as some picture books about Jewish children.

Using a reading and writing area for the humanities

There are many activities that link to the humanities which could be offered as either independent or adult-initiated tasks:

RE
Looking at books about children of different faiths
Designing invitations to celebrations
Creating menus to reflect religious eating patterns
Recounting a visit to a place of worship
Practising writing letters from other languages

Geography
Drawing and labelling maps
Describing places
Reading and talking about maps
Looking at books about far away places

History
Labelling a timeline
Looking at books about times past
Looking at old books

Using construction activities for the humanities

Having visited places in connection with the humanities, and noted their features, the children can re-create them using a variety of construction materials:

- to create places of worship with significant features;
- to create maps and routes;
- to construct a town.

Visitors

A range of visitors can help children to understand the wider world around them. It is essential that they are well prepared to work with very young children. Such people might include:

- a mum bringing in her newborn baby;
- a religious minister talking about a coming celebration;
- a parent making some food with the children;
- a traffic warden talking about their job;
- a grandparent talking about when they were a child.

Outside the classroom

The playground area is the first place outside that offers a context for learning in the humanities. Mapping skills can be developed, routes can be designed, games that explore compass points can be played.

Beyond the school gates, history, geography and RE lie on the doorstep and can be fruitfully used to help children explore their local area. A visit to the shops, to the local park, to a place of worship or a museum, all offer children a lived experience of the humanities subjects.

Providing experiences in citizenship as part of 'Personal, social and emotional development'

While the guidance for citizenship as a subject does not apply, of course, in the early years, there are ELGs within the area of 'Personal, social and emotional development' which lay the foundations for future understanding in this aspect of the humanities. For example, one of the ELGs is to *work as part of a group or class, taking turns and sharing fairly...*

> *Children must be provided with experiences and support which will help them to develop a positive sense of themselves and of others; respect for others; social skills; and a positive disposition to learn.*

(DCSF, 2008)

There are many ways in which you can focus on the development of social skills and awareness, such as turn-taking and sharing. You might point out the need for this during circle time, when children may want to speak. You can give the speaker an object or toy to hold, and then establish a pattern of behaviour so that this is passed to the next child who wishes to speak, thus providing a visual and tactile reminder of the need to wait to take your turn in conversation. You might also establish a routine for birthdays, and arrange for a cake to be shared between the children on each occasion. The children can then see the real purpose and benefits of sharing within a group.

PRACTICAL TASK PRACTICAL TASK PRACTICAL TASK PRACTICAL TASK PRACTICAL TASK

Sharing toys is always an issue with young children, particularly during periods of individual activity. Take the opportunity when you are working in an early years setting to try out different ways of encouraging children to share their toys, while at the same time avoiding any upset. To begin with, you will need to observe closely so that you are aware which children do not naturally allow others to play with their favourite toys.

Monitoring and assessing the Early Learning Goals with a humanities focus

Assessment in the Foundation Stage is largely formative and diagnostic and focuses entirely on the stage of learning and the developmental needs of each child. Practitioners' observations of children enable them to build up a detailed picture of the child – a learning journey, reflecting their individual learning styles and needs. Assessments can then be based upon children's achievements in their daily activities. Practitioners can review each child's learning journey and identify where the child is in terms of their learning and development and what they need to plan and provide for next. Practitioners are expected to:

- *make systematic observations and assessments of each child's achievements, interests and learning styles;*
- *use these observations and assessments to identify learning priorities and plan relevant and motivating learning experiences for each child;*
- *match their observations to the expectations of the Early Learning Goals.*

(DCSF, 2008)

At the end of the Foundation Stage, the EYFS Profile, based on the six areas of learning, should be a summary of each child's learning and development. Judgements about the child's achievements need to be made against the 13 scales based on the ELGs and based on consistent, independent behaviour, mostly during child-initiated activities.

As has been seen above, many activities can be set up by the practitioner or initiated by the child, which touch on understanding and skill in history, geography, RE and citizenship through the six areas of learning. A key factor in the development of individual play and learning in 'Knowledge and understanding of the world' and 'Personal, social and emotional development' is the organisation and on-going evaluation of an enabling learning environment. In order to stimulate skills in observation, enquiry, investigation, communication and decision-making, a wide range of resources and interaction is needed. Firstly, you will need to be an effective role model, asking questions, observing, investigating and using appropriate vocabulary as a model for the children to learn from. In discussion, the use of open-ended questions enables the children to explore different possibilities and encourages them to talk about their ideas. The provision of a changing home corner, objects, pictures and stories from the past, different toys, models and picture books, visits outside the setting, observation and talk about weather, or observation of distances between objects or areas in the setting, can all enable the children to initiate their own activities from which assessments can be made on children's progress in these two areas of learning.

REFLECTIVE TASK

Consider the strategies you might use and opportunities you could create to observe and record children's responses in different situations, for example when engaging in role play or exploring artefacts. These observations are critically important to take into account when planning the next steps in their learning.

Think about how you would evaluate your planning and preparation of the learning environment to further develop and enhance its potential to stimulate children's independent learning.

A SUMMARY OF KEY POINTS

> While the Early Years Foundation Stage curriculum does not explicitly include the humanities subjects, several of the areas of learning have direct links with history, geography and RE.

> Many of the topics, approaches and resources that are commonly found in the early years setting can be pursued to develop children's understanding of the humanities subjects.

> The humanities subjects offer a suitable vehicle for developing some key skills and attitudes.

MOVING ON > > > > > > MOVING ON > > > > > > MOVING ON

Consider your own knowledge and understanding of the Early Year Foundation Stage. How confident are you in your understanding of children's development at this age? Consider what you would need to do to ensure that you are secure in your knowledge of what is appropriate for this age group in relation to the humanities subjects.

FURTHER READING FURTHER READING FURTHER READING FURTHER READING

Ashton, E. (1999) *RE in the Early Years.* London: Routledge.

Boys, R. and Spink, E. (Eds.) (2008) *Teaching the Foundation Subjects.* London: Continuum.

Breuilly, E. and Palmer, S. (2001) *Teaching with Text. Religious Education 5–7.* Leamington Spa: Scholastic.

Grimmitt, M. (1991) *A Gift to the Child.* London: Simon and Schuster.

Grimmitt, M. (2000) *Pedagogies of Religious Education* Great Wakering: McCrimmon.

Hoodless, P. (1997) 'Why Teach about Time in the Primary School?', *Primary History*, Issue 17, Nov: 11–12.

Linden, J. (1999) *Understanding World Religions in Early Years Practice.* London: Hodder and Stoughton.

Martin, F. and Owens, P. (2004) 'Young children making sense of their place in the world'. Chapter 5 in Scoffham (2004) op. cit.

McCreery, E., Palmer, S. and Voeils, V. (2008) *Teaching Religious Education.* Exeter: Learning Matters.

Nesbitt, E. (2002) *Intercultural Education. Ethnographic and Religious Approaches.* London: Hodder and Stoughton.

Thornton, L. and Brunton, P. (2004) *The Little Book of Time and Place*: ed by Featherstone, S.: Featherstone.

Useful websites

www.everychildmatters.gov.uk

www.surestart.gov.uk/research/keyresearch/eppe

www.dcsf.gov.uk/
   Websites with information and guidance on Early Years.

http://nationalstrategies.standards.dcsf.gov.uk/earlyyears
   Government website which gives an outline of requirements for Early Years education.

www.teachernet.gov.uk/teachingandlearning/EYFS/
   Guidance and comment on the EYFS.

www.bbc.co.uk/schools/websites/eyfs/
   List of links for pre-school 18 months to 5 year old children.

www.magazines.scholastic.co.uk/forums/
   An example of an on-line discussion page on Early Years.

www.ncma.org.uk/
   Provides links to a number of EYFS resources.

4
Planning for progression in the humanities at Key Stage 1 and Key Stage 2

By the end of this chapter you will have:

• developed your understanding of the planning process;
• begun to understand how to plan for progression in children's learning;
• continued to extend your subject knowledge in the humanities.

Professional Standards for QTS

Q22: Plan for progression across the age and ability range for which they are trained, designing effective learning sequences within lessons and across series of lessons and demonstrating secure subject/curriculum knowledge.

Note: Standards 23 and 24 will be developed more fully in subsequent chapters.

Introduction

Planning needs to show how children's knowledge, skills and understanding will all develop and progress over their primary school years. This is known as 'planning for progression'. Progression in children's learning also needs to be shown in your medium-term plans (see below). As part of ensuring each child progresses, targets need to be set. These targets may be set for a class, group or individual child, and must reflect the highest possible expectations on the part of the teacher. However, whatever the scale of the target-setting and expectations, these must be achievable. This will ensure motivation rather than frustration!

Considerable research has taken place into the numerous aspects of the planning process in recent decades. Bloom (1964) produced a taxonomy of educational objectives which has remained influential in planning theory and practice to this day. During the 1970s and 1980s, there was growing criticism of the lack of adequate planning and clear direction in teaching. This was highlighted by HMI in 1985 (DES/HMI, 1985). Issues surrounding the effectiveness of group work were reviewed in the ORACLE project (Galton, Simon and Croll, 1980) and current methods were harshly criticised by Alexander, Rose and Woodhead (1992) in their 'Three wise men' report. Since that time, the requirements for rigour in the planning and assessment process have grown and are embodied in the National Curriculum and the Standards for the Award of QTS.

The planning process is complex and consists of two major areas: firstly, the planning, teaching, assessment and evaluation cycle; and secondly, the long-, medium- and short-term planning which is necessary for a whole school plan. The written plans can vary considerably, as can be seen from the examples used by schools which are illustrated below. However, this is to be expected, since the ways in which schools work to suit their own particular needs varies too and the plans must fit these needs.

The planning cycle

It is fundamentally important to understand the planning, teaching, assessment and evaluation cycle. What this means is that each part of the process is linked to the next one and that new plans make use of evaluation of what has gone before.

Planning must take place before teaching can begin. Planning for a particular age group in a particular locality must relate to this context. Therefore before any planning can begin, the context for teaching and learning activities needs to be analysed. Why is this? Young children have been shown to learn best when that learning is related to their own experiences or their surroundings (Bruner, 1960; Friedman, 1982). Although it is not necessarily possible to do this for all teaching and learning, there are numerous opportunities to relate real-life experience to work in the humanities (see Table 4.1, page 53).

A key aspect in planning is the setting of clear objectives. Objectives are the specific things you want the children to learn. These need to be assessed at the end of the unit of work. In choosing objectives, your knowledge and understanding of the context, particularly the learning needs of the children in your class, will inform your choice of learning objectives. Additionally, your own knowledge of the subject or topic you are to teach will inform this choice.

A second key aspect of planning is the need to ensure that all parties involved in teaching and learning know what the objectives are. Therefore it is important to share your planned objectives with any other adults working with you or as part of a teaching team. This includes classroom assistants and casual helpers, such as parents and carers. Long-term, whole-school planning needs to be shared and discussed with all staff involved in teaching the course. Last but not least, you need to ensure that you also share the objectives with the children. This takes place at the beginning of each teaching session.

Once teaching has taken place it is essential to assess what the children have learned. It is also essential to review your teaching and to reflect on its effectiveness in order to evaluate it. Both of these, assessment and evaluation, should then inform the detailed planning of the next lesson. It must be recognised that good teaching and learning depend almost entirely on carefully considered, detailed planning which ensures that children's learning moves forward. Good planning, in turn, depends upon how well children's learning is assessed and how well your teaching is evaluated. Only by taking these factors into account can you hope to develop and improve the quality of your teaching. Assessment is also closely linked to planning within the Standards. This is one part of the planning process. The second major aspect is related to the stages and variety in planning which take place.

The variety of planning that takes place in schools

Figure 4.1 aims to link together the many aspects of planning that inform an individual lesson. The child is eating an apple – this represents a lesson and that the child is actively involved in his/her learning. To plan a lesson in a particular subject you need to understand the unit plan (also called a scheme of work) – the lessons leading up to this one lesson and the lessons that will follow, shown as a twig of the tree.

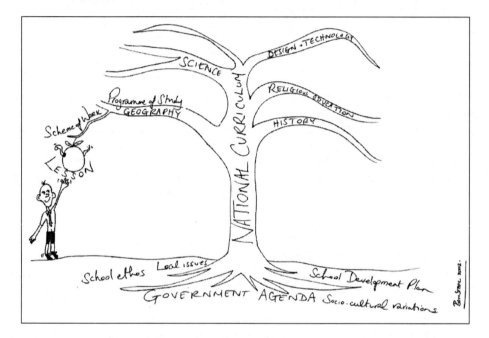

Figure 4.1 Stimulus diagram

The unit plan is part of the long-term plan for that subject's key stage in which progression over the two or three years will be carefully considered. This is represented as a branch. Each branch represents a different subject. The tree trunk holding up the branches (subjects) is the National Curriculum. Each tree is an individual school. The roots feed each unique tree and include aspects such as the school ethos and the local environment or community.

Planning is what happens before a lesson is taught. In a school there will be long-term plans for each subject providing an overview of the learning for a key stage and for each school year. There will also be medium-term plans, sometimes called 'units', and short-term plans or lesson plans. These must show clearly the teacher's learning objectives/intended learning outcomes, i.e. what the teacher wants the children to learn by the end of the term or lesson (see Chapter 7), along with the methods through which this learning will take place (see Chapter 5). Assessment and assessment methods need to be seen as an integral part of the planning process and examples of this can be seen most clearly in the medium- and short-term plans below.

Long-term plans

Long-term plans are usually drawn up by the subject co-ordinator for the whole school. Sometimes the co-ordinator for each Key Stage draws up the plan for that age phase. Tables 4.1 and 4.2 show some examples of long-term plans.

Table 4.1 Geography at a Manchester primary school

Year	Autumn	Spring	Summer
Early Years	Objectives from Early Learning Goals	Objectives from Early Learning Goals	Objectives from Early Learning Goals
Year 1	Around our school – the local area	How can we make our local area safe?	Where in the world is Barnaby Bear (Dublin)
Year 2	An island home	Where in the world is Barnaby Bear (Brittany)	Going to the seaside
Year 3	Investigating our local area	Weather around the world	How can we improve the area we can see from our window?
Year 4	Improving the environment	Zambia	Village settlers
Year 5	Should Sale Circle be closed to traffic?	Water	A contrasting UK locality – Llandudno
Year 6	Investigating rivers	What's in the news?	

Table 4.2 A history long-term plan for Key Stage 1 and Key Stage 2: A Stockport primary school

	Autumn term		Spring term		Summer term	
Rotation A*	What were homes like a long time ago?	What do we know about the Gunpowder Plot? (Visit to Tatton Hall)			What were seaside holidays like?	
Rotation B*		How are toys different from those in the past?	Why do we remember Louis Braille/ Helen Keller?			Living history/ canals. (Visit to the boat museum)
Year 3	Anglo-Saxons (QCA Unit 6B)		NONE		Romans (QCA Unit 6A)	
Visits					Chester	
Year 4	Life in Tudor times (QCA Units 7 & 8)		The Ancient Greeks (QCA Units 14 & 15)			
Visits	Bramhall Hall (Tudor Christmas)					
Year 5	Ancient Egypt (QCA Unit 10 + Adaptations)		NONE			
Visits	Manchester Museum					
Year 6	Children living in Victorian Times (QCA Unit 11)		Changes in local life in Victorian times (QCA Unit 12)			
Visits	Wigan Pier		Styal Mill			

*Years 1 and 2 follow the same syllabus on a two-yearly cycle.

The long-term plan in Table 4.1 simply shows the content to be covered across all year groups in the school to give a quick overview of what is covered by all the children. Notice how, particularly for the younger children, topics that are likely to be familiar to them are planned, such as work on the local area and work using the familiar idea of the teddy bear in Barnaby Bear. Similarly, in the history unit shown in Table 4.2, every opportunity is taken to relate topics to places nearby, such as Bramhall, or to places within the wider local area to the school, such as Chester, which will be known to the children.

Long-term planning for RE

The planning shown in Table 4.3 makes use of the QCA scheme of work for RE (QCA, 2000). It also follows the guidelines from the QCA model syllabuses (QCA, 1998) that at Key Stage 1 pupils should learn about Christianity and at least one other religion, and that at Key Stage 2 they should learn about Christianity and at least two other religions. Schools would usually use the religions represented in the school as the starting point for choosing which to include. The three themes, special people, special times and special places run through the units across the age phases. Notice here again how the topics selected for the youngest children relate almost entirely to their own personal experiences.

Long-term plans help teachers plan progression in content and skills over a period of time. They are useful in providing evidence that the National Curriculum requirements are being met and give an overview of what is covered over an entire key stage. A long-term plan lacks the detail necessary for a teacher to teach a topic in depth, however.

Table 4.3. A long-term plan for RE

Autumn 1		Autumn 2	Spring 1	Spring 2	Summer 1	Summer 2
N	Special people: myself	Special times: birthdays	None	Special times: Spring – new life	Special places: our homes	None
R	Special times: what are harvest festivals? QCA unit RA	Special people	None	Special people: who was Jesus?	Special people: who were the friends of Jesus? QCA unit RB	None
Yr 1	What does it mean to belong? QCA unit 1A	Celebrations: why do Christians give gifts at Christmas? QCA unit 1C	Special things (include objects and books from Islam and Christianity)	What can we learn from visiting a mosque?	None	Beliefs and practice (a) QCA unit 1D
Yr 2	What is the Qur'an?	Celebrations QCA unit 2C	Visiting a place of worship (church) QCA unit 2D	Why did Jesus tell stories? QCA unit 2B	None	Beliefs and practice (b) QCA unit 1D
Yr 3	What do signs and symbols mean in religion? QCA unit 3A	How and why do Hindus celebrate Divali? QCA unit 3B	What is faith and what difference does it make? QCA unit 3E	What do we know about Jesus? QCA unit 3C	What can we learn from visiting a Mandir?	What is the Bible and why is it important to Christians? QCA unit 3D

Yr 4	What religions are represented in our neighbourhood? QCA unit 4D	Growing up in Islam	What do people believe about God?	Why is Easter important to Christians? QCA unit 4C	What do we know about Mohamad?	Christianity around the world
Yr 5	What do Hindus believe about God?	Where did the Christian Bible come from? QCA unit 5C	Understanding stories from Hinduism	How do the beliefs of Christians influence their actions? QCA unit 5D	How do the beliefs of Hindus influence their actions?	How do people express their faith through the arts? QCA unit 6F
Yr 6	Worship and community QCA unit 6B	Why are sacred texts important? QCA unit 6C (focus on Christianity and the nativity stories)	What is the Qur'an and why is it important for Muslims? QCA unit 6D	What do people believe happens to us when we die?	Worship and community QCA unit 6A (focus on Islam)	Religion in the world today

REFLECTIVE TASK

Review the above examples of planning and consider how long-term plans might cover each of the knowledge, skills and understanding (concepts) required by the National Curriculum.

Medium-term plans

From the long-term plan, teachers devise medium-term plans for each topic, e.g. RE Year 6: 'What is the Qur'an and why is it important for Muslims?' or History Year 5: 'Ancient Egypt', or Geography Year 3: 'How can we improve the area we see from our window?' One of the main purposes of medium-term planning is to show how children's learning will develop and progress. Also, in recent years, many schools have begun to refer to their medium-term plans instead of drawing up separate lesson plans in order to reduce the time spent on this work.

Consequently, more detail is often needed in medium-term plans. These are often called 'schemes of work' or 'units of work'. They cover a shorter period of time, sometimes a term, half a term, or sometimes one week, e.g. in literacy or numeracy, where the subject is being taught every day. Medium-term plans are very useful in planning the work to be covered in five, six or seven weeks in the case of the humanities. If a topic is to be taught over a whole term then this must be shown in the unit of work. Medium-term plans are usually written by the class teacher or by a team of teachers working with a year group on the same theme. Teachers receive guidance in writing units of work, from the subject co-ordinator. As a trainee teacher you will be required to demonstrate your ability to draw up your own medium-term plans in humanities subjects or to contribute to a school's existing plans.

Medium-term plans can be drawn up on a spreadsheet or matrix with headings such as:

• learning objectives (linked to the National Curriculum, or in RE to the local syllabus);
• teaching and learning strategies;

- specialist subject knowledge/references;
- key vocabulary;
- key questions;
- learning tasks and activities;
- resources;
- learning outcomes;
- opportunities for assessment;
- cross-curricular links.

The most important aspect of medium-term planning is the setting of appropriate yet challenging objectives. These are derived from the National Curriculum for each subject to be taught and also from the exemplary materials in the QCA schemes of work for each subject. Objectives can be focused on knowledge, skills or children's understanding of important concepts in that subject. These objectives are also important in assessing what the children have learned. At the end of a unit of medium-term planning, schools often carry out assessments to find out how far children have met the objectives set at the planning stage. Here, the planning–assessment cycle plays a most important part.

All levels of planning require preparation, the collection of ideas and resources, and subject-specific knowledge suitable for teaching the subject and assessing children's learning. This information needs to be shown in the medium-term planning. Medium-term plans are working documents for the teacher or team of teachers to use and amend. The DfES has produced a set of medium-term plans which can be accessed by the internet.

Writing medium-term plans and long-term plans is best tackled in a group. Sharing ideas and experiences and creating together are enjoyable aspects of a teacher's work. Much of a teacher's life naturally involves working with youngsters, so when the opportunity arises to plan in a team of adults it is a fulfilling experience. We all bring different skills, knowledge and experiences to a team which helps to make the end product superior to our individual efforts. Within teams representing different year groups long-term plans can be written with the guidance of the subject co-ordinator, which creates opportunities to develop and progress children's knowledge, understanding and skills. Medium-term plans can be discussed and enhanced within smaller teams made up of year team teachers, classroom support assistants and the subject co-ordinator.

PRACTICAL TASK PRACTICAL TASK PRACTICAL TASK PRACTICAL TASK PRACTICAL TASK

While on teaching practice find out if planning teams are meeting, and offer to be involved. If school INSET days are taking place ask if you can join in.

Examples of medium-term plans designed for teaching each subject separately

These give an indication of the expected standards for children in each key stage, and al the range and content of work relevant to children of that age.

Medium-term planning in geography

When planning a unit of work to last over a few weeks, you need to include a var resources and teaching and learning strategies, plus opportunities to check chi progress. In creating lively, interesting geography schemes of work it is worth brains the topic first. The following two planning tools help teachers to consider breadth and depth while planning a geography topic.

Planning tool 1

This tool uses the key geography enquiry questions – What? Where? When? Why? and How? For example: what is being studied? (the research question, hypothesis, issue, event, process); where is this taking place? (the location, places); when? (the rate of change, key dates); why is it happening? (the processes or decision makers involved); how is it changing? (what is likely to happen in the future due to factors such as new legislation, management strategies, development).

This sequence of questions is useful when studying changes such as events in the news.

Planning tool 2

The development compass rose (Figure 4.2) can be used as an aid to planning. It reminds teachers to consider different viewpoints when studying a place or issue:

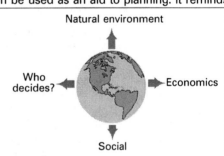

- North – the natural environmental features including plants, animals, water, hills.
- South – the social features including people's lifestyles – clothes, food, religion, family life, hobbies, etc.
- East – the economic features including work, shopping, buildings and transport.
- West – the 'who decides', i.e. political features of a location.

Figure 4.2 Development compass rose

PRACTICAL TASK PRACTICAL TASK PRACTICAL TASK PRACTICAL TASK PRACTICAL TASK

See if you can identify the influence of the two planning tools on the geography schemes of work in Tables 4.4 and 4.5.

Table 4.4 Example of a medium-term plan for geography

Duration: 10 hours	Age group: Year 2		
Learning objectives	**Teaching and learning activities**	**Achievement criteria**	**Resources**
Children should learn to: • use geographical terms in exploring their surroundings • investigate physical and human features of their surroundings and contrast these with other places	What can I find in different rooms in my house? • Show children household objects and ask which room they belong in. • Sort pictures of household objects into sets according to which rooms furniture belongs in and why it belongs there.	Most children will understand that there are different types of houses, and that within houses we have similar rooms. They will be able to describe some of the materials used to build a house, and explain that buildings are designed to protect people from the weather.	• Household objects • Pictures of household objects • Selection of materials – textures, e.g. brick • Photographs of buildings • Video/photographs of houses around the world

• make observations about where things are located • classify information • draw maps and plans • undertake fieldwork activities in the locality of the school • be aware that the world extends beyond their locality • describe similarities and differences between localities (extension – KS 2) • describe how land and buildings are used	• Discuss which rooms/ facilities are essential, which are a luxury. **What type of house do I live in?** • Children to make detailed drawings of their own home. Discuss terms such as detached, semi-detached, terraced etc. • Record type of homes children live in on a database. **What are houses and other buildings made of?** • Field trip to observe and record types of buildings in the vicinity of the school. Look and see the materials used. • Hands-on session touching and describing different materials, e.g. brick, tile, sand etc. Make crayon rubbings of textures. • Sorting exercise of photographs of different buildings – identifying houses from other buildings. **What are houses like in other parts of the world?** • Study photographs and videos. • Discuss the building materials, and the influence of the weather, e.g. use of shutters to keep out sunshine, steep roofs in snowy countries etc. **What about people on the move?** • Investigate the different types of travelling homes and the reasons why people move e.g. Nomads in the desert.	Some children will not have made so much progress and will: • be able to describe their own house • be able to point to features on a house, e.g. roof, window • be able to identify a house from other types of buildings. Some children will have progressed further and will also: • use a range of geographical terms to describe houses.	

Table 4.5 Example of a unit of work for geography

Duration: 12 hours	Age group: Year 5		
Learning objectives	**Teaching and learning activities**	**Achievement criteria**	**Resources**
Children should learn to: • investigate a place • undertake fieldwork • collect and record data about local traffic issues • undertake a decision-making exercise • look at changes in the environment • look at an issue arising from how land is used • consider how places can be managed and improved • offer solutions	**What is Sale Circle Like today?** • Study photographs of Sale Circle and the surrounding area. • Children in groups study a photo. They think of a title and words to describe what they can see, then share ideas with class. **Where is Sale Circle?** • Locate Sale Circle and school on A–Z extract. • Children use differentiated writing frames to describe area using photographs. **What problems does Sale Circle have?** • Using photos and map extracts, children brainstorm problems that could arise from traffic on Sale Circle. Share with class. • Field trip to local high-street area to collect data about traffic issues, e.g. volume of traffic, parking problems, varying needs of different high-street users like shopkeepers, children, senior citizens, businesses. Use a questionnaire to survey people's views. Listen to the sounds they can hear – try to identify. • Collate data by sharing results and recording on worksheets. Produce graphs to demonstrate patterns. **When did the problems arise?** • Interpret statistics on increasing car ownership. • Compare images from 100 years, 50 years, 10 years to present day. • Talk from community police about road safety issues. **Who is affected by the problems?** • Discussion of results. **How can Sale Circle be improved?** • Study large-scale map extract; in groups plan possible solutions. • Explore a range of possible solutions used in other locations – photographs. • Make a decision on how to improve the local area – share results by a letter to the paper/ council **or** annotate a map, etc.	Most children will investigate the issue of traffic management in a specific area and use the evidence to make a reasoned decision about the outcome. Some children will not have made so much progress and will: • carry out a more structured survey • debate the merits of a small number of provided solutions, choosing one as the best answer. Some children will have progressed further and will also: • write a letter to the local paper / council offering solutions for comment • design some elements of a plan to improve the high street.	• Photographs of Sale Circle • A–Z maps of Greater Manchester • Writing frames to aid description of photographs • Questionnaire for people's views • Data collection worksheets • Statistics on car ownership • Visit from community police • Large-scale map of Sale Circle

Medium-term planning in history

History unit of work: Key Stage 1 – Seaside holidays in the past

The preparation of resources, particularly historical sources to enable you to address your learning objectives in the activities outlined in the history units below, is of fundamental importance. Plenty of time needs to be allocated to the finding and organisation of resources such as photographs, written material, ICT resources, eyewitness accounts and artefacts. You will find it helpful first to ask the history co-ordinator in your school. They may have already spent a considerable amount of time ensuring that each unit is resourced and may have a collection ready to hand. Failing this, you will need to begin a search yourself. A useful starting point, if you have allowed time, is to write to parents and carers. They will usually send in large quantities of useful materials for the children to use. Care must be taken, however, to list all the items and to ensure their return to their rightful owners!

Other useful sources of teaching materials include the local teachers' centre, library or museum. Many of these will allow you to borrow a loan collection for a period of time if you apply very early for it. Good loan collections are well known and teachers book well in advance! The items in the collections may not be exactly what you would wish for, but they will provide you with a starting point for planning some good interactive learning. Final resorts include asking your family and friends or visiting the local antique fairs or junk shops. Although time-consuming, visits to these places can sometimes be quite rewarding. Failing all of these strategies, try to obtain at least one or two sources. These can be used for whole-class lessons or they can be rotated around groups to ensure that all children have one or two opportunities to do some first-hand learning.

REFLECTIVE TASK

Identify the range of resources you would need to carry out the plan shown in Table 4.6 on seaside holidays (pages 61–62) and that shown in Table 4.7 on the Tudors (page 63). Consider the type of resources that would best enable you to address the lesson objectives.

PRACTICAL TASK

Develop one of the suggested activities for history. Decide on a particular year group and work on the assumption that you will have 40 minutes for your lesson. Write a simple outline showing how you would divide up this time and what the children will be asked to do. Try to ensure that the content you choose matches that outlined in the National Curriculum for history. Give references to the National Curriculum in your plan.

Medium-term planning in RE: Introducing Judaism at Key Stage 2

The unit outlined in Table 4.8 (page 64) aims to introduce children to aspects of Jewish tradition through the character of a Jewish boy. Rather than try to introduce children to a whole faith tradition, it is easier to identify a child of similar age and pick out features of their lives which may have some resonance with other children's lives. The unit is aimed at Key Stage 2. The learning outcomes listed below are linked to Attainment Targets 1 (learning about religion) and 2 (learning from religion) from the QCA model syllabuses (QCA, 1998).

Table 4.6 Example of a medium-term plan for Key Stage 1 history: seaside holidays

Duration: 7 × 1 hour lessons   **Age group**: Year 2

Learning objectives Children should learn to:	Teaching and learning activities	Assessment opportunities	Resources
Lesson 1 • identify key features of seaside holidays • know when the main holiday periods occur during the year • find out information from photographs • talk about seaside holidays using their past experiences	**What are seaside holidays, when and why do we have them?** • Show the children a large photograph of a seaside resort. Discuss the sort of holiday depicted. • Ask them to talk about holidays or visits they have made to the seaside. Where did they go? What did they do? • Using a large map of the British Isles, identify seaside resorts visited by the children. • Explore with children what are holidays? Why do we have them? When do they normally take place? • Children can produce a simple time line showing main school holiday periods.	• Contribution to discussion about seaside holidays. • Finding out information using photographs. • Producing a time line showing main holiday periods.	• Large photograph of a seaside resort • Large map of the British Isles to identify seaside resorts • Activity sheets (graded) focusing on a holiday timeline, seaside vocabulary, etc. • Holiday resort websites
Lesson 2 • identify differences between travel to the seaside now, in the 1950s and in the 1900s • find out information about travel to the seaside from various sources of information such as photographs and reference books • communicate their knowledge of travel to the seaside using pictorial and written materials	**How do people travel to the seaside now and how did they travel in the past?** • Discuss with children how they travel to the seaside today. • Look at travel in the 1950s and 1900s using photographs and video material. • Children produce a poster showing transport to the seaside over time.	• Contribution to discussion about travel to the seaside in the past • Children produce a poster with annotated drawings showing travel to the seaside now, in the 1950s and in the 1900s	• Photographs and video material showing travel to the seaside now, in the 1950s and in the 1900s • Reference books
Lesson 3 • identify differences between seaside holidays now and in the 1900s • recognise that some aspects of seaside holidays have remained the same • find out information from photographs and other sources of information	**What are the differences and similarities between seaside holidays now and then?** • Use packs of photographs and video extracts to show seaside holidays now and in the 1900s. • Working in groups, children identify specific similarities and differences, e.g. clothing, bathing, beach, pier, etc.	• Identify and write about similarities and differences between seaside holidays now and those in the 1900s • Through whole-class and group discussion demonstrate knowledge about seaside holidays in the 1900s and an ability to ask questions about the topic	• Photographs and video material • Reference books • Activity sheets (graded) for similarities and differences • Written task

Lesson 4 • find out about the past from a range of sources of information • identify key features of seaside holidays in the 1900s using sorting and classification skills • communicate their knowledge of seaside holidays in the past by writing, talking and using ICT	**What were the key features of seaside holidays in the 1900s?** • Children identify key features: entertainment, beach, promenade, pier, etc. • Groups of children research one of these topics. Outcomes to be group presentations and written/pictorial work suitable for a class display. Word processing to be encouraged.	• Oral and visual presentation by each group. • Written/pictorial materials for class display.	• Resource packs for each topic, e.g. photographs, reference books, video material. • Internet-based research
Lesson 5 • place photographs in chronological order • use vocabulary relating to the passing of time • identify differences between seaside holidays now and in past time	**What were seaside holidays like for parents and grandparents?** • Ask children to look at photographs showing seaside holidays now and when their parents (1970s) and grandparents (1950s) were young. • Children sequence photographs into chronological order. Discuss reasons for sequencing. • Encourage children to use appropriate time-related vocabulary, e.g. recent, modern, older, oldest.	• Sequencing photographs into chronological order and explaining the reasons. • Children produce a chart showing key features of seaside holidays now, in the 1970s and in the 1950s.	• Pictures/photographs of seaside holidays now, in the 1970s and in the 1950s
Lesson 6 • find out about seaside holidays in the past by listening to an eyewitness account and by looking at artefacts • ask questions about the past • write simple notes	**What can grandparents tell us about seaside holidays when they were young?** • Arrange for a grandparent to visit the class and to talk about their seaside holidays as a child in the 1950s using photographs, souvenirs etc. • Encourage children to ask questions and to make simple notes. • Use a cassette recorder. • Draw and identify souvenirs brought in by the visitor, explaining what they tell us about seaside holidays in the past.	• Listening to the adult visitor and asking questions. • Identifying key points in simple note form. • Drawing a souvenir and explaining what it tells us about the past.	• Adult visitor, photographs, souvenirs, cassette recorder
Lesson 7 • summarise key issues they have learned about seaside holidays in the past	**What have we learned about seaside holidays in the past?** • Conclude topic by focusing on the classroom display of children's work, photographs, posters and artefacts. • Encourage children to summarise the key issues.	• Contribution to discussion about key issues of the topic.	• Seaside holidays in the past classroom display

Table 4.7 Example of a unit of work for Key Stage 2 history:
Britain and the wider world in Tudor times

Learning objectives	Key questions	Activities	Resources	Differentiation	Assessment
Lesson 1 Chronological understanding 1a To distinguish between wealth and poverty in Tudor times 2d	What was different about rich and poor people in Tudor times?	Place the Tudor period on a general timeline of British history. Compare pictures of the rich and poor; discuss the differences.	Timeline, pictures, portraits, woodcuts.	• Differentiate questioning in whole class group.	• Note children who could accurately place the period in time
Lesson 2 Knowledge and understanding of people in the past: key features of lives of the rich 2a	What were the lives of the rich like?	Use pictures and texts to read, discuss and write about the key features.	Portraits and pictures of stately homes and palaces	• Differentiate questioning in whole class group. • Provide more structured writing frames for less able.	• Note children who could accurately identify key features • Written work – by outcome
Lesson 3 Historical enquiry: to use a range of sources to ask and answer questions 4a; 4b	How can we find out about the lives of the rich?	Discuss the question 'How do we know?' using a variety of sources. Children record their ideas.	Pictures, portraits, wills, banquet menus, illustrations of buildings and houses	• Differentiate questioning in whole-class group. • Select appropriate sources for the various ability groups.	• Recording work – by outcome
Lesson 4 Knowledge and understanding of people in the past: key features of lives of the poor 2a To use sources to find out about the lives of the poor 4a	What were the lives of the poor like?	Discuss the question 'How do we know?' using a variety of sources. Children record their ideas.	Inventories, woodcuts, extracts from plays, e.g. Shakespeare	• Differentiate questioning in whole-class group. • Select appropriate sources for the various ability groups.	• Recording work – by outcome
Lesson 5 Organisation and communication: to select and organise information to answer a key question about the past 5a	How different were the lives of the rich and the poor?	Review all the sources used and work produced e.g. through group presentation. Children pick out key differences.	Pictures, notes and writing, drawings	• Select appropriate materials for the various ability groups to refer to and use.	• Presentation of ideas – by outcome

Table 4.8 Example of a medium-term plan for Key Stage 2 RE: Introducing Judaism

Learning objectives	Content and activities	Resources/organisation	Differentiation	Assessment
Session 1: Introducing David Children will be able to: ● identify features distinctive of a Jewish lifestyle ● compare aspects of David's life to their own 45 minutes	Display of available resources. Teacher selects from these to introduce the class to David. Teacher asks questions about what the children can see and encourages them to speculate what images might show. Draw on children's previous knowledge of Judaism correcting any misconceptions. Children draw up a list of questions they would like to ask David about his life.	Children's books introducing aspects of Judaism. Posters showing Jewish family. Prepared notes highlighting aspects of Judaism using available resources. Picture/poster of a Jewish boy wearing some distinctive artefacts or taking part in Jewish observance.	Some children may need support when writing their questions to David. Some children may have an awareness of Judaism as a religion and should be encouraged to share this as much as they can.	Most children should be able to recognise Judaism as a religion and that Jewish people live and work in Britain today. Look for the more able children demonstrating an understanding of the implications of differences in lifestyle. Some children may not be aware of other religious traditions in the country.
Session 2: Daily routines Children will be able to: ● identify common practices within Judaism ● compare daily routines to their own 1 hour	Children are asked to talk about/make a note of how they spend a typical day. Compare with each other's days. Introduce a day in David's life focusing on times of prayer, use of artefacts, perhaps attending a Jewish school. Consider the notion of pattern within our daily routines, the value of it, the constraints of it. Emphasise the purpose and reasons behind certain practices. Children design and make a kippah.	Kippah (skull cap) Tefillin (boxes tied to forehead and arm containing prayers) Tallith (prayer shawl) Poster showing a boy wearing the items Book/video clip which takes children through 'a day in the life of…'	Some children may need help in sequencing their daily routine or with the times they do things. In discussion, the more able children may need specific questions which allow them to consider the implications of particular routines.	Most children should be able to take part in discussion and show understanding of the part routine plays in everyday life. Some may be able to discuss the implications of such routines. In the kippah designs, look for appropriate use of symbolism and colour.

Session 3: David's home

Children will be able to:
- understand the role and value of the home within Jewish tradition
- appreciate the value and purpose of prayer in Jewish tradition
- discuss how beliefs about God affect daily life

1 hour

Explore the notion of prayer to ensure children have some understanding of what it is.
Discuss why using the home as a place to worship God is valuable.
Discuss the physical differences there might be between the children's homes and David's home, e.g. kitchen arrangements.
Introduce the children to the mezuzah and explain its content and role.
Children design and make a model of a mezuzah and write part of the Shema in Hebrew and English to go inside.

Pictures/video clips of Jewish family at home
Mezuzah (small box containing a prayer)
Materials for making small boxes e.g. card, plastic, paper etc

Allow for different levels of understanding of notion of prayer.
Some children may need support in their writing and may not need to write lengthy sections.

Look for more and less sophisticated understanding of what prayer means to David.
Look for careful observation and attempts to reproduce similar copies of a mezuzah.
Look for an awareness of how the home can be a special place.

Session 4: Shabbat

Children will be able to:
- identify key features of Shabbat
- reflect on importance of Shabbat for Jews
- recognise special times in their own lives

1 hour 15 mins.

Talk through some of the rituals of Shabbat using available resources to help.
Use books/videos to support the learning.
Talk about how David might spend Shabbat.
Children talk about how they spend the weekend and then record the similarities and differences between their and David's experience.

2 candlesticks, white candles
2 challot (plaited bread) and knife, salt
Wine and glass
White tablecloth
Havdalah candle, spice box (as available)
Videos clips/books about Shabbat

Children should be allowed to respond according to their writing/drawing strengths.
Some specific vocabulary will need to be on display for some children.
Some children will need to be encouraged to consider the wider implications of observing Shabbat.

Most children should be able to record the differences between their own lives and David's.
Some children may be able to consider the wider implications.
Some children may only be able to recall a few features of Shabbat.

Session 5: Food

Children will be able to:
- understand that Jewish eating patterns are governed by rules of Kashrut
- consider the implications of Kashrut
- reflect on their own eating patterns and diet

45 minutes

Children write down everything they ate yesterday. Compare with each other to see similarities and differences. Are there any particular reasons for the differences?
- Children see an example of David's food from yesterday – again, look at similarities and differences.
- Children study Bible sections relating to food. Identify how these are apparent in David's food.
- Use knowledge to say whether the packages brought in would be suitable for David or not.

Food packaging showing KOSHER guarantee
A range of different foods including milk and meat products and those containing both e.g. lasagne
Sheet containing 'David's food'
Sections of Bible text containing rules relating to food

Some children may be able to work independently when matching David's food to Jewish requirements and when classifying the packages. Others may need support in the form of careful questioning.

Look for clear understanding of the rules of kashrut and accurate application to specific foods.
Look for ability to recognise that their own diet is influenced by cultural traditions.

Session 6: Preparation for Bar Mitzvah Children will be able to: ● understand the significance of Bar Mitzvah ● recognise some features of preparation for Bar Mitzvah ● reflect upon issues of growing up in their own experiences 45 minutes	Activity to identify key moments in the children's lives, e.g. drawing memories of important occasions/key birthdays. Discuss how life changes as they grow. Tell the children David will soon have a Bar Mitzvah celebration and explain what this means. Look at cards. Talk about the implications for David of this new stage in his life. Children design a Bar Mitzvah card for David.	Greetings cards for Bar/Bat Mitzvah Pictures of boys reading from scrolls/video of Bar Mitzvah ceremonies	Some children may need help identifying key stages in life. Some children will need extra questioning to draw out implications of different life stages.	Most children should be able to talk about growing up and the changes it brings. Some children will have a more sophisticated understanding of this. In their cards look for appropriate greetings and use of Jewish symbolism and features relating to Bar Mitzvah.
Session 7: Reflection on learning Children will be able to: ● demonstrate their understanding of aspects of Jewish experience ● demonstrate their ability to reflect on their own experiences in the light of their study. 45 minutes	Look at the questions the children wanted to ask David at the beginning – how many have been answered? Which remain? Discuss how we could find out the answers to these. Discuss what further questions we might have for David. Children write/draw a booklet pretending to be David explaining his life to non-Jewish children. Make assessment criteria explicit to the children.	Materials for making greetings cards Materials for making a small booklet including colouring materials Key Jewish words encountered during unit	Some children will be able to work independently and should be encouraged to do so. Some children may need support in writing or remembering details. Children should be allowed to produce their booklet in whichever way they feel suitable.	Look for: ● recall of significant features ● attempts to explain traditions ● comparison to other children's lives ● appropriate balance of pictures and writing according to children's strengths
Links to other areas	Literacy Art Design and technology Science PSHE			

Learning outcomes for the unit:

Attainment Target 1
By the end of the unit the children will:

- recognise and understand some key terms within Judaism;
- understand the implications of belonging to Judaism on one's daily life.

Attainment Target 2
By the end of the unit the children will:

- be able to reflect on significant features of their own lives;
- understand how one's beliefs affect daily life.

The medium-term plan shown in Table 4.8 links with QCA scheme of work for RE units:

- 2A What is the Torah and why is it important to Jewish people?
- 3A What do signs and symbols mean in religion?
- 3E What is faith and what difference does it make?
- 4D What religions are represented in our neighbourhood?
- 6A Worship and community
- 6C Why are sacred texts important?

This unit of work demonstrates a consideration of many of the requirements of the Professional Standards. The learning objectives cover both AT1 and AT2 type learning outcomes as described in the QCA model syllabuses in that they focus not only on the acquisition of new knowledge, but on the development of skills and attitudes too. For example, 'children will appreciate the value and purpose of prayer within Jewish tradition'.

Children's past achievements are accounted for in the differentiation that is built in, for example, 'some children may need support...'. The content of the work reflects that which appears in the Judaism section of many local authority Agreed Syllabuses and has close links with units in the QCA scheme of work for RE.

The work also takes into account the expectations of achievement in RE; for example, level four of the QCA expectations include the requirement that children 'describe the impact of religion on people's lives' (QCA, 2004, p36). There is clear evidence of progression throughout the unit of work, starting with an introduction to the boy, David, and developing into some detailed study of aspects of his life. Assessment opportunities can be seen throughout the unit, giving clear indications of what the teacher should be looking for, e.g. 'in their cards look for appropriate greetings, use of Jewish symbolism and features relating to Bar Mitzvah'.

Use is made of a range of resources (posters, religious artefacts, food, video, books, materials) and the unit also draws upon children's own backgrounds and experiences as a context for the study.

The unit displays careful consideration of the learning needs of the children and the development of these into a coherent, stimulating focus for study.

REFLECTIVE TASK
ᴿᴱᶠᴸᴱᶜᵀᴵⱽᴱ ᵀᴬˢᴷ

REFLECTIVE TASK

Critically review the different medium-term plans shown above and consider the various headings they include. Reflect on the range of headings which you think would provide the most useful information for this stage in the planning process.

Lesson plans

Lesson plans are just what they say. They are teachers' own detailed plans for each lesson of forty minutes, one or two hours. They include similar headings as the medium-term plans, but will also have detailed timings for each activity, key vocabulary to be introduced or explained, differentiation strategies for particular pupils, classroom management strategies, children's activities and an indication of how children's learning will be assessed and recorded. These plans are specific to a particular lesson for a particular time of day. In the humanities, the key questions that the teacher may wish to ask will be an important aspect of lesson planning.

However, while recent practice has seen a reduction in the amount of detailed planning in the humanities, trainee teachers may need to demonstrate that they can write appropriate, detailed lesson plans such as that shown in Table 4.10. These lesson plans will need to show clear objectives. Objectives are the knowledge, skills or understanding (concepts) which you will want the children to have learned by the end of the lesson. These are the learning outcomes that you will be able to assess to see which children have met your objectives, which have not met them and which have exceeded them. Trainees will also need to evaluate their lessons and their planning. In evaluating a lesson, you will need to say how effective your teaching strategies, classroom management and use of resources were, as well as commenting on how far the children met your objectives. Lesson evaluations help you plan future lessons.

PRACTICAL TASK PRACTICAL TASK PRACTICAL TASK PRACTICAL TASK PRACTICAL TASK

Look at the QCA schemes of work for geography at Key Stage 1 – these are medium-term plans. Choose one of the schemes of work and draw up a detailed lesson plan including your own ideas on activities and resources as shown in Table 4.9. Ensure that your lesson plan has one or two very clear objectives, showing what you want the children to have learnt by the end of the lesson. Refer to the National Curriculum for geography in your planning.

Table 4.9 A lesson plan for geography

Session: Mapping our classroom	Age group: year 1
Learning objectives:	Children will be able to: • draw a plan of our classroom • identify key features within the classroom – developing their observation skills about where things are located.
Previous learning:	Designing a bedroom Introduction to maps
Key vocabulary:	Map, plan, view, key, furniture, window, door, desks, whiteboard, bookshelves, sink

Resources:	Drawing paper, pencils, rulers Pre-prepared large-scale map of room, cut out coloured shapes ready for placing on map. Each colour a different feature, e.g. desks, bookshelves. Large labels ready prepared to put onto classroom features.
Session outline: *Introduction*	Class on carpet. Discuss the words, maps and plans. Remind children of previous lessons on maps and designing their own bedroom. Display the large-scale outline of the classroom – ask if anyone knows what it shows. Orientate the outline pointing out windows, walls and door.
Development	Explain to children that today we are going to make a plan drawing of our classroom. Demonstrate the difference between 3D drawings of furniture and a plan view. Discuss which style goes onto a plan map. Use samples of 3D pictures to match to plan shapes.
Conclusion/Plenary	Show the children the different coloured shapes that together we will place on the classroom plan as accurately as possible. Remind children how important it is to listen and take part so that they will be able to complete their own plan. Encourage volunteers to place the coloured shapes on to the plan. Create a key on the board to remind children what the coloured shapes represent. Volunteers place large labels on real classroom features.
	Main task – pupils return to desks to draw their own plan. First task to draw the outline. To aid drawing the four sides of the classroom, pupils may need to move seats to gain a different view (hard to draw what is behind you). Along the four sides add windows and doors. Remind children to use a colour for each. Inside the space draw the desks. Remind pupils of birds eye view of desks and other furniture. Use a colour.
	Discuss children's plan's. What was easy/difficult to draw? Display pupil work on wall.
Differentiation:	Worksheet or card sorting exercise for those who didn't understand the difference between 3D and plan pictures of objects during carpet time. Outline plan of classroom ready drawn for those struggling with spatial awareness. English as a second language – pictures of furniture with labels in both English and home language. Extension task – to measure the sides of the classroom, and the sizes of furniture.
Assessment:	Monitoring progress during lesson Maps drawn to be marked for accuracy and understanding
Other links:	Mathematics Art and design Literacy

Table 4.10 A lesson plan for Key Stage 1 history: seaside holidays

Curriculum area: History (Seaside Holidays) **Year group**: 2 **Duration**: 1½ hours
Date: ....

Learning objectives
- To identify key features of seaside holidays in the 1900s.
- To find out about one aspect of seaside holidays in the 1900s using photographs, books, etc.
- To communicate their knowledge of seaside holidays using writing, pictures, talk and ICT.
- To promote teamwork and oral communication skills.

Key questions
What were the key features of seaside holidays in the 1900s?
What can you find out about one of these key features such as the pier or the beach?

Organisation – Whole Class/Group/Individual Mainly group work

Differentiation – By task/By outcome Support Staff (Classroom assistant, adult helper)

Activity structure
Introduction:
- Using prior learning and visual sources, children will identify key features of seaside holidays in the 1900s, e.g. accommodation, beach, promenade, pier, entertainment, etc.
- Explain that they will be working in groups to investigate one of these areas.
- Explain the outcome: a short presentation to the whole class and written/pictorial/3D material for class display.
- Task to be completed by the end of the next lesson.

Lesson development:
Children work in groups investigating their topic using resource packs.
Activity sheets are available to support and structure their investigations and written/pictorial outcomes.
Teacher, teaching assistant and adult helper give support to individual groups.
Teacher to monitor group progress and the role of individuals.

Conclusion:
Draw session to a close with a short whole-class activity.
Review progress made with brief inputs from each group.
Emphasise that group work will continue next session when materials for display/presentation will be completed.

Assessment focus
Finding out about the past using available resources/information.
Written/pictorial outcomes for class display.
Working together in a group.

Resources
Resource packs for each topic, e.g. photographs, reference books, video material, ICT facilities.

Cross-curricular links
Geography; Literacy; ICT

PRACTICAL TASK PRACTICAL TASK PRACTICAL TASK PRACTICAL TASK PRACTICAL TASK

Using the format in Table 4.11, develop another lesson plan in detail. Make sure that the level of work is appropriate for the age group you specify, and that the content is relevant for this age group. Remember to set clear objectives. Refer to the guidance you have used in your planning. Type up and print out your lesson example.

Table 4.11 A lesson plan for RE

Session 4: Shabbat	Age group: year 4
Learning Objectives: **QCA AT1** Learning about religion **QCA AT2** Learning from religion	Children will be able to: ● identify key features of Shabbat; ● reflect on importance of Shabbat for Jewish children; ● recognise special times in their own lives; ● reflect on time spent with their own family.
Previous learning:	Introduction to David, his family, daily routines and prayer.
Key vocabulary:	Challot, Havdalah, Shabbat, Synagogue
Resources:	2 candlesticks, white candles 2 challot (plaited bread) and knife, salt Wine and glass White tablecloth Havdalah candle, spice box (as available) Writing/drawing materials Video about Shabbat (as available)
Session outline: *Introduction* *Development* *Conclusion*	1. Revision of work of previous lesson. What does the group remember? 2. Talk group through some of the rituals of Shabbat using available resources. Ask whether they recall special meals with their own family. 3. If possible show a video of Jewish families during Shabbat. 4. Have books available showing Shabbat preparations and rituals. 5. Discuss how David might spend his Shabbat, e.g. attending synagogue, being with family, reading religious texts, family meals. Discuss the kinds of things David would be unlikely to do. 6. Have the group share their thoughts of how they spend the weekend. 7. The children could then record their learning in written or pictorial form. A page could be divided in two – on one side the children draw/write about how they spend the weekend and on the other how David spends Shabbat. Alternatively, they could draw/write about the Shabbat evening meal and show their own special meal.
Differentiation:	Children could be allowed to respond according to their own drawing/writing strengths. Specific vocabulary could be supplied for those who need it. Some children might be encouraged to consider the wider implications of Shabbat observances and the value of setting a day a week aside as special.
Assessment:	It would be expected that most children would be able to produce work which showed distinct features of Shabbat and their own experience. Some children might also be able to demonstrate an understanding of the wider implications of setting a day aside as special. Others may only recall a few of the features of Shabbat.
Other links:	Literacy – specific vocabulary associated with Shabbat PSHE – thinking about special times spent with one's family

A SUMMARY OF **KEY POINTS**

> It is important to ensure that you set clear objectives, with high expectations at the medium- and short-term planning stages. This is necessary if you are to meet the Standards for QTS.

> It is important to understand the planning cycle.

> Long-, medium- and short-term planning are all used in primary schools.

> Planning needs to show progression, resources and key vocabulary, as well as children's activities.

> Objectives need to be shared with other adults in the team and also with the children.

> Objectives should be linked with assessment.

> Time needs to be allowed for personal research, preparation and the selection of suitable resources.

> The development of children's key skills and concepts needs to be shown in planning as well as lesson content.

MOVING *ON* >> >> >> > > > MOVING *ON* >> >> >> > > > MOVING *ON*

Standard C26, Standard C28

Find opportunities, within your schemes of work, to extend children's learning in the humanities by setting tasks for children to work on at home with the support of their parents or carers. For example, a structured interview with an adult might be used to develop work started in a history lesson on the Second World War and lead to further progression in children's learning. Parents might be asked to contribute their knowledge or views on particular issues; older family members or friends might be able to record or talk about their memories of this period in the past.

FURTHER READING FURTHER READING **FURTHER READING** FURTHER READING

Chambers, B. and Donert, K. (1996) *Teaching Geography at Key Stage 2*. Cambridge: Chris Kington Publishing. Chapter 2 explores the many types of planning, and gives advice on using enquiry questions to generate stimulating topics for children.

Claire, H. (2004) *Teaching Citizenship in Primary Schools*. Exeter: Learning Matters.

Cooper, H., Rowley, C. and Asquith, S. (2006) *Geography 3-11: A Guide for Teachers*. London: Fulton.

Hoodless, P. (2008a) *Teaching History in Primary Schools*. Exeter: Learning Matters.

McCreery, E., Palmer, S., and Voiels, V. (2008) *Teaching Religious Education.* Exeter: Learning Matters.

The above four books give a good overview of each subject.

DfEE/QCA (1998) *Geography. A Scheme of Work for Key Stages 1 and 2*. London: DfEE/QCA.

DfEE/QCA (1998) *History. A Scheme of Work for Key Stages 1 and 2*. London: DfEE/QCA.

DfEE/QCA (1998) *RE. A Scheme of Work for Key Stages 1 and 2*. London: DfEE/QCA.

These publications give useful examples of schemes of work in all the humanities subjects. They do not need to be followed to the letter they are merely suggested approaches to planning units of work.

Useful websites

www.ncaction.org.uk/
www.qcda.org.uk/
www.teachers.tv/
    Websites with useful examples of planning.

www.standards.dfes.gov.uk.
    This site contains examples of medium term planning.

5
Teaching strategies in the humanities

By the end of this chapter you will have:

- developed your understanding of a range of teaching and learning strategies within the humanities;
- begun to appreciate the importance of active and independent learning within the humanities;
- begun to understand how to plan for differentiation;
- recognised the importance of using a diverse range of resources within the humanities.

Professional Standards for QTS

Q10: Have a knowledge and understanding of a range of teaching, learning and behaviour management strategies and know how to use and adapt them, including how to personalise learning and provide opportunities for all learners to achieve their potential.

Q14: Have a secure knowledge and understanding of their subjects/curriculum areas and related pedagogy to enable them to teach effectively across the age and ability range for which they are trained.

Q25: Teach lessons and sequences of lessons across the age and ability range for which they are trained in which they:

(a) use a range of teaching strategies and resources, including e-learning, taking practical account of diversity and promoting equality and inclusion;

(b) build on prior knowledge, develop concepts and processes, enable learners to apply new knowledge, understanding and skills and meet learning objectives;

(c) adapt their language to suit the learners they teach, introducing new ideas and concepts clearly, and using explanations, questions, discussions and plenaries effectively;

(d) demonstrate the ability to manage the learning of individuals, groups and whole classes, modifying their teaching to suit the stage of the lesson.

Introduction

This chapter explores a range of teaching strategies that can be drawn upon in order to promote effective learning within the humanities area. History, geography, RE and citizenship are potentially exciting curriculum areas but in order to engage children's interests an emphasis needs to be placed on interactive teaching methods. Teaching strategies can vary significantly between lessons and even within lessons with both the role of the teacher and the pupil changing according to the type of organisation being used. Let us first consider the role of whole-class teaching as a strategy.

Whole-class teaching

Effective whole-class teaching is an essential part of good practice in the humanities but it is important to recognise that it can exist in a variety of forms and that it can be used in a negative manner suppressing pupil interest and learning. At its most extreme, whole-class teaching may involve the teacher talking to the pupils who listen and assimilate the information. Here there is a high level of teacher dominance and exposition with passive pupil participation. This style of teaching is based upon the traditional idea of the teacher being an instructor of knowledge. History, geography, RE and citizenship all have a substantial content base but it is important that a narrow focus on factual information is avoided and that emphasis is placed on skill and concept development.

A more acceptable style of whole-class teaching is where the teacher continues to inform and explain new knowledge and understanding but the children are encouraged to contribute more actively through discussion. Questioning by the teacher is an essential ingredient and the class learns not just from what the teacher says but also from the children's own answers and contributions. Much questioning in the classroom, however, tends to be of a closed variety testing children's factual knowledge and understanding. The use of open-ended questions that encourage children to think about a variety of viewpoints is essential if genuine dialogue is to develop. Above all effective questioning requires a positive climate in which the value of children's responses is recognised.

Whole-class teaching is particularly useful at the start of the lesson when highlighting learning objectives and introducing new content. It is also useful at the end of the lesson for reviewing and consolidating what has been learned. In the 1990s there was to some extent a reappraisal of the value of whole-class teaching and its potential value is emphasised by the significant part it now plays in both the literacy and numeracy hours. An important factor when using the whole-class approach is the length of such inputs. Children have relatively short concentration spans and may become bored and disinterested if a whole-class input is excessively prolonged. Being aware of time is critically important as well as giving children opportunity for active participation. To be an important stimulus for learning the whole-class approach requires enthusiasm, imagination and interest, but fortunately the humanities are particularly rich in the range of resources to support such activity.

Whole-class teaching is generally characterised by a high level of teacher activity through explaining and questioning with a lower level of pupil activity. It is clear, however, that if teaching is to be truly interactive and promote independent learning, then alternative approaches need to be used which are not overdirected by the teacher. Children need opportunities for discussion, to put forward their own ideas and to take some responsibility for their own learning.

Individual work

Following a whole-class teaching input at the start of the lesson, children are most likely to be given a task to be undertaken individually. A range of activities may be undertaken but commonly this will be a written task from a worksheet or textbook. Advantages of individual work are that it promotes pupil autonomy and independent learning, while allowing a more personalised approach, with differentiated work to be given to children. It can be quite demanding for teachers because of the need to monitor the class and to frequently give short inputs of support to individual children. Individual work is a vital part of humanities teaching but its effectiveness depends on the nature of the tasks set and its benefits can be undermined by an excessive diet of worksheets. A key priority must be to present children with interesting, active learning approaches, commonly referred to as enquiry-based learning.

Enquiry-based learning

Active approaches to learning are often associated with activities broadly described as enquiry-based, exploratory, investigational or problem-solving and these are at the core of good practice in the humanities. OFSTED subject reports are a useful starting point for contemporary classroom observations about what is deemed to be effective practice in relation to teaching strategies. The value of using enquiry-based work in the humanities is often highlighted, *Standards in geography* (1999), for example, concluding that g*ood geography teaching frequently uses, and encourages in pupils, an enquiry-based approach in which questions are posed about the places and themes being studied*. A strong correlation is also emphasised between effective humanities teaching and well chosen resources, the OFSTED subject report for RE (1999–2000) observing that *where RE is well taught, teachers draw on a wide variety of sources such as books, posters, pictures, music, speakers, visits and articles of faith, showing how each adds to the understanding of religions*. The importance of enquiry-based and problem-solving strategies is emphasised by National Curriculum documentation for history and geography (DfEE/QCA, 1999). In history, for example, children need to 'find evidence, weigh it up and reach their own conclusions. To do this they need to be able to research, sift through evidence and argue for their point of view – skills that are prized in adult life.' In geography children are expected to 'develop a range of investigative and problem-solving skills both inside and outside the classroom'.

A good example of an enquiry-based approach is given by Dinkele in Carter (1998) and involves a Key Stage 2 unit of work looking at local traffic problems around a school. Four key questions were investigated by the children:

- Why are journeys made?
- Where do our children come from and how do they get to school?
- What effect does our coming and leaving school have upon the village?
- What can we do to ease or solve the problem?

While whole-class teaching would be a part of this unit, using individual, paired or group work would give more scope for children to think for themselves and to manage their own learning. Undertaking a traffic count and analysing the data, for example, in a pair or small group forcefully emphasises the character of enquiry-based activities.

The acquisition of subject knowledge is clearly an important objective in the humanities but the children's acquisition of skills and understanding through process is also a key priority. The value of enquiry-based approaches for the development of process skills can be highlighted by an analysis of QCA units of work such as Geography Unit 23: Investigating Coasts. Teaching activities suggested include groups of children contributing a section to a holiday brochure on coastal destinations for tourists. Groups are allocated a particular area to investigate such as walking, beach holidays and birdwatching. Research is undertaken using a variety of resources including maps, non-fiction books, holiday information and the internet.

Clearly in this activity children will be developing specific subject knowledge about different coastal areas and their features but important process skills can also be identified including:

- collecting and recording evidence;

- communicating in different ways;
- using ICT;
- using maps;
- asking geographical questions;
- using secondary sources of information.

In the humanities area process skills developed through enquiry-based work are often not subject specific but develop through their school career. There are clear links here with current developments relating to thinking skills where the focus is about children learning how to learn. Thinking skills cover a range of areas such as communication, ICT and problem-solving. The National Curriculum 2000 has put a new emphasis on these thinking skills categorising them into information processing, reasoning, enquiry, creative thinking and evaluation skills. Wallace (2002) and Wallace and Bentley (2002) explore the practical application of thinking skills in the primary classroom and there is clearly much of relevance for humanities teachers.

The example of children's work shown in Figure 5.1 is also an illustration of an enquiry-based approach. This is the introduction to an individual project on the Royal Air Force in the Second World War undertaken by a Year 6 pupil as part of the 'Britain since 1930' history unit. The children were asked to research a topic of their choice linked to the unit, produce a written folder and also give a brief oral presentation of their findings. The children used books from home, library resources and the internet to research the topic. This particular child was also able to discuss the project with an elderly member of the family who had served in the RAF in the 1940s. Redrafting was used to produce an effective piece of writing. In this extract the child displays a clear understanding of the focus of the project and has thought carefully and empathetically about what it was like to be in the RAF during the Second World War.

MY INTRODUCTION

World War II started in 1939. The RAF was not ready when war broke out, but by the spring of 1940, the RAF had good fighters, but not enough of them. The British aircraft had to defend **and** attack. Fighters attacked incoming enemy aircraft and helped the bombers fight them off. People could see 'dogfights' from the ground. If they were lucky, the pilots and crew came home.

I chose to do this project because I have always been interested in the aircraft, especially the Spitfire, but I have found out other interesting facts, such as how important radar was, what it was like to be a pilot, and the sheer size of some of the aircraft.

I have found out just how important the aeroplanes and their crew were in World War II. I do not think that I would have liked to have been a pilot or one of the crew as it was such a dangerous job. I would have liked to have designed one of the aeroplanes or to have been one of the mechanics because I am interested in how the engines worked. The aircraft were quite beautiful in the air.

Figure 5.1 Example of enquiry-based work

Enquiry-based approaches are clearly to be encouraged and are frequently commented upon positively in OFSTED reports. Giving children more responsibility for their learning, however, can be problematic as the following OFSTED comment in Standards in history (1999) emphasises:

> Pupils undertake poorly planned historical enquiry or lack opportunities for this sort of work. Often 'research' is unfocused, with the emphasis on location and presentation of information rather than its use to answer particular questions. Poor use of ICT, and particularly of the internet, can exacerbate this problem...

Discuss these issues with fellow trainees and school mentors. What strategies might you adopt as a teacher to avoid some of the criticisms highlighted above?

Collaborative group work

Enquiry-based work and investigational activities can clearly be undertaken on an individual or paired basis but an alternative and clearly important vehicle for this is collaborative group work. This involves small groups of children being given problem-solving activities using collaborative discussion. Collaborative group work should not be confused with group seating arrangements where children sit together in groups but essentially work through tasks on their own. Group work can be a beneficial learning experience in several ways. Task-focused talk promotes thinking skills and children can learn from each other by sharing knowledge, understanding and ideas. Key skills relevant to their school career and the adult world are also promoted such as self-reliance, problem-solving and oral communication.

Successful group work depends on a number of factors:

- careful planning and preparation are required;
- good quality resources must be provided such as reference materials, maps or photographs;
- children need to be clearly briefed about the learning objectives and task;
- choosing groups is an important consideration – pupil choice? gender? mixed-ability?
- the teacher has a key role monitoring and supporting groups;
- the teacher's role is that of facilitator;
- time deadlines for group work are useful.

Waterson in Jacques and Hyland (2007) highlights many of the generic issues relating to group work.

A 'mixed economy'

Whole-class, individual, paired and group work are different ways of organising learning. All have their values and limitations but what is important is for children to experience, as Richards (1999) argues, a 'mixed economy'. With any of these strategies it is important to ensure that children are engaged in interesting and active processes which give all children an opportunity to acquire new skills, knowledge and understanding.

Select a history, geography or RE topic from the QCA schemes of work. Look through the documentation for the unit and consider where an enquiry-based approach using collaborative group work could make a positive contribution. Draw up a lesson plan in which collaborative group work is a significant feature.

Differentiation

Fundamental to any discussion of teaching strategies is the need to consider differentiation because within any primary classroom there will be a diversity of children with varying individual needs. In academic terms there may be gifted children working alongside those with learning difficulties but the needs of individual children do not just relate to their cognitive abilities. Some children are confident, enthusiastic and hard working while others may be insecure or lacking in motivation. Children's personal interests, experiences and culture vary and teachers may face a situation where English is actually the pupil's second language. Some children may have special educational needs such as a hearing impediment and can often display a preferred learning style. Matching work to the individual needs and abilities of children is clearly important in the humanities and a range of strategies can be utilised (see Figures 5.2, 5.3 and 5.4, pages 79–81).

Outcome

All children work on the same task using similar resources. The task needs to be sufficiently open-ended and designed so that it is accessible and challenging for all children. Differentiation is achieved through the response of children who will approach the task with varying levels of understanding.

Task

Tasks are designed which are graded in difficulty or stepped. Some children may only cover the easier questions allowing others to go on and tackle the more demanding tasks. Another variation might be to set the class off with a common task and then provide a range of differentiated materials such as extension work for the more able.

Resources

Differentiation can be promoted by using a wide range of resources and the humanities subjects are particularly rich in this area. To cater for children's varying levels of reading ability, it is essential that information books and worksheets that we use reflect a variety of language levels. It is important that while some resources give more help and support to children, there are also materials which challenge and demand more initiative.

Support

The level of support given to individual children plays a key role in the promotion of differentiation. Knowledge of individual children and careful monitoring during lessons is important so that the teacher can intervene whether to support a pupil with special needs or to challenge a gifted pupil.

Content

Content can be varied in a number of ways including the amount of information, the number of concepts introduced and the level of vocabulary used. Given the multi-cultural nature of our society, it is important that humanities content reflects this. In history, for example, the QCA scheme of work, 'How has life in Britain changed since 1948?', provides opportunities to explore the nature and impact of Commonwealth immigration in the 1960s. Having cultural diversity within curriculum content clearly helps to promote inclusive and differential learning.

Name: _____

Date: _____

Elizabeth I

➤ Draw Elizabeth in prison in the Tower of London

Young lady

Red hair

Big dress

Pale skin

Dark room

➤ Was Elizabeth happy in the Tower of London?

_____

_____

➤ Write or draw any facts you remember about Elizabeth I

Figure 5.2 Example of lower/middle ability activity

Name _____

Date: _____

Famous People - Elizabeth I

Use the words below to complete the sentences

London	born	Queen	sad	throne
half sister	great	England	freed	

Princess Elizabeth was _____ on the 7th

September 1533. When Elizabeth was thirteen her

_____ Mary put her in prison in the Tower of

London. Mary feared that Elizabeth wanted to take the

_____ from her. Elizabeth was very

_____ and lonely in the Tower. Elizabeth was

_____ a few years later when Mary died. In

1558 Princess Elizabeth became _____ of

England. Many people were happy. Elizabeth was a

_____ Queen and she brought peace to

_____.

Figure 5.3 Example of middle/higher ability activity

Name _____

Date: _____

Famous People - Elizabeth I

- Answer the following questions

1. When was Princess Elizabeth born?

2. How old was Elizabeth when she was put in prison?

3. Was Elizabeth happy in prison?

4. Who put her in the tower?

5. When did Elizabeth become Queen?

- Can you remember any other interesting facts about Elizabeth I?

Figure 5.4 Extension activity

In the teaching of primary humanities, there is generally less emphasis on ability groupings compared to the core subjects but differentiation is still a key issue. The distinctive nature of the humanities subjects can do much to promote a positive approach to catering for the needs of individuals. Cooper (2000) has commented how 'history can be an ideal subject for adapting to meet the diverse needs of children from a variety of social and cultural backgrounds, different ethnic groups and linguistic backgrounds and those with a range of special educational needs or disabilities'. Cooper argues how the use of a range of strategies including stories, oral sources, role play, drama, simulations and CD-Roms can make the subject highly accessible to all children, comments which can equally apply to geography and RE.

REFLECTIVE TASK

Consider the strategies for differentiation discussed above in relation to the issue of teacher workload. To what extent do you think it is practical to individualise pupils' work within a humanities lesson? Talking with experienced teachers will provide interesting insights into this important issue.

PRACTICAL TASK PRACTICAL TASK PRACTICAL TASK PRACTICAL TASK PRACTICAL TASK

Carefully observe a humanities lesson analysing the strategies used to promote differentiation such as outcome, task, resource and support. Can you suggest any other ways of enhancing differentiaton in the lesson observed?

Active learning in the humanities: useful strategies and resources

Whether using whole-class, individual, paired or collaborative group work strategies, humanities teachers have a wide range of activities and resources to draw upon to promote interactive teaching and some of these are presented below. It is important to emphasise, however, that how the teacher uses the resource or activity can influence the quality of the learning process. Television programmes, for example, are potentially very valuable resources for geography, history and RE but without careful planning, for example, using short extracts, they can easily develop into a passive, ineffective learning experience.

The importance of using a wide range of teaching strategies which help accommodate pupils' diverse learning styles is a point emphasized by Howard Gardner's work on multiple intelligences (1993). Wallace (2003) has interestingly used this concept of seven different learning areas to devise an excellent range of creative activities for a history topic on Ancient Egypt, an approach which clearly has much wider application within the humanities area.

Activities and resources
- Brainstorming sessions.
- Posing open-ended questions.
- Discussion in pairs, small groups and whole class.
- Group presentations to the whole class.
- Information-gathering and research using non-fiction materials and the internet.
- Conducting interviews and surveys.

- Giving a variety of writing experiences including diary accounts, newspaper reports, stories, letters and poems.
- Using pictorial responses as well as purely written work such as annotated sketches.
- Handling and analysing data.
- Using written documentary sources.
- Investigating artefacts and objects.
- Maps.
- Fieldwork including local studies.
- Visits to places like museums, libraries, religious buildings.
- Adult visitors to the classroom, for example to generate oral history.
- Interpreting photographs and pictures.
- Using a digital camera.
- Role play and drama.
- Storytelling.
- Music and dance.
- Artwork.
- Making a classroom display.
- Practical activities such as model making and cooking.
- Using ICT such as simulations and links with other schools via e-mail.
- Television, film and radio material, making a video.

REFLECTIVE TASK

Consider your own experiences as a learner in history, geography or RE. Which activities did you enjoy and learn best from? Which activities do you think can help bring the humanities alive? Compare your ideas and findings with those listed above.

Interpreting and analysing sources

In history, for example, a fundamental objective in many lessons would be to develop children's ability to interpret and analyse historical sources. These sources would include artefacts, visual sources, texts, music, art and historic sites. Children need to be taught how to pose appropriate questions and derive information from sources such as these. In using a Tudor portrait, for example, a wide range of questions would need to be asked:

- Is this a painting or a photograph?
- Does it look modern or is it from the past?
- Have they seen a picture like this before?
- How long ago was it made? Can they name the period it is from? (Responses to questions like these will, of course, vary greatly depending on the age and previous learning experiences of the children.)
- Can they recognise the figure in the portrait (e.g. Henry VIII)?
- How is he dressed?
- What does the style and quality of his dress tell us about him?
- Are there other clues about his importance (e.g. regalia, jewellery, attitude, expression)?
- Why did he have this portrait made?

Discussions based around questions such as these will model for the children the process of analysing historical evidence and hopefully they will eventually be able to carry out this process more independently. The same questioning process can be applied to other sources, such as historical documents or architecture from the past. It is also an appropriate approach to the use of source materials relating to other humanities subjects, such as geography and RE.

PRACTICAL TASK PRACTICAL TASK PRACTICAL TASK PRACTICAL TASK PRACTICAL TASK

Choose a geography, history or RE unit from the QCA schemes of work. Look carefully through the content and identify opportunities for using some of the teaching approaches and resources listed above.

When on school placement seek an opportunity to teach a unit of work from the humanities. In your planning and preparation incorporate some of the ideas from above. Develop some new resources and approaches to the topic which will be of value to yourself and the school, for example, making effective use of a new geography software program or in RE organising a visit to a local religious building.

CLASSROOM STORY
Key Stage 1 history

A class of Year 1 children were studying the unit: 'What were homes like a long time ago?' The teacher had assembled a collection of household objects of the late nineteenth and early twentieth centuries. Parents had also been asked for items and a few had offered to assist in the activity as adult helpers. An interesting range of objects were available for the activity including a flat iron, oil lamp, ginger beer bottle, candle holder, an old blue bottle and a trivet. The children were clearly excited by the sight of so many unusual objects on their tables and the classroom was soon filled with lively discussion about the items. 'I like this old lamp but how does it work?' 'This bottle says "Not to be taken", something nasty must have been in here!' After a short while the teacher brought the class together and focusing on one object encouraged the children to think about questions they could ask about it. Soon a set of questions were on the whiteboard. The children were asked in their groups to investigate the objects using these questions and to prepare a short presentation about their findings. Additionally the teacher provided some books with pictures of the artefacts in their working setting. During this group work task the teacher supported the children, praising good ideas and prompting where necessary. Following the short presentations, the children were given a task sheet framework on which they made an annotated sketch of one of the objects and wrote comments against key questions.

This case study highlights a number of issues including the value of using artefacts within the humanities area for promoting active learning. It also emphasises the role of the teacher as a facilitator who has planned a clearly structured lesson, prepared a range of resources but encouraged the children to take some responsibility for their own learning. Children working together to investigate the objects and to present their findings is clearly an example of 'interactive teaching methods and collaborative group work'. A particularly important aspect of this activity is the potential through group work for promoting oral language which is a powerful vehicle for developing thinking skills.

This activity is based on mixed-ability group work but what about differentiation? Within the groups children will provide mutual support, for example, in clarifying ideas about the objects. The teacher also has a key role giving support on a group or individual basis in response to the monitoring and knowledge of individual children. The task sheet framework supports less able children while also allowing more able children to be challenged. Much of the differentiation, whether in the presentation or written work, will be achieved through outcome.

Careful selection of artefacts is important in order to take into account any 'children from different cultural and ethnic groups'. For example, if traveller children were present it would be useful to include an artefact associated with traveller homes in the past such as an old water container and traveller education services might be of use here at least with the provision of suitable photographs.

CLASSROOM STORY
Key Stage 2 religious education

A Year 4 class was studying the QCA unit: 'Why is Easter important for Christians?' One of the lessons focused on the events which led to the arrest of Jesus within the garden of Gethsemane. The teacher told the story of the events at Gethsemane by reading what was written in Mark's Gospel (Mark 14:32–52). The text of the story had been enlarged onto a poster which the children could easily see. Questioning was used by the teacher to highlight key features of the story, for example, why was Jesus disappointed with his disciples and what does it feel like to be disappointed? Children were then split into small groups and given a copy of a well-known painting depicting events in Gethsemane. They were asked to discuss what was taking place in the picture and to identify the people involved. They were also encouraged to study closely the faces of the people in the painting and to suggest what feelings were being shown. Key questions relating to the activity were displayed on the board and also on a worksheet for each group. A strict deadline of 20 minutes was set for the activity. During the group work task the teacher monitored the discussion ensuring the children were task focused and supported and prompted as appropriate. The teacher observed how a few children made little contribution to the discussion. In the plenary each group reported their findings, a lively discussion taking place. Children were then asked to write a newspaper report linked to the painting and story as told in Mark's account (see Figure 5.5).

This case study highlights a number of important issues. Whole-class teaching is used to introduce and to structure the lesson. Skilful questioning is used to encourage pupil participation and discussion. The lesson also includes a good example of collaborative group work where children are given opportunity to make their own conclusions about the painting. Careful attention, however, is given to the management of time. Some of the difficulties of group work are also highlighted such as children who can become marginalised and the teacher's role which requires careful balancing. Too much intervention can impede pupil thinking, while discussion can drift aimlessly if the teacher adopts too low a profile. Notice how the lesson is underpinned by a careful use of resources including the painting, which emphasises the value of visual stimulus material as well as written sources. The use of a newspaper report format shows how written outcomes can be imaginative and there is scope here to use commonly available ICT software.

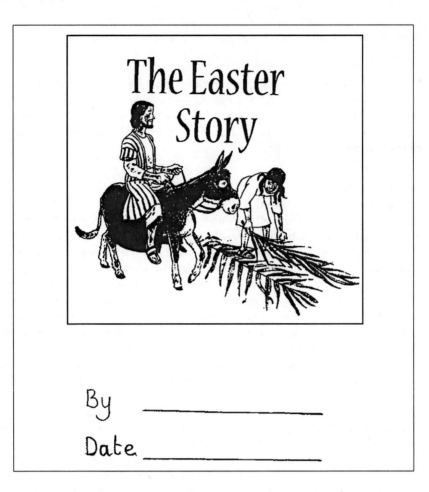

Figure 5.5 Cover of child's report of the Easter story

CLASSROOM STORY
Key Stage 1 geography

Simon taught a Reception class in a suburban primary school. He wanted to help the children explore their school grounds as he felt they had great potential for teaching and learning in geography.

He used the story *We're Going on a Bear Hunt* by Michael Rosen as a starting point. He hid a teddy bear in a corner of the playing field and encouraged the children to think of where it might be and to plan their route to find it. On the day of the 'Bear Hunt' Simon divided the class into groups of six, each with a parent helper. He gave each group an outline map of the school grounds and a compass. The children were encouraged to follow the route on the map as Simon led them 'wading through grass' and past numerous other obstacles on their hunt for the hidden bear!

This activity gave the children the experience of following a map and stimulated a great deal of purposeful talk about the school environment and about journeys. On their return to the classroom each child made a story book about their 'Bear Hunt' to enable them to share their experience.

> **CLASSROOM STORY**
> **Key Stage 2 Geography**
> Peter taught a Year 4 class and he decided to use the school grounds as a starting
> point for learning about the environment. He began with the children working in
> groups in the classroom. Each group was assigned to a window of the classroom and
> they had to comment on the view. They were asked, 'How can we improve the area we
> can see from our window?' They had to consider the main features they could see, the
> quality of the environment, their likes and dislikes and how the area could be
> improved. The book *Window* by Jeannie Baker was used to encourage the children to
> imagine how the area might look in the future.

A SUMMARY OF KEY POINTS

> Humanities lessons benefit from using a range of teaching approaches including whole-class, individual and group work.

> Make whole-class teaching effective with clear explanation, skilful questioning, lively presentation and interactive dialogue.

> An enquiry-based philosophy should permeate work in the humanities.

> Collaborative group work should be encouraged in the humanities.

> There are a variety of strategies for differentiating work in primary humanities.

> Active learning in the humanities is promoted by the use of a wide range of interesting resources and strategies.

MOVING *ON* > > > **> > >** MOVING *ON* > > > **> > >** MOVING *ON*

Standard C10

The selection of appropriate teaching strategies and resources is fundamental to effective teaching in the humanities. To develop expertise in this area, it is clearly important to plan and teach humanities lessons in a classroom context and to critically evaluate the outcomes. This practical experience, however, needs to be underpinned by a developing knowledge and understanding which can be acquired by relevant, up-to-date reading. One of the best ways to do this is by using professional journals such as *Primary History* and *Primary Geographer*, where there are numerous articles which describe a wide variety of teaching strategies.

FURTHER READING FURTHER READING **FURTHER READING** FURTHER READING

Bastide, D. (1999) *Co-ordinating Religious Education across the Primary School.* London: Falmer Press. A thorough exploration of the teaching and organisation of RE in the primary school with a strong emphasis on the importance of resources to support effective and interesting activities.

Bastide, D (2004) *Religious Education 4–11*, 2nd edn, Abingdon: Routledge. A good survey of key aspects of Primary RE.

Brown, E. (1996) *Religious Education for All.* London: David Fulton. This book provides some excellent ideas for practical activities and learning experiences in RE with all major religions being considered. It is strong in relation to differentiation and making RE relevant to all pupils.

Cooper, H. (2007) *History 3–11: A Guide for Teachers.* Abingdon: David Fulton. A comprehensive and up-to-date discussion of key aspects of Primary history.

Cox, K., Goddard, G. and Hughes, P. (2000) *Primary Curriculum Guide*. London: David Fulton. This is a useful introduction to history teaching for primary trainees. Firmly rooted in classroom practice, there is a strong emphasis on using a wide range of resources such as artefacts, photographs and music to promote stimulating and interactive lessons.

Fines, J. and Nichol, J. (1997) *Teaching Primary History*. Oxford: Heinemann. A product of The Nuffield Primary History Project, this text provides a detailed discussion of teaching strategies. Enquiry based methods are highlighted and there are numerous examples of interesting and imaginative classroom based activities.

Foley, M. and Janikoun, J.(1996) *The Really Practical Guide to Primary Geography.* Cheltenham: Stanley Thornes. A very useful introduction to geography teaching for the primary trainee. Resources and teaching activities such as fieldwork are thoroughly explored with an enquiry-based model of learning prominent.

Hayes, D. (1999) *Foundations of Primary Teaching* (2nd edn). London: David Fulton. A detailed and comprehensive core text for trainees. Chapters 6 and 7 include a very rigorous consideration of teaching and learning strategies, which are clearly applicable to the humanities area.

Marsden, B. and Hughes, J. (eds) (1994) *Primary School Geography.* London: David Fulton. This book provides a critical and philosophical discussion of geography within the National Curriculum. There is a particularly interesting section on links between geography and other curriculum areas.

Primary Geographer (Journal of the Geographical Association).

Primary History (Journal of the Historical Association).

Useful websites

www.bbc.co.uk
Useful for a variety of different sources.

www.ohs.org.uk/
www.shop.bl.uk/
Websites which provide useful sound recordings.

www.qca.org.uk/history/innovating
A useful reference website for looking up the new schemes of work and for making modifications to create your own schemes and strategies.

www.pcet.co.uk
This educational supplier produces a wide range of charts, maps, timelines and photo packs for use in humanities teaching.

6
Creativity and cross-curricular planning

By the end of this chapter you will have:

- developed your understanding of ways of introducing cross-curricular work in the humanities;
- begun to develop skills in recognising the benefits of innovative practice where it is appropriate;
- begun to develop skills in constructive criticism of innovative approaches and ideas.

Professional Standards for QTS

Q8: Have a creative and constructively critical approach towards innovation, being prepared to adapt their practice where benefits and improvements are identified.

Introduction

This chapter aims to illustrate the potential of local studies as an opportunity for creativity in planning cross-curricular work in the humanities. The contribution of Professor Aline Bless (1976, 1990) to both debate and research in this area has been lasting and influential. This research focused on the key concepts (mentioned in Chapter 2) through which real, meaningful links could be made between the humanities disciplines, without detracting from them as subjects in their own right. Much of this work was published as a Schools Council Project 'Place, time and society' (1976), and was finally written up in the book, *Making the Grade for Primary Humanities* (1990). These ideas and aspects of creativity in developing the curriculum can be traced through in the discussion of creative links across the curriculum in the NACCCE Report, *All Our Futures* (2001).

It is well known that many young children learn in a holistic way rather than in subject areas (see, for example, Buck, Inman and Moorse, 1994). Local studies provide an excellent opportunity to present learning in a manner which is meaningful to primary children, and which will therefore interest and motivate them (see Issue 52, *Primary History*). It is through the study of the local environment that many disciplines meet and converge. There is scope for the development of skills in all the core and foundation subjects, but the role of history, geography, RE and citizenship is most significant in work on local studies.

Each humanities subject has its own valuable contribution to make to local studies in terms of approaches, strategies, concepts, skills and resources. However, it is an area of the curriculum which, although rich in many senses, requires individual preparation of a kind not needed when teaching other topics. For example, whereas for a study of Egypt, its geography, history and religious background could fairly easily be resourced from book and non-book published materials, this is not necessarily the case with local studies. Occasionally, there is a publication produced by a local individual with a particular interest, such as the parish priest, and there is often a brief guide to local history. Most resources of interest at primary school level, however, will need to be found and prepared to suit their immediate purpose.

Background: selecting and preparing resources

Unless you are fortunate in teaching in a school where local resources have already been well researched, you will need to begin by finding out about your new locality for yourself. There is, however, a vast range of material obtainable for any local study and much of it is readily available in local libraries and local record offices, where staff will help in the location and copying of any useful materials. The following checklist of resources you could borrow, copy, collect or make will help you to get started:

- maps, both current and historical;
- street plans;
- photographs, both old and present-day, which you could take yourself with a digital camera;
- census data and street directories;
- artefacts;
- oral accounts which could be recorded;
- newspapers;
- parish records.

Other resources include places of local interest which you would need to visit, such as:

- the library;
- record office – both town and county have materials suitable for schools;
- church, cathedral, mosque, synagogue;
- museum;
- art gallery;
- historic sites such as stately homes, industrial archaeology;
- tourist information offices.

There are also local groups that might be able to loan resources, such as:

- a local history society;
- a drama group;
- a music group.

REFLECTIVE TASK

After thinking about your own locality, consider which feature might be most effectively used as a focus for an environmental study. Such features might be a local shopping street, a place of interest, a park or a place of worship. Consider whether it might provide material relevant to the humanities subjects and whether it would provide sufficient interest for the age group using it.

Example of a medium-term plan for a local study: Key Stage 1

Local studies can begin at home or at school. For children at Key Stage 1, their own learning context will form probably the most understandable environment to begin this kind of work. At both Key Stage 1 and Key Stage 2, there are numerous opportunities to link or combine work in history, geography, RE and citizenship, or a combination of two of these. In the example below, history and geography have been combined to create a comprehensible initial local study for a Year 2 class.

CLASSROOM STORY
Key Stage 1 history

Linda was the class teacher for a Year 2 class. She taught in an old school building, dating from 1910. At the beginning of the Spring term one year she decided that the school itself could provide a new way of working, which would stimulate interest, variety and challenge for her lively class. Starting with their immediate surroundings, she decided to develop a unit of work based around the notion of exploration – they would begin by exploring their own school to see if they could find something new. There could be opportunities for all kinds of cross-curricular work, including not only mathematics and English of course, but also history, geography and RE.

Before she could draw up her unit of work, Linda had to take a walk around the school herself and identify points of interest and potential educational value. She realised, once she started to talk about her ideas in the staff room, that the people associated with the school were a great resource in themselves. The caretaker had worked at the school all her life, several teachers had been there for many years and the deputy headteacher had even attended the school himself as a child. He could remember his experiences at school during the war. The headteacher also showed her a wonderful collection of old school log books, the earliest of which were leather bound and were locked with a heavy padlock.

Starting with the classroom where she worked, Linda realised that the old black-lead fireplace in the corner of the room must date from the original building. She decided that this would be one focus of the children's study. She then noticed an unusual pipe coming down from the middle of the ceiling. She was informed by the caretaker that this was what was left of the old gas lighting which had originally been installed throughout the school. The high windows were unusual, and Linda decided she would need to do some research into why a school should have been built with such high windows that no one could see out. She could see plenty of opportunity to link work on the history of the room with some simple mapping and plans of the room to show where these old items could be found.

Linda then went to look along the corridors and up the stairs. Here she noticed the same high windows and beautifully carved wooden handrails running up each staircase. Outside the heavy wooden outside doors, she knew that there were inscriptions. At one end of the school the inscription read 'Boys' Entrance', and at the other, 'Girls' Entrance'. Here was scope for plenty of work related to citizenship and equality, she thought.

While she was investigating these details, she came across an open door leading down a very dark staircase. Although it was hard to see and also smelled very musty, Linda found her way down and managed to discover a light switch. To her amazement, there was a huge old black cooking range, still with the ashes in it, and large pipes leading up into the ceiling. Yet another dark room revealed all manner of old-fashioned school items: a huge old easel and blackboard, an old wooden teacher's desk, and various old pots and pans. Linda quickly realised that this cellar held many secrets which would enthral her class. After some research and discussion with her school colleagues, Linda was able to draw up the unit of work shown in Table 6.1.

Table 6.1 Medium-term plan for a history-led cross-curricular topic: our school

Learning objectives	Key questions	Activities	Resources	Cross-curricular links	Assessment
Lesson 1 Find out about the past from a range of sources of information – buildings: Hi 4a	How do we find out about the past?	Discuss the notion of 'clues' which can tell us things about the past. Look around the classroom and identify clues themselves.	Classroom; example of detective story	English	Be able to point out old-fashioned features and objects
Lesson 2 Fieldwork skills: record information on a classroom plan: Geo b Place objects in chronological order: Hi 1a	How can we show what we have found?	Using an outline plan of the classroom, discuss where things could be drawn on it and add items of interest. Place labels and drawings at the appropriate point on a simple timeline.	Simple classroom plan; outline timeline	Geography; Mathematics	Place items appropriately on a plan Begin to understand that objects can be placed in time
Lesson 3 Find out about the past from a range of sources of information: buildings: Hi 4a; Geo. 2c; Art 1c Select from their knowledge of history and communicate it in a variety of ways – ICT: Hi 5; Geo 1d	What can we find out about our school?	Walk around the school as a whole class, noticing 'clues' from the past. In the classroom, discuss and list on the computer all the old-fashioned things they have noticed.	Jotters, pencils; computer and large video screen/OHP	English; ICT; Geography; Art	Be able to point out a wider range of old-fashioned features and objects Select items for discussion and recording
Lesson 4 Ask and answer questions about the past: Hi 4b	What questions do we have about our school?	Shared writing: a list of questions they want to find out about.	Paper and pencils; computer	English; ICT	Be able to suggest and frame simple questions about the past
Lesson 5 Ask and answer questions about the past: Hi 4b	How can we find the answers to our questions?	In groups, at chosen places of interest, make sketches and notes, and finally question staff in the school. Add their work to the list of questions printed off and displayed.	Note-pads; sketching paper; coloured pencils; drawing pencils; lists of questions to ask	English; Art; ICT	Be able to use questions about the past and suggest answers

Lesson 6 Select from their knowledge of history and communicate it in a variety of ways – talking: Hi 5; Geo 1d Follow route on map: Geo 2c	How can we share our findings?	Talk about their findings to the rest of the class, and then hear Linda's adventures 'down in the cellar'. In small groups, use maps to find the secret door, and investigate the cellar themselves.	Sketching equipment; digital camera	Geography; ICT	Be able to communicate their findings in discussion
Lesson 7 Select from their knowledge of history and communicate it in a variety of ways – writing: Hi 5; Geo 1d	How can we share our findings?	Write, draw and paint about what they found in the cellar for class display. Print off photographs from the computer.	Writing, drawing and painting materials; computer and printer	English; Art; ICT	Be able to communicate their findings in a variety of ways
Lesson 8 Ask and answer questions about the past: Hi 4b Identify differences between ways of life at different times: Hi 2b	How can we find the answers to our questions?	Visit of caretaker and deputy headteacher to talk about memories of school, and to answer questions.	List of questions to ask	English	Be able to ask appropriate questions; be aware of some things that were different in schools in the past
Lesson 9 Select from their knowledge of history and geography and communicate it in a variety of ways – writing, ICT: Hi 5; Geo 1d	How can we share our findings?	Make a class book, including a simple timeline, about the history of the school.	Book-making materials; writing and drawing materials	English; Art; Geography; ICT; Mathematics	Be able to communicate their findings in a variety of ways

PRACTICAL TASK PRACTICAL TASK PRACTICAL TASK PRACTICAL TASK PRACTICAL TASK

Devise an idea for unit of work for a Year 1 class, based on a school you are familiar with. Try to combine two or three of the humanities subjects in your unit. If possible, discuss your ideas with teachers and other support staff at the school. Think about your own role during the walk around the buildings and/or grounds. Carry out a pre-visit to the places you plan to take the children and note any hazards and specific points you would want to teach. Which subjects do you think you could sensibly combine for the activities to have more meaning for the children? Consider whether you would need any additional support staff.

CLASSROOM STORY
Key Stage 2

Meera taught a Year 4 class in a school housed in a Victorian building on the outskirts of a small industrial town. During the Summer term the class would be undertaking a local study, which would combine both history and geography.

Meera wanted to find a focus that would capture the children's imagination and she realised that the class had become interested in a building site near the school where an area of derelict land was being cleared to make way for a small retail park. She felt that this would make an excellent starting point to consider how places change, what they were like in the past and what they might look like in the future.

As a newcomer to the area, Meera realised that she would need to improve her own local knowledge before she could begin to plan the term's work in any detail. She started by spending time walking round the area, taking photographs of the building site with its half erected shops and the contrasting terraces of Victorian houses and other buildings nearby. She also visited the library and the town's planning department which both supplied her with a variety of information and up to date maps.

Back at school, Meera asked in the staff room for any useful local contacts, including school governors who might be happy to share their local knowledge with the children. She also checked out websites that were suitable for the children's use. She found that there was a considerable amount of research and preparation needed for teaching a unit of work based on a local study.

Example of a medium-term plan for a local study focusing on geography at Key Stage 2

Meera used the QCA scheme of work for geography as a starting point for planning her local study (see Table 6.2). She adapted Unit 6, 'Investigating our Local Area'. Most of the Key Questions and Learning Objectives remained the same but many of the teaching activities had to be changed to suit the local circumstances (e.g. the unit was based on a village whereas her school was on the edge of a town). Meera wanted to the children to be aware of how their area was changing and to consider the effects of those changes on people's lives. She also wanted to include some local history and to compare the present geography with the past.

REFLECTIVE TASK

Consider ways in which aspects of citizenship education might be effectively incorporated into a local study. Reflect critically on the issue of whether attempts to combine several subjects within one topic might be inappropriate or unhelpful in furthering children's learning. For example, will their work cover more aspects of the topic at the expense of depth and quality?

Table 6.2. A medium-term plan for a geography-focused cross-curricular theme

Learning objectives	Key questions	Possible teaching activities	Learning outcomes	Resources
Introduction				
Lesson 1 • To investigate places • To learn about the wider context of places • To make maps and plans • To use and interpret maps	• Where is our locality in relation to other places? • Where is our school?	• Ask the children to locate the UK on a globe and then, on progressively larger scale maps, to locate region, county, town. • Ask the children to find the school site on a map and aerial photographs of the town. Ask them to give directions from the school to specific points in the town, recording their directions on a map and identifying features in sequence.	• Locate their town and school on maps at a range of scales • Plan routes around the town on a base map	• Globes • Atlases • Local street maps • OS maps (1:10,000 and 1:25,000) • Aerial photographs • Postcards • Other photographs
Lesson 2 • To learn about physical and human features • To learn about land use in settlements • To use and interpret maps • To use secondary sources	• What is our part of the town like? • What was it like in the past?	• Help the children to match ground photographs of the main human and physical features to a base map of the area, naming features and listing questions for further research. Produce a class word bank. • Ask the children to study an oblique aerial photograph of the area. Ask them to use the word bank to identify the main land uses and features and then label an outline plan showing key land use boundaries. • Discuss with the children the layout of the settlement and reasons for why it is like it is. • Discuss what the area might have looked like in the past. • Locate old buildings on the old map.	• Identify main human and physical features of the area • Develop awareness and understanding of land use in the area • Develop an awareness of any recent changes to the area	• Recent photographs of the area (these could be digital photographs) • Large base map of local area • Aerial photographs • Old maps (e.g. 100 years old) • Old photographs
Lesson 3 • To collect evidence • To use fieldwork techniques • To learn about physical and human features • To learn about land use in settlements • To use ICT to handle data	• What are the main land uses in the local area? • How was land used in the past?	• Before finding out about the land use in the village, ask the children how they think land use can be recorded. • In the field, divide the children into pairs. Ask each pair to identify land use, e.g. *houses, shops, roads, services, farm land*, within a small area and mark it on a base map using a colour-coded key. • In class, collate the children's results and ask the children to present their findings using ICT, e.g. in databases, as simple graphs, as simple pie charts. • Study an old map of the area and discuss how the land was used in the past. • Discuss the findings with the children. Identify which parts of the area have changed and which have remained the same.	• Identify and understand different land uses • Record land use on a map using a key • Present findings using ICT • Understand how land use changes over time	• Clip boards • Photocopied map for each child • Coloured pencils • Large base map of local area • Old maps (e.g. 100 years old) • Old photographs • ICT programmes

	Key questions	Activities	Learning outcomes	Resources
Lesson 4 • To collect and record evidence • To learn about how the locality is linked with other places • To use and interpret maps	• What jobs do people do? How do they get to work? What services does the town provide? • What jobs did local people have in the past?	• With the children's help, design and conduct a class survey to identify adult jobs within and beyond the school. List the jobs and ask the children to sort them into categories and investigate where and how far people travel to work. • Ask the children where their families would go to buy certain goods, e.g. furniture, clothes. Ask them to use a local map to work out how they would get to these shops. • Use census data to discover what jobs local people had in the past (100 years ago). • Discuss how jobs have changed.	• Classify types of work • Understand the relationship between work and travel • Describe a journey, including the route and type of transport • Draw a simple map to show a route • Learn about the past	• Local maps • Old maps • Census data (100 years ago)
Lesson 5 • To use fieldwork techniques • To use secondary sources • To learn about environmental impact • To learn about sustainability	• What changes have taken place in the local area? • What was the area like in the past? • What might it be like in the future?	• Ask the children about the building site for the new shopping centre. What had been there before? • Ask the children to think of what effect the new shopping centre would have on local people. • Discuss the impact on the environment of the new shopping centre.	• Identify damage to the environment • Describe improvements to the environment • Know about other environmental concerns and how they might be addressed	• Local maps • Photographs of the new shopping centre

Value of using a place of worship

Most schools are within striking distance of a place of worship from at least one religious tradition. The presence of such places will reflect the religious and cultural make-up of the local community and offer a rich resource for investigating the beliefs and practices of that community. A place of worship is the source of a first-hand learning experience in which children can begin to recognise that their community is made up of diverse groups of people. Their learning can be experiential in that they can reflect on their own responses to such a visit and how it helps them understand both their own and perhaps someone else's traditions. The key purpose of such a visit will be to encourage the children to reflect on the significance of the place for that particular community: why is it important to them, what makes it special?

Preparing for a visit

There are practical and educational implications when preparing for a visit to a place of worship. Both must be addressed if the visit is to be a rewarding and positive experience for the children.

- As with all school visits, parental permission and support is needed. Parents may be sensitive to the religious context of the visit and may need reassuring of the educational purpose and learning outcomes of the visit. This might be explained in a letter and parents could be invited along. Often they may be needed anyway to improve the ratio of adults to children, but it also gives those who have concerns an opportunity to see the place for themselves.
- You should always visit the place first yourself to check out both the practical situation and to ensure that the place is suitable for a visit. Visits provide accurate information but be aware that some may reinforce negative perceptions and prejudices. For example, some religious leaders may not wish to speak to boys and girls together. Some places of worship may not offer much in the way of visual resources if they are very plain or they are in buildings which have been converted from other uses.
- Check whether there will be someone at the place who will be available to talk to the children, or whether you will need to lead the visit yourself. Sometimes places of worship have an education adviser for this purpose; more often it will be a member of the community or a religious leader. Use your judgement as to whether this person will be able to pitch a talk at a level the children will understand, and that their English is clear enough if it is not their first language. It is often wise to give the person a particular topic to talk to the children about, for example how the building is used or what happens during services.
- Prepare the children for the visit. This may include looking at examples of other places of worship from within the same tradition. This enables them to learn some of the terms associated with the place and they can also compare the real thing to the version they have seen in pictures or videos. Further preparation needs to include discussion of any dress or behaviour requirements relating to that place. For example, children may be required to cover their heads or remove shoes before entering the building. It may not be appropriate to touch certain items or go into particular areas.
- Some places of worship may charge for an educational visit, others welcome donations. It would be appropriate, for example, to take flowers or fruit to a Hindu temple, or money to a Sikh gurdwara.

Studying a place of worship in the locality

Table 6.3 shows the medium-term plan for an RE-led cross-curricular theme. This unit of work aims to show children how religion is evident in their locality. The most obvious evidence will be places of worship, but there may be other places that demonstrate the

Table 6.3 A medium-term plan for RE-led cross-curricular theme

Learning objectives	Content and activities	Resources/organisation	Differentiation	Assessment
Session 1: Special places Children will be able to: • reflect on their own special places to identify why they are special • explain why places of worship are special to particular groups	• Silent reflection: children asked to think of their own special place. When do they go there? How do they prepare to go? Who with? Why do they go? What do they do there? How do they feel when they are there? Children can then share their thoughts with their neighbours. • Reflection on why someone might wish to visit a place of worship. Encourage speculation about the various reasons why someone might go. Use above questions to help.	• Room layout suitable for silent reflection, e.g. circle of chairs. • Focus for reflection, e.g. candle.	• Allow for different responses, particularly if children are new to this type of work.	Look for: • children being able to express thoughts and explain choices • careful listening to others

Session 2: A place for worship
Children will be able to:
 	
• identify key features of a place of worship and explain their significance
• understand some of the traditions and observances relating to the place
• identify further issues of enquiry
	• Research from books to identify some of the features of the place of worship to be visited. Focus on specific terminology. These might include:
	The building – its age, history, architecture, orientation.
	How it is used – in worship, for festivals, for rites of passage, for learning, meeting, socialising.
	Who uses it and when – children, adults, particular groups.
	• Discuss use/significance of features:
	  symbolism artefacts
	  decoration focal point
	  sacred writings use of music
	  furniture
		• Books on places of worship, specific religion in focus
		• Video material
		• Posters
		• Photos
		• ICT – internet research
			• Provide a range of material matched to reading abilities of children.
			• Allow for a range of responses including written work, visual work and oral response.
				Look for:
				
				• accuracy in use of language and terminology
				• understanding of use/significance of features

Session 3: The visit Children will be able to: • consider their response to the place • identify and record key features • use interview skills to add to knowledge	• Discuss any observances required at the place, e.g. removing shoes. • Generate questions to be answered on visit. • Silent reflection. Spend first part of visit allowing time for children's immediate responses. Discuss. • Explore place gathering information in written and visual form and using ICT equipment. • Interview member of the community relating to questions raised in school.	• Drawing materials • Writing materials • Clip boards • Cameras (including digital) • Tape recorders	• Distribute tasks allowing for children's individual strengths. • Allow for a variety of responses in relation to each activity.	Look for: • ability to link classroom and field work • careful focus on key features of place • sensitive and interested questioning skills
Session 4: Follow up Children will be able to: • present gathered data in a variety of forms • explain significance of the place of worship for the community	• Use material gathered to present to a wider audience in a variety of forms, e.g.: – in an assembly – on a wall display – in a book – on a web page • Develop sketches and drawings into models and paintings.	• Art materials • Computer • Book making materials	• Distribute tasks allowing for children's individual strengths. • Make expectations for work clear to all children. • Group children according to individual strengths.	Look for: • focus on key features • ability to explain significance of place of worship and key features • awareness of audience

presence of different religious groups. The unit might form part of a wider one on the locality, which might also include work in history and geography. It is based on four sessions, including a visit to a place of worship. The learning outcomes below are based on the QCA model syllabus attainment targets (QCA, 1998) and there are links with the QCA Unit 2D 'Visiting a Place of Worship' (QCA, 2000).

Learning outcomes

Attainment Target 1: Learning about religion

By the end of the unit the children will be able to:

- identify a religious tradition represented in the area;
- describe the main features of a place of worship they have
- understand the role that the place of worship plays in the lif

Attainment Target 2: Learning from religion

By the end of the unit the children will be able to:

- consider the link between places of worship and their own special places;
- understand that religion plays a significant part in some people's lives;
- respond sensitively to issues of commitment.

PRACTICAL TASK PRACTICAL TASK PRACTICAL TASK PRACTICAL TASK PRACTICAL TASK

In your own local area, identify a place of worship which you might choose as the initial focus for local studies work with a class of primary children. Carry out the necessary background research which you would need to do if you were to teach about this place or set work based on it. Write a summary of 500 words of your findings.

Cross-curricular lesson planning

A lesson can easily be designed to retain a key focus on one curriculum subject while making use of the real links with others. Young children will relate closely to this way of working on the whole, since they naturally learn in a holistic way rather than about subjects in separate compartments. The examples below illustrate some ways of achieving this approach. They also indicate potential opportunities to address the *Every Child Matters* agenda through personalised learning.

CLASSROOM STORY
Geography
Lindsey took her Year 6 class into the local area to study shopping patterns. The children visited a local shopping centre of five shops in Little Hulton and a larger shopping centre at Walkden. Both shopping centres took about 7 to 10 minutes for children to walk to.

Prior to the visit the children discussed types of shops, e.g. food shops, take-aways, services (banks, dentists and medical centres), etc. Also before the trip the children created mental maps of their local area. This helped Lindsey to understand her children's spatial skills and local knowledge. During her teaching placements she noticed that boys are far better than girls at local mental maps. She explored this by asking children how far they are allowed to go on their own around their home. One able girl who regularly achieved a level 5 across all subjects couldn't make a mental map. When Lindsey chatted to her, she discovered that her parents drove her everywhere, to school, to her friends, etc.

On the field trip children carried a sketch map of the shopping centre to annotate. A hand-held tape recorder helped with interviewing shoppers to find out:

- how far they had travelled;
- mode of transport;
- which shops they were visiting.

After the trip children analysed their results back at school. They compared the types of shops found in the two shopping centres, e.g. how many food shops there were in Little Hulton and how many at Walkden. They questioned the types found, e.g. they saw a furniture shop in Walkden but was there one in Little Hulton? They discovered how far people travelled and whether their mode of transport was linked to the distance travelled.

Most people visiting Little Hulton walked less than 1 km and were buying small quantities of food shopping or a paper at the newsagent's, etc. At Walkden the shoppers travelled mainly by car or bus. They bought their food shopping for the whole week, or clothes or furniture.

Numeracy skills were developed by drawing bar graphs of the types and quantities of shops and the mode of transport. Literacy skills were developed in the process of asking questions, listening and analysing responses.

Building on the experiences

CLASSROOM STORY
Lindsey had the opportunity of assisting the Year 6 class on a week's residential to Lledr Hall (Salford's outdoor pursuits centre) near Betws-y-coed. The annual residential experience gave children the chance to compare their local area with a very different locality.

The trip cost £130 for a week. All the Year 6 were given this valuable learning opportunity. Monies were collected from September to just before the visit in July. Most could afford the trip; if they qualified for free school dinners then the trip was further subsidised.

PRACTICAL TASK PRACTICAL TASK PRACTICAL TASK PRACTICAL TASK PRACTICAL TASK

Decide on another more distant locality that would provide a good contrast with your own. Visit this locality and make notes about the features you might wish to compare. Carry out some background research into the area. Finally, make a note of the most useful sources of information and resources which enabled you to familiarise yourself fairly quickly with this new area.

Cross-curricular lesson plan for a history topic

The lesson plan in Table 6.4, which shows cross-curricular links within a history-led topic, develops in more detail one part of the medium-term plan for a topic on 'Our school'. It illustrates how an activity originally seen as a history one can naturally involve other curriculum areas.

Table 6.4 A cross-curricular lesson plan based on history

Lesson: part of a local studies topic on 'Our school' Age group: Year 3 Duration: one hour							
A school walk	Objectives	Prior learning	Activities	Resources	Differentiation	Key vocabulary	Assessment opportunities
History	4a: find out about changes from buildings	The class have looked at their own classroom for clues about its history	Search for clues about the school's past and its age	Clipboard and pencil	Challenge the more able children with questioning; support for less able from parent helper	clue source observe	Discussion during activities
Geography	2c: use a plan and key	They have made plans of the classroom	Follow plan of walk around the school	Plan showing route of walk, with simple key	Challenge the more able children with questioning; support for less able from parent helper	plan key route	Observation during activities
Art	1c: collect visual information using a sketchbook	They have sketched artefacts	Observational sketches	Soft pencils or charcoal and drawing paper	Work with different groups to support development of skills	sketch detail observation	Marking work
Citizenship	1e: know about the range of jobs carried out by people they know	They have talked about the work of the dinner ladies	Observe and note the work of the caretaker	Clipboard and pencil	Work with groups to support observations	Caretaker Safety Secure	Observation during activities

REFLECTIVE TASK

Review the above examples of planning and reflect on the potential opportunities within them to develop personalised learning.

PRACTICAL TASK PRACTICAL TASK PRACTICAL TASK PRACTICAL TASK PRACTICAL TASK

Using one of the medium-term plans for cross-curricular work in Tables 6.1 to 6.4, develop your own lesson plan in more detail, showing what links could logically be made with other subjects.

Lesson plan: RE topic with cross-curricular links

Very often, it is easy to see the links between RE topics and other areas of the curriculum. However, it is important to remember that any links with other subjects must be natural and logical and must not compromise the meaning and understanding of the religious content. For example, we must avoid making tenuous links with subjects which are meaningless. The story of Noah's Ark from Jewish and Christian tradition probably suffers most from this, having been linked to topics such as: water, floating and sinking, colours, animals, 2× table, transport, the seaside, rainbows, the weather – to name but a few! The result is that children are not given the opportunity to study the story in its own right to discover *why* it is an important story for Jews and Christians.

In the lesson plan shown in Table 6.5 the links between RE and three other subjects are described. We must be aware of how we are using each of the subjects and how far children's knowledge and understanding of each are being developed. Here, the primary aims of the lesson relate to RE, and the other subjects, literacy, drama and music, are vehicles which are being used to convey religious understanding. At the same time, some learning objectives relating to these subjects are also being covered.

Note that the timing covers two hours, which might be an afternoon session. This can be justified due to the number of subjects being covered.

A further note needs to be added here about covering Creation as a topic in school. The major world religions have stories that tell of the creation of the world, but there is a wide

Table 6.5 A cross-curricular lesson plan for RE

Lesson: Creation myths	Age group: Year 3 Spring term
RE learning objectives: *AT1*	Children will make links between stories they have heard about Creation myths.
AT2	Children will use knowledge of creation myths to inform a dramatic representation of Creation.
Learning objectives: *Literacy, Drama, Music*	**Literacy: Year 3** *Text level work* to identify typical story themes, e.g. trials and forfeits, good over evil, weak over strong, wise over foolish. *Text level work* to write a plan for own myth, fable or traditional tale, using story theme from reading but substituting different characters or changing setting. **Drama Key Stage 2** *Speaking and listening:* use character, action and narrative to convey story, themes, emotions, ideas in plays they devise and script. *Speaking and listening* – improvisation and working in role, scripting and performing in plays, responding to performances. **Music: Key Stage 2** 1. Pupils should be taught how to: b. play tuned and untuned instruments with control and rhythmic accuracy; c. practise, rehearse and present performances with an awareness of audience; 3. c. improve their own and others' work in relation to its intended effect.
Previous learning:	The children have been exploring myths from ancient religions and world religions. They have discussed what these stories say about the world we live in and our relationships with each other and the natural world. The focus has been on what we can learn from the myths and what they tell us about how humans see the world.
Key vocabulary	Myth, origins, creation
Resources	Musical instruments, writing materials, fabric and other items for dressing in.
Session outline: *Introduction 20 mins* *Development:* *50 mins* *30 mins* *Conclusion: 20 mins*	Remind the class of the work they have been doing on myths. Identify the distinctive features and themes. Group the children and ask them to devise their own myth which helps explain a feature of our world. 1. Children compose myth together. Teacher's role is to ask questions about the myths to see if children are thinking about meaning as well as action and dialogue. 2. Children then rehearse their scene, using instruments to add sound. Teacher's role to supervise and advise where necessary. Children perform to each other when they feel ready. Each group to discuss the ones they see and give feedback.
Differentiation Mixed ability grouping may allow those with better developed writing skills to be the scribe. Some children may need help articulating the meaning behind the story.	**Assessment** Performances could be recorded, written versions kept and feedback from both teacher and peers collected. The teacher will be looking for how far children have absorbed the narrative style of myths and how far they have understood that the most important part of a myth is the meaning that people take from it.

range of differences between beliefs within each tradition. The teacher needs to be sensitive to the children's own beliefs about Creation, which for some will be informed by religious beliefs and for others will be informed by explanations offered from science.

A SUMMARY OF **KEY POINTS**

> The humanities provide opportunities for creative cross-curricular planning.

> Local studies is a major theme where meaningful cross-curricular links can be used.

> Time needs to be allowed for personal research, preparation and the selection of suitable resources.

> Two or more humanities subjects may be combined in a cross-curricular topic or unit of work.

> Clear objectives are needed for each subject involved at the medium- and short-term planning stages.

> Valuable links can be made with the core subjects and the humanities.

> Aspects of the *Every Child Matters* agenda may be addressed in a local study.

MOVING *ON* > > > > > > MOVING *ON* > > > > > > MOVING *ON*

Standard C8
Identify opportunities to address the agenda of *Every Child Matters* through the humanities-based work which you are responsible for planning, such as opportunities to develop personalised learning.

FURTHER READING FURTHER READING **FURTHER READING** FURTHER READING

Blyth, W.A.L. (1990) *Making the Grade for Primary Humanities.* Milton Keynes: Open University Press.

Cooper, H. (2007a) *Geography 3–11: A Guide for Teachers*. London: Fulton.

Cooper, H. (2007b) *History 3–11: A Guide for Teachers*. London: Fulton.

These are detailed guides to history and geography.

NACCCE DfEE (2001) *All Our Futures: Creativity, Culture and Education. Report.* London: DfEE. This report tries to break away from the somewhat rigid structure imposed by the National Curriculum and suggests ways forward which involve forging creative links between, for example, schools and sporting or cultural institutions.

Primary History, Issue 52, summer, 2009. This whole issue is devoted to the use of the environment in humanities teaching.

Turner-Bisset, R. (2005) *Creative Teaching: History in the Primary Classroom.* London: Fulton. This book takes a fresh look at creative practice in primary history.

Useful websites

www.showme.uk/
> UK museums and galleries for children.

www.english-heritage.org.uk
> The website of English Heritage.

www.tlfe.org.uk/clicker/historyks1.htm
> Useful for humanities topics.

www.ncaction.org.uk/creativity/
www.teachers.tv/
> Sites with useful ideas for innovative lessons.

7
Monitoring and assessment

By the end of this chapter you will have:

- developed an understanding of the monitoring and assessment process within the humanities;
- developed a knowledge of teacher assessment activities including marking of work;
- begun to understand the use of level descriptions;
- considered various ways of recording assessment evidence;
- begun to recognise the value of pupil self-assessment.

Professional Standards for QTS

Q11: Know the assessment requirements and arrangements for the subjects/curriculum areas they are trained to teach, including those relating to public examinations and qualifications.

Q12: Know a range of approaches to assessment, including the importance of formative assessment.

Q26: (a) Make effective use of a range of assessment, monitoring and recording strategies.

(b) Assess the learning needs of those they teach in order to set challenging learning objectives.

Q27: Provide timely, accurate and constructive feedback on learners' attainment, progress and areas for development.

Q28: Support and guide learners to reflect on their learning, identify the progress they have made and identify their emerging learning needs.

Introduction

This chapter aims to support you in assessing and recording the progress and attainment of children in geography, history and RE.

Since the introduction of the National Curriculum through the Education Reform Act of 1988, an increased emphasis has been placed on the assessment process with national tests in the core subjects at the end of the key stages. Although foundation subjects like geography and history are exempt from formal testing in the primary school, pupil progress must be reported to parents annually. This statutory requirement does not apply to RE which is governed by a locally agreed syllabus, but this usually outlines similar responsibilities on teachers for assessment and reporting.

Evidence about the current state of assessment in primary humanities can be found in recent OFSTED primary subject reports in history, geography and RE which emphasise that despite some progress humanities assessment remains a major weakness. In OFSTED's 1999–2000 report on primary RE it was noted that *assessment remains a major weakness in RE teaching and lack of assessment information is associated with teacher's low expectations of what pupils can achieve*, while in the 2000–1 history report it was observed that *even in many of the schools where history is thriving, assessment is an area of relative weakness*. The Standards in geography (1999) report concluded *an improvement in teacher assess-*

ment but still an unsatisfactory situation in over a third of schools. To improve standards schools were urged *to continue to develop better assessment strategies both at the whole school and individual pupil's level*. In the light of these comments it is important for trainees to develop a good practical working knowledge of humanities assessment at the earliest opportunity. Analysis of the OFSTED subject reports highlights the elements of good practice. In relation to history, for example, OFSTED observed in the 2000–1 report that *where assessment is good marking provides pupils and teachers with useful information, and there is some sort of periodic assessment, such as an end-of-unit assessment, yielding information that can be used to gauge pupils progress and the success of the teaching of that unit of work*. This school-based evidence again emphasises the importance of both good quality formative and simulated assessment activities.

It is important to remember that assessment is a central part of the overall teaching and learning process. By making judgements about what children know, understand and can do, teachers are then in a better position to plan for the next stages of learning. The overall assessment process covers a range of activities which are important to clarify. Analysis of the standards highlights four key features:

- *Monitoring* involves the teacher on a day-to-day basis carefully observing children and their progress during the learning process.
- *Assessment* is using a range of strategies to collect evidence about a child's progress.
- *Recording* is the development of written documentation showing the progress of children.
- *Reporting* involves giving feedback to parents whether through written reports or orally at parents' evenings.

There are also different types and functions of assessment which need to be highlighted.

- *Formative*. Arguably this is the most important type of assessment used by humanities teachers and involves the day-to-day assessment of children's progress. The marking of children's written work and regular feedback to them which indicates how they can improve their work is a key aspect of formative assessment.
- *Diagnostic*. This type of assessment identifies specific strengths and weaknesses with a view to identifying development strategies and targets. It is clearly important in the process of identifying children with special educational needs.
- *Summative*. This type of assessment which summarises children's attainments takes place at the end of the year or key stage when a significant stage of learning has been completed. Examples of this in geography and history would be the assessment of children against the National Curriculum level descriptions at the end of Key Stages 1 and 2, providing information which could be passed onto parents or the next teacher.
- *Evaluative*. This type of assessment dimension is concerned with evaluating the overall effectiveness of the teaching and learning processes. Assessment results of individual children and their feedback would be a significant source of evidence which could help to inform future planning. A review of the content and delivery of Key Stage 2 geography units would be an example of evaluative assessment but this could also extend to reviewing the effectiveness of a whole curriculum area within a school such as religious education.

Consider and reflect upon any humanities lessons which you have observed or even taught. In particular, can you think of any monitoring, assessment or recording activities which took place? Make a note of any examples and compare them with those that subsequently are discussed in this chapter.

Monitoring

An important task for the teacher during the lesson involves monitoring the performance of both the class and individual children in relation to the activities and learning objectives. Effective monitoring skills take time to develop but it is important for trainee teachers to be aware of the teacher's role in this area. Monitoring can take place in a whole-class teaching situation where a priority is to ensure that children understand new knowledge and understanding. Careful observation of children's body language and analysis of their answers or questions can give an indication of how the lesson content and activities are being received by the class. Evidence of misunderstanding or difficulty on the part of the whole class, groups or individuals will need the teacher to respond by a possible change in teaching method. If the children are working individually or in groups, monitoring can again take place by looking at examples of work and talking with the children to ascertain their level of understanding. Here there is an opportunity for the teacher to give individual or group support and to deal with any misconceptions. Constructive feedback and discussion which supports the children in their learning is an important part of the overall monitoring process.

The importance of monitoring but also its complexity is clearly emphasised by Kyriacou (1995, see also 2007) who notes:

> What makes teaching a particularly demanding activity is the need to monitor the whole variety of concerns that need to be taken account of if pupils' attentiveness and receptiveness and the appropriateness of the learning experience are to be maintained. Such concerns include whether the pupils are becoming bored; whether the lesson has been pitched at too difficult a level; whether some or all of the pupils are completing the set work faster than expected; whether pupils are encountering problems or making errors..

Effective monitoring takes time to develop because it involves careful observation of children and quick interpretation of the signals which they give out. During a lesson it is natural for the physical process of teaching to dominate the teacher's mind but simultaneously monitoring skills must be applied as part of the teaching process. Monitoring has both short- and longer-term value for the teacher which may involve changing strategy during a lesson or amending subsequent planning.

CLASSROOM STORY
Key Stage 2 religious education

A Year 3/4 class was studying the unit 'What do we know about Jesus?' The planning and teaching was being undertaken by a PGCE trainee teacher on final placement. For the third lesson three learning objectives had been identified which were for the children to become more familiar with the structure of the Bible, to interpret readings from the Bible and to consider what the Bible readings informed us about the character of Jesus. The lesson began with the class discussing the previous session which had focused on pictures of Jesus including the controversial Turin Shroud. Using overhead projector transparencies, the structure of the Bible was explained and how to access it. Three stories about Jesus were introduced to the class in the form of extracts from the gospels of Matthew, Luke and John. Children were set to work in pairs using these extracts with the task of discussing the meaning of the story and what it said about Jesus. A worksheet with a writing frame was provided for the children to record their findings. Children were expected to report back their interpretations of the stories in a brief plenary.

When the children started working in pairs using the Bible extracts, a queue soon developed around the teacher for help, a significant number having difficulty making sense of the readings. The trainee teacher quickly became alert to this and changed the lesson organisation by going through the stories with the whole class, supporting them in relation to language issues and what the stories meant. Key ideas about the character of Jesus were identified but not in the way that had been intended.

Although the lesson had been carefully planned, structured and resourced, the teacher realised that children were struggling with the task. Instead of carrying on with the planned activity, the teacher quickly responded and adopted a different approach using whole-class teaching and giving the children more teacher support. The trainee teacher demonstrated a perceptive awareness of how the children were coping with the learning activity. Prompt, assertive and positive action was implemented to try and ensure an effective learning experience. This scenario clearly emphasises the importance of teachers using monitoring skills to identify problems and to respond to them both during and after lessons. Following the lesson the trainee's evaluation identified several practical strategies to address the problems encountered including more emphasis on differentiated work.

Setting assessment tasks for children

In Chapter 5 it was argued that good practice in humanities teaching is promoted by drawing upon a wide variety of teaching and learning styles supported by resources. A similar philosophy which advocates variety of approach needs to apply to the selection of assessment tasks so that the full ability range of children are able to demonstrate what they know and what they can understand. Plenty of imagination and a clear focus on subject learning objectives are important assets in devising assessment tasks. Hillary in Carter (1998) shows how in geography it is very feasible to use an interesting range of assessment activities which are not solely dependent on written work. In Key Stage 1, for example, activities suggested include assessing children's ability to observe and record objects in the playground and a group discussion of photographs and posters produced as part of a local environment survey. As Hillary comments, 'a range of assessment techniques is necessary to assess a child's full range of ability. Some children are better at mapwork, others may find oral presentations easier.' Some creative and interesting assessment activities in geography are also highlighted in *The Primary Geographer Assessment Special* (Geographical Association, 2001). Examples given include:

- an annotated picture-map of a fieldwork visit to a new locality;
- a newspaper report on an environmental issue;
- presentation of ideas about improving the school playground followed by a class discussion.

A similar assessment activity philosophy with plenty of variety allowing children to respond in different ways is advocated in history by Bage (2000). Key Stage 1 assessment activities suggested include children using the class timeline or display to explain what is different from today and asking the children to write a book caption, museum notice or label about an artefact explaining what this evidence tells us about how it was used. Bage (2000) emphasises how history assessment activities should allow children to *talk and explain, interpret pictures and objects, research, sort and sequence, draw, pose questions as well as writing*. Likewise, a variety of approaches need to be applied to the selection of assessment tasks so that the full ability range of children are able to demonstrate what they know and what they can understand.

PRACTICAL TASK   PRACTICAL TASK   PRACTICAL TASK   PRACTICAL TASK   PRACTICAL TASK

Choose a unit of work from the QCA schemes of work for geography, history, RE or citizenship (www.standards.dfee.gov.uk/schemes). Look carefully through the content of the unit including the section on learning outcomes and devise a range of assessment activities.

Teacher assessment activities

Teacher assessment of children can operate in a number of ways and some of these will now be discussed. The marking of children's day-to-day work is clearly important but observation of children when on task in the classroom is also a valuable strategy. These examples of formative assessment need to be reinforced by longer-term more summative assessment, for example, using level descriptions to judge attainment at the end of a key stage. Turner-Bisset (2005) highlights a range of interesting approaches to history assessment including drama, concept webs, writing frames and even oral recordings of children's thinking, emphasising the importance of diversity in humanities assessment.

Marking of work

In the humanities the day-to-day marking of children's work is arguably the most important aspect of the assessment process providing information to child and parent as well as the teacher.

- Before marking work in a school discuss the school marking policy with the class teacher or mentor. Schools will usually have a clear marking policy giving guidance to teachers in order to promote consistency across the school. The subject policy document and subject co-ordinator should also be consulted regarding marking policies.
- With any piece of work the teacher should make it clear to the children what will be the focus for marking. This will of course clearly relate to the learning objectives of the lesson or series of lessons. Children need to know what is expected of them! Comments on work should relate to specific learning objectives.
- Marking should be positive, recognising the achievement of learning objectives but also identifying any weaknesses or misconceptions which can be translated into subject targets.
- Try to avoid writing general comments on their own like 'good work' or 'satisfactory' but be analytical and include comments which are subject specific and related to the learning objectives. Focus on the

history, geography or RE content and not just use of English. Highlight why the piece of work is good or what the child needs to do to improve their work. Children need clear advice on how they can move forward.

- Ensure that written comments are legible and can be clearly seen by the children. Use a contrasting colour pen to the children.
- Children need to be clear about your expectations in relation to presentation of written work and use of English such as spelling and punctuation. Clearly these are important issues to consider when marking but subject content must not be neglected.
- Avoid excessive alterations when marking which might undermine the child's confidence. If necessary see the child on an individual basis to discuss the work and any problems.
- Marking should focus on the individual child and his or her previous performance, not how well the overall class has performed.
- Remember that marking should be a two-way process, a dialogue between child and teacher. Although time is a limited resource, opportunities should be created for review and discussion with individual children about marked work. Children need time to reflect and respond to marked work.
- For humanities teachers marking provides excellent opportunity for gathering evidence about children's progress and attainment. Areas of difficulty and misconceptions may be identified which can inform short-term future planning and teaching.
- When marking children's work it is important to recognise the possible effect on their motivation and self-esteem – marking, and indeed other forms of formative assessment needs to be positive and constructive so that the child is encouraged as opposed to being demotivated. The display of marked work is clearly important in this context.

REFLECTIVE TASK

The marking of work in the humanities is clearly an important undertaking. Consider how you might balance the demands of marking within your overall role as a teacher. What strategies might one adopt to achieve effective, but time-efficient, marking? Discussing this issue with the class teacher or humanities co-ordinator will provide some useful guidance.

PRACTICAL TASK PRACTICAL TASK PRACTICAL TASK PRACTICAL TASK PRACTICAL TASK

Look at the examples of marked work in Figure 7.1 and 7.2 (pages 110 and 111). Assess the quality of the marking using the guidance points highlighted above.

Photocopy examples of children's work in geography, history and RE. If necessary there is an interesting choice on the QCA website (www.ncaction.org.uk) which illustrates children's work at different ages and key stages. Clearly establish the learning objectives covered by the piece of work. QCA unit documents will be useful here as well as the subject programme of study. Using this information as well as the guidance points above, mark the examples of work remembering to focus on the child's subject knowledge, understanding and skills. Identify any difficulties you faced in this marking activity.

Observation of children

While most assessment in the humanities relates to written work, the observation of children, whether in groups, individually or in whole-class activity, is a valuable form of teacher assessment. Apart from purely watching children work, assessment observations can be made by questioning children in the teaching situation and assessing their responses or listening to them talking about their work. Observation can cover a number of issues includ-

25th September Tuesday
Food and Farming

There was not a lot of good farming land in Ancient Greece because it was not very flat and there is not a lot of grass. The Ancient Greeks grew barley, fruit and vegetables. They kept mountain goats and sheep for their milk and wool. They did not eat a lot of meat.

The Ancient Greek diet was made up of barley bread and porridge, fish and lots of vegetables and fruit. They made cheese from goat's milk and flavoured thier food with olive oil.

Super. You have shown a good knowledge of a typical diet for an Ancient Greek!

Figure 7.1 Example of marked work

ing subject knowledge, skills and understanding, attitude and behaviour, oral communication skills and working as a member of a team. Brief written notes can be recorded using an appropriate recording sheet and the example in Figure 7.3 shows a possible format.

CLASSROOM STORY
Key Stage 2 history

A Year 6 class studying the history unit, Britain since 1930, focused on 'The Home Front during World War 2'. An important component of the unit was the use of small groups to research key aspects such as the Blitz, the experiences of children, the role of women and food. To support the activity a wide range of resources were used including library books, wallcharts, video material, CD-Roms and the internet. Several lessons were allocated to this activity. In the first session the teacher spent much time helping to set up the project and supporting the groups, for example, giving advice on research methods. In the third lesson the groups were well established and working relatively independently. While of course monitoring the whole class at all times, the teacher spent about 20 minutes focusing on an individual group. Careful observations were targeted at both the group as a whole and individual children. The teacher was keen to observe how each child worked as a member of the group. The teacher was also interested in the historical knowledge, understanding and skills demonstrated by the child as well as transferable skills such as research ability and oral communication. Conversations within the group were carefully listened to and the teacher engaged in discussion with individual children to assess their understanding. The teacher made written notes about the children using a structured observation sheet. The teacher then moved to another table in order to begin observations of a new group of children.

Life in chembakoila   8 wednesday
                          May

5:00 Am   chanda wakes up and ~~sta~~ start~~ting~~
          ~~make~~ making papaya and rice.
          After breakfast chanda get dressed
          and sets of for work. ✓

6:30 Am   She needs to colleds some water
          for her famaily ands fulleds it for
          it will last for two days now. ✓

7:00 Am
          Chanda sets of to return to home
          a Monkey runs past her making
          her spill half the water! ✓

7:30 Am
          At last Chanda returns and
          sweeps the floor to get ready
          for her his band to come home. ✓

8:00 Am
          It is getting awfuly hot so she cooked~~s~~
          Stuffed parters with melon, her best meal,
          her husband ~~of~~ comes and eats lunch
          ~~togeth~~ alone. But chanda has to wait for
          her lunch. ✓

9:00 Am   Chand~~as~~ go's to market for food
          needs
          and ~~s~~ to ~~get~~ get home before Kulus
          dockters ~~opurtns~~ kulu has tummy ace

          ~~Chan~~ Chanda and Kulu go to docter
          Ropa and his st·ser Devan ✓

          Well written   you
          have captured the spirit of
          India with the heat and
          the food. It certainly
          sounds like a hard life.

Figure 7.2 Example of marked work

RECORD OF OBSERVATIONS

SUBJECT:_____

LEARNING OBJECTIVES:_____

NAME:	NAME:
NAME:	**NAME:**

Some suggestions for observation:

- attitude towards lesson
- behaviour
- concentration level
- work rate
- knowledge, understanding and skills demonstrated
- communication skills (oral and written)
- how the child coped with new learning
- any evidence of learning difficulties

Figure 7.3 Example of a record sheet for pupil observation

This scenario emphasises that assessment is not just about written outcomes but that children's performance can also be assessed by observing and listening to them in the learning situation. This form of assessment is a challenging activity for the teacher but nevertheless an important one giving insights into skills not demonstrated in written work such as the ability to discuss. The use of structured observations (see Figure 7.3) clearly helps to provide a more thorough assessment profile for the child which has benefits, for example, in relation to target setting and reporting to parents. Clearly such an assessment strategy needs to be discussed and negotiated with the children. An alternative approach would be to use a video camera to record group work thus allowing the teacher to analyse and reflect upon the work of the children in a less pressured situation.

Level descriptions and end of key stage attainment

Day-to-day formative assessment needs to be underpinned by longer-term summative assessment and to facilitate this attainment targets and level descriptions can be used. For geography and history the National Curriculum provides level descriptions as a basis for making judgements about pupil performance at the end of the key stages. Level descriptions describe the subject knowledge, skills and understanding which children working at that level should be demonstrating. At Key Stage 1 the majority of children are expected to work between levels 1 and 3, achieving a level 2 at the end of the key stage. At Key Stage 2 the majority of children are expected to work between levels 2 and 5 and attain a level 4 at the end of the key stage. In using level descriptions at the end of the key stage, it is necessary for teachers to judge the description which best fits the children's performance. When deciding on a particular level description, careful consideration needs to be given to the adjacent levels so that the 'best fit' is achieved. It is also important that judgements about level descriptions are based upon several pieces of the child's work. An indication of the nature of level descriptions can be seen in the geography and history examples below which describe the performance of the majority of children at the end of Key Stage 2.

Geography level 4
Children show their knowledge, skills and understanding in studies of a range of places and environments at more than one scale and in different parts of the world. They begin to recognise and describe geographical patterns and to appreciate the importance of wider geographical location in understanding places. They recognise and describe physical and human processes. They begin to understand how these can change the features of places, and how these changes affect the lives and activities of people living there. They understand how people can both improve and damage the environment. They explain their own views and the views that other people hold about an environmental change. Drawing on their knowledge and understanding, they suggest suitable geographical questions, and use a range of geographical skills from the Key Stage 2 or 3 programme to help them investigate places and environments. They use primary and secondary sources of evidence in their investigations and communicate their findings using appropriate vocabulary.

History level 4
Children show factual knowledge and understanding of aspects of Britain and the wider world. They use this to describe characteristic features of past societies and periods, and to identify changes within and across different periods. They describe some of the main events, people and changes. They give some reasons for, and results of, the main events and changes. They show some understanding that aspects of the past have been represented and interpreted in different ways. They are beginning to select and combine information from different sources. They are beginning to produce structured work, making appropriate use of dates and terms.

(The National Curriculum attainment targets in DfEE/QCA (1999), pp31, 29)

As RE is not part of the National Curriculum, there are no statutory level descriptions but locally agreed syllabuses often include end of key stage statements of attainment and non-statutory national expectations have been produced by DfEE/QCA. Some examples of level 4 expectations are given below:

Attainment Target 1: Learning about religion
Knowledge and understanding of expression and language:
Children 'show, using technical terminology, how religious beliefs, ideas and feelings can be expressed in a variety of forms, giving meanings for some symbols, stories and language'.

Attainment Target 2: Learning from religion
Response, evaluation and application of questions of values and commitment:
Children 'ask questions about matters of right and wrong and suggest answers that show understanding of moral and religious issues'.

DfEE/QCA (2000), Appendix 4: Non-statutory national expectations in religious education (levels 1–5)

The importance of level descriptions

A good working knowledge of level descriptions is important to teachers because a key part of the assessment process is ensuring that a child is performing at an appropriate level commensurate with his or her age and ability. OFSTED primary subject reports have voiced concerns about this area; for example, in relation to history in the 2000–1 report it was observed that 'some teachers have only a vague idea of what may reasonably be expected of pupils at different levels of attainment, and so do not question underachievement or raise the stakes'. Nevertheless, the use of level descriptions is not always straightforward. For example, Turner-Bisset (2005) has highlighted how the five key elements of National Curriculum history are unevenly spread across the various levels.

PRACTICAL TASK PRACTICAL TASK PRACTICAL TASK PRACTICAL TASK PRACTICAL TASK

Look carefully at the examples in Figures 7.4 and 7.5 of work done by Year 6 children. Using the level descriptions for history (DfEE/QCA, 1999, p29), try and find the 'best fit' for these pieces of work. Which level best matches the evidence in the work? Have you encountered any difficulties in undertaking this levelling activity? Remember, however, that a piece of work on its own should not be used as an indicator of the child's overall performance. This would need to be used alongside other examples of the child's work.

Now find some examples of children's work in geography and RE. Using the geography levels of description (DfEE/QCA, 1999, p31) and the expectations in RE (QCA, 2000, p25), again try and find the 'best fit' for each piece of work.

Recording

The development of an effective record-keeping system is important for a number of reasons:

- to record pupil progress and achievement in relation to the learning objectives;
- to record particular problems or misconceptions which children have experienced;
- to have a record of assessment evidence which can be used as a basis for modifying future lesson planning;
- to provide easily accessible and structured information about individual children which can be used for report writing.

Comparing maps of Cheshire Street.

We noticed: We looked at maps dated 1843, 1880, 1902 and

that in the 1843   1926.

map's had a Market House and it was where they sold good. They also

had a Police Station and the Tudor House (Pub) They had a Oak (Pub)

and a Raven (Pub) we think. The police station was on the pavement

of the street on the left hand side if you come from the

Market House. The Tudor House was built but we don't know

what it was used as.   ✓

We noticed that in the 1880 map there is a bank which kept

the money and the Market House is still their and they still

sell good. They also had a brewery where they made beer and

the police station is still there like in the 1843 but the changed

market house into Market Hall. There was an Eagles foundry

which worked with metal making things like gates.   ✓

In the 1902 map there was a public House which we don't

know who the owners of and it was a pub. There was the Raven

foundry which made things out of metal. The Police Station

had moved in between cheshire Street and Frogmore Road.

The brewery had been moved up the street. There was still

one bank and the market Hall was still their. There was

the Town Hall and the Railway Hotel and there was

pump. The Railway Hotel was built for all of the Railway

travellers. The Pump we think was used for water. ✓

We noticed that on the 1926 map (then) there were two banks and the Police Station and the market Hall. There were a Sunday school and the Town Hall was still there. There was also a Post office and the War Memorial because the war had finished. The public house was a pub. The War memorial had all of the names of the men killed from Market Drayton. ✓

There has been a police station on every map. The Market House or Hall has always been there. There has been two brewery because one was on 1880 and one on 1902.

✓

Good research.

Figure 7.4 Example of work by a Year 6 child

Balancing these needs against creating a system that is manageable in terms of workload is not easy! There is also the issue of school policy. The subject co-ordinator in, say, geography will have responsibility for assessment and record-keeping within the subject and hence will be a key point of contact for the trainee.

Nevertheless, there will also be a requirement for subject record-keeping to be integrated with the whole school policy. What then should be realistically recorded? Consider the following suggestions.

- Develop a portfolio of children's work demonstrating progression of the class in the subject area across a range of abilities.
- Individual pupil achievement in relation to learning objectives needs to be recorded and 'tick sheets' are a popular method.
- Some facility for making occasional written comments about individual children would also be sensible. An example of a record sheet for humanities use is given in Figure 7.6. Children's achievement of key learning objectives can be entered by ticking the relevant section but there is also space for supporting observations, for example, to denote a particularly good standard of work or to highlight learning difficulties. Although there are dangers of such a system being too time consuming, if used sensibly to record significant areas of progress and difficulty, it would provide a valuable resource for report writing. Various record sheet formats are in use within the humanities and the class record sheet and individual pupil record sheet found in Lomas et al (1996) are interesting history examples which can be applied across the humanities area.

I am a Scullery maid

I am 11-years-old and I'm a scullery maid for Mrs Yold.
Mrs Yold is the house keeper for Marwell Mannor, my ma was so pleased when I got the job of the new scullery maid, but I for one was not.

Every fortnight on a Sunday I get paid 6/2d and given a tart for my family, straight after that I go to Ma's and Papa's to give them the little money I earn, to help feed the family. Even though my three sisters and brother bring in quite a lot. Well, my sisters do on the other hand my brother works down in the pit earning less than me, he is now suffering from bronchitis, and will get worse and worse as he gets older

Figure 7.5 Example of work by a Year 6 child

ASSESSMENT RECORD

SUBJECT: HISTORY   **UNIT:** SEASIDE HOLIDAYS   **YEAR** 2

LEARNING OBJECTIVES

NAME	Identify differences + similarities between holidays now and in the past	Chronological understanding	Finding out about the past using a range of sources	Communicating knowledge · writing · talking
Colin	Recognised some key differences especially using visual sources.	Understands now and the 1900s. Less confident when 1950s are included. Able to use terms like a long time ago.	Worked hard using ref. books but reading ? difficult. Slower progress. Big books helpful. Used photos and not effectively	Again worked hard but struggles with sentence, structure, writing frames useful. More motivated using ICT
Aisha	Good recognition of both differences and similarities. Able to give reasons for change. Good with vocab. like modern, olden etc.	Clear grasp of different time periods and can sequence. Understands reasons. Confident.	An enthusiastic researcher. Worked well with a range of books and internet. Keen to ask questions about the evidence.	Writes well. Communicated with using captions or photos.

Figure 7.6 Assessment record sheet

Figure 7.7 Example of annotated work

PRACTICAL TASK PRACTICAL TASK PRACTICAL TASK PRACTICAL TASK PRACTICAL TASK

Develop a portfolio of children's work for one of the humanities subjects. Choose work from different year groups to show progression and also from different abilities within the same year group to show differentiation. Annotate examples of children's work to highlight new knowledge, skills and under-standing achieved as well as any learning difficulties and misconceptions. Comment on how the work could be improved and identify targets. (An example of annotated work is given in Figure 7.7.)

Reports

The production of reports is an important part of the overall assessment process. Normally the reports for the humanities areas will be relatively short compared with those for the core curriculum but nevertheless comments need careful consideration. Reports can be presented in a variety of different ways including using computer based programs, tick lists and traditional written reports.

- Report writing, as with the marking of children's work, should be supportive and positive.
- Use of language is an important consideration. Reports need to be written in a style which is informative and easily accessible to parents without use of jargon.
- A key focus should be reference to pupil progress in relation to subject knowledge, skills and understanding. Areas of difficulty should be highlighted and targets identified. Levels descriptions may be used as a basis to describe pupil progress.
- Subject discussion can be supplemented by comments about issues such as presentation of work, attitude and behaviour but remember that a report needs to be subject specific and clearly identified as a geography, history or RE report.

PRACTICAL TASK PRACTICAL TASK PRACTICAL TASK PRACTICAL TASK PRACTICAL TASK

Some examples of reports for the humanities are given below. In the light of the above discussion, critically evaluate these reports identifying both positive and negative features.

- **Year 3 geography**
  The topic 'Far Away Places' involved comparisons of climate, land use, habitats and tourism within our country. Richard contributed well to the topic. He did his own research at home and presented it to the class. He can use maps, atlases and grid references. He is aware of direction and has a good geographical knowledge.

- **Year 6 RE**
  Work has included studies of belief, worship and lifestyle in the context of Christianity, Judaism, Hinduism and Buddhism. We have looked at religious symbols and their significance. Susan thinks very carefully and can often see other points of view. She is tolerant and weighs up opinions carefully.

- **Year 5 history**
  Andrew organised and communicated historical knowledge skilfully, responding enthusiastically to our Victorian topic. He asked searching questions and enjoyed acquiring the relevant knowledge.

- **Year 5 history and geography combined**
  Tom is developing a good range of historical skills and shows an understanding of the chronology of historical events. He can recognise the similarities and differences between natural and human geographical features on the various stages of a river.

- **Year 3 history**
  The main topic this year has been Tudors. A visit to Little Moreton Hall was very worthwhile. Julie worked very hard throughout. She was very interested in artefacts and used reference materials effectively in her work. She appreciates that the past is relevant to the present.

- **Year 3 history and geography combined**
  Michael has shown a real interest. He is beginning to develop a sense of history and an understanding of the chronology of historical events. He is demonstrating an interest and awareness of the local area and the wider world.

Children's self-assessment

The current emphasis on giving children some responsibility for their own learning and developing independent learning skills has also influenced assessment practice where there is increasing evidence of children participating in some form of self-assessment. This process involves children reflecting upon what they have done and making some assessment of what they think they have achieved. As part of an overall assessment policy for humanities subject areas, children's self-assessment is clearly good practice which should be encouraged, allowing them some ownership of what is a key aspect of the learning cycle. Self-assessment for children, however, needs to be kept simple and manageable. One of the more popular and time-effective approaches is for children to indicate if they have coped well with a piece of work by drawing a smiley face and by indicating otherwise if the task has proved difficult. A more sophisticated approach, particularly for Key Stage 2, is for children to comment at the end of a unit on what they think they have learned in terms of new knowledge and skills. Through this approach children are encouraged to identify not only their strengths but also areas for development which can be translated into targets. For self-assessment to be effective the teacher has a key role to play ensuring that the children are continuously made aware of the learning objectives.

REFLECTIVE TASK

Look carefully at the example of the project assessment sheet in Figure 7.8. Apart from the comments of the teacher, there is also some evidence of the child being asked to contribute to the assessment process. What are your opinions on the use of self-assessment at primary level? If possible draw upon your own experiences as an observer or teacher in the primary classroom of pupil self-assessment. Make a list of what you consider to be the advantages and disadvantages. What do you think about the format of the project assessment sheet? Suggest ways in which the format could be improved to give the child even more effective opportunity for self-assessment.

PRACTICAL TASK

During your school experience discuss the issue of report writing with your mentor. Towards the end of the placement seek the opportunity with the support of your mentor to practise report writing. You could, for example, choose three children across the ability range and draft reports for them in whatever humanities area you have taught them.

Name .... Date 21st. 1 : 02

My project and talk to the class was about
British ~~aircraft~~ air crash

To do this work I used information from the following sources
Books – own ...✓............ Library ✓............
Computer programmes .... Internet ✓..........
Interviews - with grandparents .... other people ....

The most useful source was ..... library ..... what about the museum?

I included - pictures ...✓......... photographs....................
other artefacts ....

Did you find the research ?   difficult ✓....   easy ✗.....
interesting...✓... enjoyable .... fun .... boring......

Did you find preparing the project ?   difficult ....   easy ......
interesting....... enjoyable ✓...... fun .... boring.~~~~

Why did you present your project in the way you did ? ..because
that was the order in my file

Any other comments you want to make ? I think I could of
done the gallery of world war two planes better by puting there
names.

Teacher comments A clearly presented project containing
interesting information. It needs a bibliography.
Your talk was quiet, but clear and organised
It had a clear introduction and developed in a
controlled way. Well done!

Figure 7.8 Project assessment sheet

A SUMMARY OF **KEY POINTS**

> Assessment is a fundamental part of the teaching and learning process and should not be an add-on activity.

> Monitoring skills need to be used during lessons to identify pupil progress and difficulties.

> Assessment informs teachers about the effectiveness of their own teaching as well as the progress of children.

> Within the humanities a variety of assessment strategies should be used including marking of written work, observations of children and pupil self-assessment.

> Marking of work needs to be positive, clearly related to subject learning objectives and identify development points.

> Record-keeping systems need to be manageable and efficient but contain sufficient subject attainment information for purposes such as reporting.

> Reports to parents need to be subject specific, clearly identifying pupil achievements as well as targets for the future.

MOVING *ON* > > > > > > MOVING *ON* > > > > > > MOVING *ON*

Standard C31, Standard C32, Standard C33, Standard C34

Developing effective strategies in the humanities can be challenging for trainee teachers. A key early focus should be the quality marking of written work, targeting specific subject-related learning objectives. Practical experience of pupil self-assessment and written observations of a small group of children could then be developed. Simple, straightforward record keeping documentation needs to be experimented with. Skills in assessment can clearly be helped by observing other teachers at work in this area and discussing with them their own approaches to monitoring, assessing and recording within the humanities in order to raise levels of attainment.

FURTHER READING FURTHER READING FURTHER READING FURTHER READING

Bastide, D. (1999) *Co-ordinating Religious Education across the Primary School.* London: Falmer Press.

Davies, J. and Redmond, J. (1998) *Coordinating History across the Primary School.* London: Falmer Press.

Halocha, J. (1998) *Co-ordinating Geography Across the Primary School*. London: Falmer Press.

Although explicitly aimed at subject co-ordinators, these three books provide valuable information for trainees about the teaching and organisation of RE, history and geography. All contain useful ideas and practical suggestions for effective assessment and record-keeping.

Cooper, H. (2007) *History 3–11: A Guide for Teachers*. Abingdon: David Fulton. A very thorough, up-to-date guide for primary history with useful assessment advice.

Hayes, D. (1999) *Foundations of Primary Teaching, (2nd. edn.)* London: David Fulton. A perceptive discussion of key aspects of primary school teaching with a detailed and insightful section on assessment issues.

Jacques, K. and Hyland, R. (eds) (2007) *Professional Studies: Primary and Early Years.* Exeter: Learning Matters. This book is a useful core text for trainee primary teachers. Although adopting a generic approach, the chapter on assessment, recording and reporting includes much good practice which is relevant to the humanities.

DfEE QCA (2000) *Expectations in Religious Education at Key Stages 1 and 2.* London: QCA.

SCAA (1997) *Expectations in History at Key Stages 1 and 2.* London: SCAA.

SCAA (1997) *Expectations in Geography at Key Stages 1 and 2.* London: SCAA.

These publications provide useful examples of children's work which seek to illustrate subject expectations in Key Stages 1 and 2. They are a useful resource from an assessment perspective forming a focus for discussion in relation to assessment tasks, marking, level descriptions and portfolio development.

Useful websites

www.ncaction.org.uk

www.standards.dfee.gov.uk/schemes

8
Equality, inclusion and diversity in the humanities curriculum

By the end of this chapter you will have:

- developed your understanding of factors which can affect children's learning;
- begun to acquire knowledge and understanding of how to make provision for personalised learning in the humanities;
- developed your understanding of ways of promoting equality and inclusion in your humanities teaching;
- begun to acquire knowledge and understanding of the roles of other professional colleagues.

Professional Standards for QTS

Q18: Understand how...the progress and well-being of learners are affected by a range of developmental, social, religious, ethnic, cultural and linguistic influences.

Q19: Know how to make effective personalised provision for those they teach, including those for whom English is an additional language or who have special educational needs or disabilities, and how to take practical account of diversity and promote equality and inclusion in their teaching.

Q20: Know and understand the roles of colleagues with specific responsibilities, including those with responsibility for learners with special educational needs and disabilities and other individual learning needs.

Introduction

Learning in the humanities, as in all other areas of the curriculum, is affected by a wide range of factors. The ECM agenda requires that we address the needs of individual children and this means that, in order to plan appropriate differentiation, the different factors which may be influencing the learning of each child need to be taken into account. These factors can include cognitive and maturational development. The knowledge and understanding of children of the same age can vary greatly, due to differences in their intellectual development or general maturation. These factors may in turn affect their interest levels, an issue which needs to be taken into account when planning and resourcing lessons. Social, religious, ethnic, cultural and linguistic differences may also affect children's knowledge and understanding of different curricula areas, as well as their motivation and interest levels. In many multicultural classrooms, there is a wide diversity of needs, therefore, and this chapter will begin to assist you in recognising these and in making provision for them.

Hilary Claire (1996, 2001, 2004a) has written extensively on issues of equality, inclusion and diversity. She sees these issues as of central importance in the education of the young child. Her research into issues such as equality and inclusion in history shows how the curriculum need not marginalise women, minority groups or those with disabilities. She suggests further reading and a wide range of resources to assist you in planning for an inclusive curriculum. Helena Gilespie has drawn together useful work on special needs in history, which can be found on the History Initial Teacher Training (HITT) website (www.history itt.org.uk/).

Establishing an enabling learning environment

The school and classroom environment can significantly affect the quality of children's learning. Consequently, an important factor in effective learning is the establishment of a purposeful, enabling environment. Levels of interest, pace of learning and conceptual under-standing are all influenced by the classroom context. There are many factors that cannot be controlled by the teacher, such as the degree of support provided for the child out of school, their emotional and physical well-being when they arrive in school, or their stage of intel-lectual development. However, a secure working atmosphere, achieved through sound relationships, security, comfort and good classroom management are fundamental. The physical organisation of learning resources can affect the flow of lessons and in turn, chil-dren's motivation to learn. This is particularly true of the humanities, where the accessibility of resources such as globes, maps, books, pictures, charts, timelines and ICT resources may, in themselves, motivate and contribute to learning. Their careful organisation and accessibility, however, is crucial in independent, personalised learning.

Personalised learning

A particular feature of meeting the needs of every child is the adoption of methods which enable personalised learning to take place, along with skill in making good use of other professionals who may be able to support this approach. As most teachers and educational theorists would agree, children of all ages and abilities respond positively to high expecta-tions and a supportive learning environment. There are many ways of developing personalised work in the humanities, such as research and enquiry into an individually chosen topic, book making, diary writing, or creating ICT presentations. However, children of all ages and abilities require guidance, structure and support in differing degrees. They particularly need guidance in how to find information for their humanities topics and then how to use it. They will need to have suitable websites selected for them and have help in finding relevant material in children's books on history, geography and religious education.

They will also need guidance in devising questions to guide their enquiry work in the humanities. The following example of a mind-map, drawn up by a Year 2 child, shows how this process can start at Key Stage One. A verbal form of this kind of reasoning and enquiry might be useful for children in the Foundation Stage.

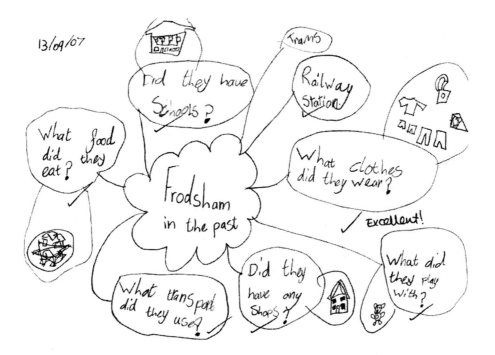

Figure 8.1 Mind map (Year 2 work)

The KWL grid is another useful form of support in guiding children to frame useful questions for their enquiries in any aspect of the humanities. The grid also enables them to evaluate what they have found out and involves them in self-assessment. Different levels of support will be needed in helping the children complete their grids, from helping the children formulate and write down their questions to giving them freedom and choice to compose their own independently, depending on their different abilities.

K (What I know already)	W (What I want to know)	L (What I have learned)

Figure 8.2 Example of a KWL grid

In communicating their findings, they will need support and direction. For example, if creating their own book or website, they will need guidance and direct teaching of the necessary skills. The strength of this approach is that it is completely open-ended and allows any level of response to be valued, as long as it is the child's best work.

Children realise the value of producing a really well presented booklet of their work in the humanities. If, for example, they have been carrying out some research into a humanities theme such as local studies, there is little more that they enjoy than making their own book about the subject. Paul Johnson (see, for example, Johnson, 1998) has written several excellent guides about how to teach children to make and bind books of their own, many of which are truly beautiful. Once a child has invested great energy and time into producing their own book, they will inevitably strive to ensure that only their best quality work will fill its pages. An added incentive is to allow the children to keep these topic or project books and to encourage family members and carers to take an interest in the child's work. Further examples of how the full potential of all children can be achieved are described in the following classroom story.

CLASSROOM STORY
High expectations in local and environmental studies

John was working on a local studies topic with his Year 6 class in a school situated in an education action zone. The major problem John had faced when he began to teach in this school was the general lack of motivation among the children and the lack of pride in their work. He had noticed that, somehow, this atmosphere pervaded the school, and that some of the teachers who had been there for many years had begun to accept these standards. During the term, his class had been looking at the local area as part of a cross-curricular humanities theme. The work the children had produced in their exercise books, however, seemed scrappy, and John was convinced that the children could improve on this. He devised a number of ways to try to motivate the children to become more involved.

Apart from altering the focus of the study to ensure it was more child-centred, John decided to look at how the children's work was presented. Clearly just putting small pieces of information into an exercise book did not interest them. He studied books about book-making and display, and drafted out a letter inviting the children's parents to the school later in the term to see their work. He then explained his plans to the class. The children worked hard to produce some books for their local studies, designing their own individual covers using printing, collage, wax resist and various other media. Some incorporated photographs into their front cover designs.

The children were interested in John's ideas about a display of their work in the school hall. He had negotiated with the headteacher some space for this and explained what he thought the class could do. These ideas included large-scale painting, collage and three-dimensional models. The children were again excited by his ideas and quickly set to drawing out the background scene of the location of their old school. They printed off labels and captions on the computer for their display. They then put together, using large cartons and boxes, a model of their old school building, along with trees, lamp-posts and other street furniture. Once painted and with the finishing details added, the scene looked really impressive.

Producing the display was only a start, however, for John now wanted them to give presentations about the things they had learned in the course of the local studies topic. Each child worked at a separate area, such as what they could find from the school logbooks, census data or street directories. Others found out about the children that attended the old school, or asked people like older members of staff to talk about their memories. All these contributions were then put together to form a class presentation for the school and for the parents of the children in John's class. John was amazed at how many people came: compared with parents' evenings, the turnout was very good. He realised that it was because the parents and carers had become involved and interested in what the children were doing. They also wanted to show their support for their children on the day. Of course, it was a great success, with staff, parents and children in the rest of the school impressed at how much John's class had found out. What had impressed the other staff was the high quality of the work and the individual presentations that John's class had managed to produce. Although exhausted at the end of the day, John realised that these methods had succeeded in motivating his class and raising their attainment in many ways.

REFLECTIVE TASK

After reading the classroom story above, look back on classes and settings where you have previous experience. Reflect on the potential difficulties you might encounter in using the methods described with groups such as these.

Differentiation

In addition to providing opportunities for personalised learning through open-ended tasks, differentiation is a vitally important part of provision in the humanities. The Warnock Report in 1978 said:

> *The purpose of education for all children is the same, the goals are the same but the help that individual children need in progressing towards them will be different.*

(DES, 1978)

Children's learning and behaviour both rely heavily on the provision of work set at an appropriate level for them to be challenged, yet at the same time for them to also have a sense of achievement. It is in the area of social learning that Vygotsky (1962) made one of his most important contributions. He introduced the notion of a 'zone of proximal development', where children are able to achieve more with appropriate adult support in the form of 'scaffolding'. You can 'scaffold' tasks set for children to complete by providing verbal support, working alongside the child and encouraging them to follow your example, or, in the case of independent written work, by providing 'sentence starters'. For example, following lessons on the lives of children in the Second World War, instead of giving a Year 4 child with reading and writing difficulties a set of questions to answer, you could provide sentence starters such as the following:

- Children in the Second World War often felt very . . . .
- In the Blitz, children would hear . . . .
- Because of the rationing, children did not eat many . . . . .or . . . .
- People in Canada used to send children things such as . . . .

This type of scaffolding can, of course, be modified to suit the needs of more or less able children, with those with more severe difficulties using drawing or tape-recording to respond to set tasks. Writing frames are also useful as a form of scaffolding. These can be adapted in endless ways, such as proving sentence beginnings and in another column, sentence endings, which the children match and write out or cut out and join together. They can also be used to provide relevant key vocabulary or phrases to support children in their own writing.

See Chapter 6 for more detailed discussion of strategies for differentiation and examples of differentiated work.

Supporting children with English as an additional language (EAL)

This is a very important aspect of work in humanities in modern classrooms, especially in inner-city, multicultural schools, where there is a school population which is constantly changing, with refugees, immigrants or children arriving with their families for extended visits. The position of the child who has recently arrived, for example, from Bosnia or Afghanistan is perhaps the most problematic. Having experienced at first hand possibly traumatic scenes, then to have lost their home, and finally to find themselves in a strange classroom, not able to understand very much at all is a terrible situation for young children to find themselves in. Their learning must be considerably affected, and it is the responsibility of the humanities teacher to alleviate the child's difficulties as much as is possible.

The teacher, therefore, needs to have some general knowledge about language acquisition and some understanding of the nature of bilingualism and the role the first language plays in learning (see Baker, 1988, 2000a, 2000b, 2001). A key aspect of the teacher's knowledge, however, is an awareness of the factors that impact on the acquisition of an additional language.

- Cultural diversity.
- The language of different subject areas.
- Different writing systems.
- Ways of accessing specialist help.
- Current legislation.
- Ways of liaising with families.
- Saturday or evening schools and the impact of these on the child's learning.

The QCA point to the need for sensitivity in working with children who have recently arrived in Britain. Care is needed when dealing with emotive topics such as those studies in the humanities, particularly in history, involving war, refugees or movements of people and families from their homes:

> The experiences of children who have lived overseas can be an asset to the history class. However, it is important to understand that some children may wish to put their experiences behind them and might feel uncomfortable if required to draw on recent traumatic events as part of their learning in school. Drawing on children's past personal experience requires appropriate professional judgement and sensitivity. Even work in history that does not appear to be directly related to the experiences of the child may raise difficult issues.
>
> (www.qca.org.uk)

On the other hand, children's past experiences of education might not relate to their present learning context.

- Class sizes might be different in their home country.
- Teaching and learning styles might be different.
- Concepts of the subject or topic might be different. For example, in their home culture, history might not be broken down into different 'periods' as it is in Britain.
- Prevalent beliefs, views and attitudes might be different for children coming from parts of the world where there are different religious traditions.
- Children will not be familiar with common aspects of British life in the present or the past.
- They will experience difficulties in using and interpreting sources.

These are only a few of the challenges faced by children arriving from other parts of the world, but they need to be taken into consideration in your planning and teaching of humanities topics. What is important is to maintain high expectations. You can achieve more with children with EAL by planning jointly with specialist ethnic minority achievement staff, who will provide ideas for enabling these children to access your lessons. To assist children with EAL in speaking, reading and writing in humanities lessons, you can make use of:

- modelling, which allows children to rehearse and explore the language they will need;
- shared reading and writing;
- collaborative reading and writing with peers;
- scaffolding, using writing frames, for example;
- additional support staff to assist with speaking and writing activities;
- adaptation of curriculum topics to include work on an aspect more familiar to them. For example, children newly arrived from Pakistan might find work on the theme of the Indus Valley interesting and meaningful.

However, above all, lessons need to be engaging and to make use of visual, auditory and kinaesthetic approaches as well as language to assist children with EAL to participate fully.

There are groups and organisations which provide support in the form of materials for children and teachers facing these difficulties. These include EMAG (Ethnic Minority Achievement Grant) and NALDIC (National Association for Language Development in the Curriculum). The section on 'pathways to learning for new arrivals', found at www.qca.org.uk, has many useful ideas, along with a DfES publication, *Access and Engagement in History* (2002, also available at http://publications.teachernet.gov.uk).

Assessment is an issue which needs careful consideration in particular. For example, a child may have a good understanding of a subject but not have the language skill to communicate this knowledge. The regular use of diagnostic assessment will enable you to target frequent or common errors in a child's use of English. Therefore, assessment tasks need to be accessible to the child. The teacher also needs to be aware that they are not assessing skill in language use, but in the subject.

Inclusion

Inclusion refers to the act of including children from different backgrounds. It applies both in the social and the intellectual sense, since children need to be considered full members of the class and school community, and they also need to feel involved in the content of lessons and the curriculum in general. Children from all different backgrounds and abilities have an equal right to full access to the curriculum. Therefore, to ensure equality of opportunity, the teacher must use strategies designed to ensure inclusion and access to the curriculum for all.

An inclusive classroom

Inclusive practice requires that individual children, whatever their circumstances or background, are treated equally and with respect. Such practice involves a detailed knowledge of the abilities, interests and backgrounds of each child, in other words, a child profile. This profile might include the results of assessments and continuous monitoring of their progress. It might also include comments on their personal progress and interests, both in and out of school. Individual Education Plans would be included in building up these child profiles. This detailed knowledge and understanding of each child will then support you in providing a more personalised learning experience for the children in your class.

An inclusive curriculum

While the curriculum for most of the humanities subjects is wide-ranging, encompassing different places, people and faiths from around the world, the curriculum for history seems to focus heavily on Britain. However, there are many ways of ensuring that the curriculum for history is also culturally rich and varied. For example, there are resources such as story books which could be used in teaching history in the early years or at Key Stage 1, which draw on the lives of families from widely different backgrounds. Examples of significant people could be drawn from cultures across the world, both black and white, such as Mary Seacole's career as a nurse during the Crimean War (see Seacole 1857/1999).

At Key Stage 2, the multi-cultural nature of British history can be emphasised. For example, the Romans, Saxons, Vikings, Danes and Norman French brought to Britain many different cultures. In the Victorian period there was considerable emigration and immigration, which included Jewish and Asian populations. The period of the Second World War provides excellent examples of how multi-cultural history really is, when people from Asia, Africa, Australia and the Caribbean all volunteered to join the British forces. Following the Rose Review of primary education (DCSF, 2009), there is likely to be a greater focus on cross-curricular work and the combination of humanities subjects to form themes or topics. In these themes there will be an excellent opportunity to forge a truly inclusive curriculum which can better meet the needs of those children and those families who have recently arrived as new members of local communities in Britain.

REFLECTIVE TASK

Reflect on aspects of the humanities curriculum and identify further opportunities to include examples of the roles played in the history of Britain by members of different cultural and ethnic communities.

What do we mean by special educational needs?

Special educational needs can include an enormous variety of different kinds of need. Some of the major categories that you may encounter in school are listed below:

- the needs of the gifted and very able child;
- specific learning difficulties (SLD);
- hearing or visual difficulties;
- moderate learning difficulties (MLD);

- physical or medical difficulties;
- emotional and behavioural difficulties (EBD).

Teaching the gifted and very able child in the humanities

Our task as teachers is to meet the needs of all the children we teach. We need to create opportunities to interest, motivate and challenge all to help them reach their potential. Freeman (2002) discusses the changing view of how to teach the most able over the last fifteen years. Prior to 1994, the needs of the brightest were not officially catered for. The author stresses that meeting the needs of the most able has a positive knock-on effect to all children. The major principles of the gifted and talented programme are identify, accelerate and enrich. These three principles are clarified and examples are given.

The author also gives details of the support that is available; for example, a toolkit for teaching the gifted is at present being developed for all teachers and BPRS research grants are available to teachers to research giftedness in their classroom.

In this research Eyre et al. (2002) have two main aims.

- To identify the repertoire of strategies used in effective teaching of able pupils.
- To work towards a pedagogical understanding of the effective teaching of able pupils.

The article reminds us of Bloom's (1964) taxonomy of thinking from low order to high. It is shocking to read of research carried out in Year 1 of secondary schools showing that 85 per cent of tasks are low order. This makes the reader question whether primary school pupils are entitled to develop a range of skills beyond those of a low order. The authors quote from HMI reviews on the variety of factors which makes an effective teacher of able pupils, including paying close attention to the needs of the individual pupil through the differentiation of tasks. The research studies five teachers over two terms. The data is categorised and discussed under four headings.

- Teacher beliefs about learning.
- Classroom climate.
- Teacher-pupil interaction.
- Task setting.

In conclusion, Eyre et al. (2002) summarise the extra qualities that effective teachers of able pupils seem to possess.

Typical characteristics of gifted and talented pupils include the following. According to Owen and Ryan (2001), they:

- have a thirst for knowledge and learn quickly;
- have a very retentive memory;
- can concentrate for long periods on subjects of interest;
- have a wide general knowledge and interest in the world;
- enjoy problem solving;
- have an unusual imagination;
- show strong feelings and opinions and have an odd sense of humour;
- set high standards and are perfectionists;
- possess keen powers of observation and reasoning, seeing relationships and generalising from a few given facts.

You will need to adapt lessons and teaching styles to encourage and challenge the very able child. Having within the classroom a selection of resources from the next key stage is a good idea to help extend individual children's research skills, such as asking a child to compare a place studied by the whole class, e.g. Chembakolli village in India, to another place, e.g. a village in Morocco, such as Imahl.

Increased responsibility can be allowed the very able child in choosing and directing their own enquiries, such as deciding upon their own questions to answer, or the form that they will use to put their information together at the end. You will be able to expect wider reading, longer and more skilful written pieces and good contributions to classroom discussions. The very able child will need to be challenged more extensively to go further than their peers in their thinking and communication. They may wish to develop creative topic work of their own which they can work on at home as well as in school, and can then share with the class.

Over recent decades, there has been considerable interest and literature on the teaching of the gifted and very able child. Freeman (2002) argues that meeting the needs of the most able has a positive effect on all children in a class. Issue 47 of the journal, *Primary History*, on history for the gifted and talented, contains much useful information and ideas for practice (Historical Association, 2007).

Figure 8.3 Year 5 work on the Second World War. An example of children's work which combines history, English and ICT

Specific learning difficulties

These occur commonly in most mainstream classes and can include the following features. Children of normal intellect sometimes have difficulties in specific areas:

- poor drawing and writing skills;
- clumsiness and poor body organisation;
- poor spelling, maths/reading skills;
- difficulties with right/left disorientation;
- emotional immaturity;
- language difficulties – either in understanding verbal instructions or in expressing self adequately.

Children with specific learning difficulties may go on to develop behavioural problems such as anxiety, withdrawal or aggressive behaviour, particularly if their needs are not addressed.

Specific learning disability – dyslexia

Dyslexia is thought to be a neurological disorder which results in difficulty in reading and deciphering text of all kinds. It might also relate to organisational problems in reading, writing or general activities. Dyslexia can easily remain undetected for many years, especially if the child has already begun to use strategies to overcome aspects of their difficulties. Dyslexia can affect children's memory, speech, reading, spelling, handwriting, story writing and study skills. It often manifests itself in the form of untidy writing, apparently careless mistakes in reading and spelling, and the child is often criticised for a careless attitude towards the presentation of their work. Children with dyslexia or dyspraxia may find that their thinking outpaces their ability to write. This can quickly lead to loss of motivation and a rejection of the standards that are expected of a particular age or ability group. Eventually, if unchecked, the accumulated effects can result in antisocial or aggressive behaviour, since the child can become frustrated by constant lack of reward and a sense of continual under-achievement. Dyslexia can, of course affect progress in humanities subjects in school. In all subjects, reading speed and accuracy can lead to lack of comprehension and a failure to meet the learning objectives. This can affect learning in history in particular, where there is a heavy emphasis upon the use of written sources. It can also affect a child's ability to read and comprehend numbers, particularly in the form of tables or charts. This clearly has implications for a considerable amount of work, for example in geography, which may rely on the effective interpretation of data.

The teacher, therefore, needs to be aware of potential difficulties in this area, being constantly alert to the fact that a child with dyslexia may not have been identified. Children with statements need support in reading and structured, scaffolded tasks. Such scaffolding should include text in a large font size, preferably on a pale coloured background, and a marker to help the child follow lines of text. These techniques are thought to aid the child who suffers from difficulties in searching for visual clues to decipher text. Positive adult support and encouragement are important, since it is vital that the child does not suffer loss of self-esteem. Other strategies you might find useful include the following.

- Encourage children to use a scribe or dictaphone to record their ideas.
- Show children how to create simple mind-maps, which can be sequenced and written up in sentences later.

- Use colour coding and the sense of touch, such as letters and words created in different textures. Older or more able children might write on coloured slips of paper.
- Teach children how to cut and paste on the computer to help them sequence their ideas.

Appropriately scaffolded 'sentence starters', as previously mentioned, and writing frames will also support the child with dyslexia. You might, for example, ask a child with dyslexia to write two words or phrases under each heading in the following writing frame.

All about me		
What I look like	My house	My school
•	•	•
•	•	•

Figure 8.4 Writing frame

Writing frames can, of course, be adapted to suit the needs and stage of development of each child. However, a key principle to remember is that children with learning difficulties benefit from very clear organisation, headings and specific guidance on what they need to do. This helps them to focus on the task in hand and reduces the burden of having to struggle with organisation as well as other problems with spelling and letter formation.

A variety of tasks need to be planned, which do not exclusively rely on skill in reading, writing or using data. It is important to be clear on the purpose of the children's activities; if writing is not the main focus of demonstrating understanding then other methods could be used to achieve the same outcome, such as using a camcorder, oral presentation, word-processing, or cut and paste exercises. Story, role-play and drama based on humanities themes can enable the dyslexic child to achieve their potential and greatly build their self-esteem.

An essential issue, however, is in the marking of written work, where account must be taken of specific difficulties. Care must be taken not to confuse the child's lack of skill in aspects identified as areas of difficulty with their real skill in understanding the content of the work. Other methods of assessment, such as talking, artwork, presentations, drama and display may enable the child with these difficulties to fully demonstrate their abilities in the humanities.

Hearing difficulties

Hearing is the ability to perceive sound. It is a passive process, since you cannot learn how to hear. Listening, however, means paying attention and attaching meaning to what has been heard. This is an active process, and you can learn how to listen. Listening is a vital skill. Research shows that teacher talk is the most commonly used teaching method, on average occupying at least 60 per cent of most lessons! *Most people talk at about 100 to 200 words a minute. At that rate, a one-hour lecture could contain up to 12,000 words – a short book!'* (Petty, 1993, p109).

Factors affecting the ability to listen include:

● classroom noise level;
● classroom management;
● teaching style.

Listening in the classroom is different to home life. For many children it will be like learning a new language – they will need to learn how to:

● adjust to a whole-class situation;
● develop skills of extended listening;
● develop the ability to extract information from what they have heard.

Creating a listening classroom

The humanities provide a wide range of opportunities to develop a listening classroom. For example, history lessons will make use of sound recordings and videos, stories, oral accounts, interviews, drama, role play and children talking about their research. However, you need to work at creating a listening environment. Be aware of your classroom – open areas with hard floors, high ceilings and reverberating sound makes it hard for children to listen. Use quiet corners for listening and small group work. Wherever possible, children with poor hearing/listening skills should sit near to the teacher and away from corridors/doorways, buzzing computers and other sources of noise.

● *Enhancing communication* – remind children that they need to listen. Ensure all children can see you. Avoid having the light behind you as it puts your face in shadow. Try not to speak to the board, many children need to lip read. Give listening breaks – children can only actively listen for up to ten minutes, while for the hearing impaired make this five minutes. Recap previous lessons. Have an outline of today's lesson on the board to help children to cue into what is going on. Visual clues help – pictures, key words, flash cards, objects, etc.
● *Enhancing understanding* – check comprehension often. Use open questions. Say children's names before asking a question – some children need: 'Darren, I am going to ask you a question next, are you ready?' Some children need to be encouraged to listen by giving them a specific task, e.g. 'Sally, in the passage, listen carefully for the name of the river'. Another strategy would be to get children to do a simple action every time they hear a specific word, e.g. 'Listen to this passage about life in a tropical rainforest, make a tick for every plant or animal I say'. Once instructions have been given to the whole class, ask a pupil to retell. With 'question and answer' sessions, the teacher should repeat an answer for all children to hear.
● *Positive marking*:
  – Marking should be specific and related to the task set.
  – Ideally marking should take place with the pupil present.
  – Praise and reward work, e.g. smiley faces, stickers, merits, certificates.
  – Corrections should be clearly written to enable a child to copy.
● *Positive lessons* – think about the following:
  – Seating – where should the pupil sit? should they be near the board? away from doors or windows? next to a well motivated pupil?
  – Instructions – should be clear and concise. Set only one task at a time. Make eye contact.
  – Encouragement – often those with the biggest problems are reluctant to ask for help. Create a climate which encourages all to ask.
  – Avoid – ridicule, sarcasm, put downs. Do not compare to others in the class. Do not compare to other relatives.

- Improve children's self-esteem – many children with behavioural problems have low self-esteem. If showing displeasure, label the action rather than the pupil.
- A variety of teaching and learning strategies should be used – multi-sensory methods are great for dyslexic children.

CLASSROOM STORY

Sally was on her final teaching placement and was being challenged as a teacher by the unique needs of a Year 1 child with Asperger's Syndrome. In order to include this child within lessons, Sally needed to research this particular special educational need. By speaking to the class teacher and looking on the internet, Sally adapted her teaching style to ensure all her children were on task.

The child's particular needs required attention to:

- short-term planning – creating a school to parent diary to aid organisation;
- drawing skills – providing outlines ready drawn, helping with layout, providing space in which to work;
- social skills – organisation of children's groupings as Sally could not rely on friendship groups including the child. She needed to keep monitoring the progress of groups and to provide clear tasks;
- moving from tasks – constant reminders and encouragement were needed. For example, at the start of day she described what she would be doing that day and when. At the start of each lesson she provided clear teaming objectives and timings;
- Sally planned exactly what she intended saying.

In addition to these considerations, Sally ensured that during her lessons she provided extra support for this particular child. She made sure that she herself could provide help if the classroom assistant was not available.

PRACTICAL TASK PRACTICAL TASK PRACTICAL TASK PRACTICAL TASK PRACTICAL TASK

Safran (2002) provides a useful starting point for any teacher wishing to know more about Asperger's Syndrome. The child with Asperger's generally has average or above average intelligence but lacks social awareness and skills. The typical characteristics are also discussed, e.g. an inability to appreciate non-verbal behaviour. The article reassures teachers by offering strategies for helping pupils develop social/team skills. The Asperger's child needs very clear instructions and routines, e.g. the use of an egg timer to control contributions within discussions.

Search on the internet for Asperger's Syndrome. Make a list of key characteristics. What can the teacher do to maximise the learning potential of children with this special need?

Teaching visually impaired children

'Visually impaired' refers to children who have little or no sight. This can have serious consequences for their learning in the humanities if not fully taken into account. The British Journal of Visual Impairment includes a wide variety of articles of direct relevance to the teaching of humanities. Lewis et al. (2002) discuss research into how blind children develop spatial awareness and an understanding of the relationships between places. Euclidean understanding is the 'ability to think in straight-line directions, e.g. sitting in your kitchen and pointing out the straight-line' direction to your bathroom upstairs. The authors carried out research with both sighted and blind children to find out if they could point to places (rooms) in their own home both using straight-line directions and pointing out the route they would take. For example, pupils were taken to their bathroom and asked if the bath overflowed into which room would the water flow down to. Lewis's conclusion is that a lack of sight does not stop pupils developing spatial understanding.

All humanities subjects include as a normal part of planned activities visits out of school and the use of a considerable amount of visual material. Clearly the implications of these activities for children with visual impairment will need careful thought. The classroom story below provides an example.

Examples of different types of visual impairment include:

- *Myopia (nearsightedness)*. If a child has myopia they cannot focus on distant objects including the teacher. The body language of the teacher may be missed. It is important to stand near the pupil, and not with a light source behind you.
- *Astigmatism*. This involves an uneven curve to the eye and is generally corrected by wearing glasses. Children would appreciate clear bold black print on a matt surface. Some students may also be light sensitive.
- *Nystagmus*. This involves involuntary movement of one or both eyes. Near vision tasks are very tiring, and children may need to tilt their head to obtain the best focus. Printed tasks need to be well spaced to avoid blurring.
- *Retinitis pigmentosa*. This involves the degeneration of the retina. These children need well lit environments.
- *Retrolental fibroplasia*. This occurs when the developing eye receives too much oxygen and scar tissue may exist on the retina. Intense light helps these children.

Some children may have difficulty in discriminating between colours. This doesn't have a solution and wearing glasses doesn't solve the problem. Teachers need to think in black and white and avoid colour coding within tasks. Within geography, colouring maps is a normal activity, so teachers need to be more adventurous and use different symbols, shapes and textures instead of colours. When coloured pencils and paints need to be used ensure these have labels on them to aid the pupil.

CLASSROOM STORY

Susan, an experienced teacher, was taking over a mixed ability Year 6 class which included Marie, a student with no sight. Susan was looking forward to this new challenge, but was naturally apprehensive about how to adapt her teaching style and resources to enable Marie to fully participate in class.

Lessons became more orally focused. When work was written on the board, Susan read aloud the information. Showing a video of a rainforest in a geography lesson, the sounds of the forest were accessible to all. Regularly during the video, pauses were made, and volunteer children recapped the visual clues about the rainforest.

Nas was to begin teaching practice at a school in Derbyshire and met with the classroom teacher beforehand. The mixed-ability Year 5 class contained a girl with visual impairment. As well as being diagnosed with nystagmus, the child also had 6/36 vision and tunnel vision. This condition meant that the detail the child could see at 6 metres was the level of detail most of us could see at 36 metres. With only a sixth of the distance vision problems were caused when using OHPs or board work and facial expressions of the teacher could not be seen. The other conditions meant this reduced vision would also be flickering and limited on the periphery.

The classroom teacher outlined the following strategies for teaching humanities.

- Never allow the child to share worksheets, maps or books.
- Always make sure she is at the front for any demonstrations or video films.
- All written tasks and reading needs to be in large print, font size 16 or above (black on white is acceptable).
- If using an OHP, give the child a hard copy of the overhead to refer to.
- Allow more time for reading instructions.
- Cue the child in for questions by using her name.
- Avoid black and white diagrams, as colour helps to distinguish features.

Nas found these strategies helped her support the visually impaired child to enable her access to lessons in geography.

Children with moderate learning difficulties

Children with moderate learning difficulties are common in most primary classrooms, and often include pupils with a reading age below their peers. Thinking about the reading ages of textbooks and resource sheets may help the young learner. There are a variety of tests you can carry out in order to judge the reading age of a piece of text.

SMOG Index stands for 'simple measure of gobbledegook':

1. Find a section with 30 sentences.
2. Count how many words have 3 or more syllables = A.
3. Find the square root of A.
4. Add 8.
5. This is the reading age.

The FOG Index stands for 'frequency of gobbledegook':

1. Find a section with 100 words.
2. Count the number of complete sentences = B.
3. Count the number of words in each of the complete sentences = C.
4. Find the average sentence length C/B = D.
5. Count the number of words of three or more syllables = E in the 100-word section.
6. Add together D and E, multiply by 0.4 and then add 5.
7. This is the reading age.

PRACTICAL TASK   PRACTICAL TASK   PRACTICAL TASK   PRACTICAL TASK

Try out the FOG and SMOG methods on this textbook, and on a range of pupil texts.

Children with severe physical or medical difficulties

These children are likely to be taught in a separate, specially designed unit or school. However, if they are being taught within a mainstream class, they are likely to be supported by a full-time classroom assistant with special training in managing their needs. Nevertheless, whatever the situation, the features of good practice in humanities teaching identified above also apply to these children. They, like others, need stimulating, challenging, interactive methods to promote their interest and learning across the humanities.

Children with emotional and behavioural difficulties

You will need to take advice from an experienced teacher. Many will probably suggest that paying attention to particular behaviour produces or reinforces that behaviour. If you are in the classroom first, the child is entering your space which encourages them to conform to your expectations. You need to focus on the task you want the child to complete rather than focus on the behaviour, and for many children with these problems, visual sources based on the humanities provide a strong stimulus. Avoiding embarrassment for the child reduces the likelihood of confrontations, and individual attention and talk can often prove valuable for children in need of emotional support.

Children from different minority ethnic backgrounds

Humanities subjects can play an important part in the elimination of racism, sexism and other forms of discrimination by showing how they have arisen and how they can be dealt with. For example, an historical study of Commonwealth involvement in the Second World War can demonstrate the important roles of black individuals and communities, both then and now.

Figure 8.5 An African soldier: Year 4 work

The variety of cultures often found in the modern classroom provide a rich resource for learning in the humanities. However, you will need to ensure the schemes of work do not exclude particular groups of children. (See for example Lewis and Coxall, 2001.) Activities aimed at valuing our multicultural society can be on a large or small scale. For example, you could start with place names and children's names. These provide an insight into the multicultural links of our community. In the names of streets and buildings there is evidence of past societies and of recent heroes from other parts of the world, such as Nelson Mandela. Local studies in urban centres has a naturally inclusive focus, where immigrants, refugees and asylum seekers all make up local communities. There are many local community organisations which provide information, small exhibitions and resources for teaching.

All of the humanities subjects provide good opportunities to study other societies and to begin to understand the reasons for how they evolved. For example, the history of Benin might provide a way into some study of the slave trade and its eventual abolition. While the work of William Wilberforce is fundamental, children could be introduced to the work of Olaudah Equiano, a slave from Benin who won his freedom, and then assisted Wilberforce in his abolitionist work. Equiano has produced a fascinating autobiography, in which he describes his childhood memories of Benin (Equiano 1789/1995).

Resources and displays need to include people from different backgrounds, cultures and races to emphasise the fact that all are considered equally important in the curriculum. It is also worthwhile trying to use an equal number of images which give a positive view, particularly of African and Asian cultures, and which avoid stereotypes. For resources on this aspect of the curriculum, see www.nationalarchives.gov.uk/pathways/blackhistory/.

There are a number of strategies based on the humanities for introducing new arrivals into your classroom. If your school has links with another school you could plan a route through your local community for them which covers important site factors and interesting names of streets. A 'guide to our local area' could be created to help the visitor or newcomer to understand the names in the locality. A school in Exeter has created an emergency dictionary for new children translated into the languages reflected by the cultures in their locality. This is displayed in all classrooms. The pupils in the school researched the languages spoken at home, and generated a selection of about 20 words/ phrases that a non English speaker would need to know, such as 'Fire!' (Snowdon, 2001).

Gender issues

With regard to gender, there is a need to ensure the schemes of work do not exclude groups of children, either boys or girls. Certain topics, despite what we may like to see, do interest girls while others appeal more to boys. It is important, therefore, to be aware that topics which may have appealed to you as a girl or boy may not motivate all the children in your class. Topics about the Second World War, for example, will inspire Key Stage 2 boys to research all the finer details about aircraft at that time. On the other hand, dress, changing fashions and costumes from around the world or different religions may well appeal to many of the girls. When selecting aspects of a theme, therefore, it is useful to aim for a balance in the types of subject likely to motivate different children.

There is also a need to ensure that the resources children use are balanced and avoid stereotypes. You will also need to see that the use of certain types of resources is equally apportioned. This is particularly true in the Foundation Stage and Key Stage 1. At these young ages, children have already responded to much social stereotyping. This can have a significant impact on their learning in certain areas of the curriculum. For example, when using constructional toys, especially if there is free choice involved, you will need to ensure that the girls sometimes have an opportunity to play with the toys and to make models. These resources are often dominated by boys, who have been trained to assume that this is their area of expertise. These assumptions can easily spill over into history and geography activities such as model-making and map-reading.

There are a number of issues relating to gender within RE. Traditionally, many of the major world religions could be described as being male orientated. This has been expressed in a variety of ways which include:

- a male image of God;
- exclusion of women from influential roles;
- role expectations for men and women;
- absence of female role models;
- absence of women from literature and history.

These issues have been addressed in recent years within certain faith groups and a greater equality between men and women is sought in many quarters. However, issues remain and in the course of any RE study will need to be addressed in the classroom. This can be done in a variety of ways.

Notions of God

Many children from Christian backgrounds may be familiar with the notion of God as 'Father' and this male image of God is prevalent in the Christian tradition. Some Christians have concerns about this and are working towards more gender-neutral ways of referring to God. This can be modelled in the classroom where personal pronouns can be avoided so that 'God' is used where appropriate. For example, 'What do you think God would think of the way the world has developed?' rather than 'What do you think God would think of the way his world has developed?' In addition to this, children's study of other world religions will demonstrate to them that not everyone sees God in male terms. Islam, for example, prohibits any images of God and avoids describing God in human terms. Hinduism offers a completely different perspective, in which the ultimate, Brahman, is seen in a variety of forms including male and female.

The role of women

It will be obvious to older children studying religion that men and women appear to have different roles to play in religious life and that often it seems that women have a lesser role. Those within religious traditions would argue that this is not the case, and that while men and women's roles may be different, both are valued equally. Some religious traditions, for example, are critical of current society that does not consider child nurturing to be an important role. In the classroom we may take the opportunity to reflect on the roles that men and women have in our society and to ask some important questions about the messages we receive from our families and wider society in comparison to the messages received from the religious traditions. Children will need to consider, for example, why, in some traditions, men and women are separated during public worship. This might include discussion of times and places that men and women are separated in general society.

It is important that we do not stereotype religious traditions as being, for example, 'bad to women', nor that we use the situation in other countries as being the norm. What is important is that we attempt to give an honest picture of life as reflected in our families and the wider society in which we live. Alongside this we need to make the best use of the resources we have, which includes people from religious traditions. Some ways of doing this might include:

- Finding visual resources which contain images of men and women in different roles, e.g. Sikh men serving food to the congregation at the gurdwara, Muslim women teaching the Qur'an to students.
- Asking parents or local community leaders to talk about men's and women's roles.
- Locating religious writings in which women play an important role, e.g. Queen Esther in Judaism, Ruth in Judaism and Christianity.
- Identifying women in history or contemporary society who play a leading role within their tradition, e.g. women ministers in Christianity or women rabbis in Judaism.

Issues of class

Issues of class and social disadvantage can often be hidden within schools and classrooms. However, children from disadvantaged backgrounds will almost certainly be acutely aware of their disadvantages compared with their middle-class peers, and you will need to employ positive strategies to ensure these children feel fully included. The humanities offers a wide range of opportunities to achieve this aim. For example, an emphasis, in RE, on respect for all, fairness and equality will help instil an inclusive attitude on the part of the whole class.

You can also try to offer opportunities to empathise with other social economic groups. Address questioning and examples to the children's experiences. For example, if working in a deprived area foreign holidays may not be part of their prior knowledge. Access to the internet and resources such as books need to be available in school time, as many families do not have these. The cost of trips may be an issue, and alternative plans may need to be considered if fieldwork is a very regular feature of the school's work in the humanities.

Organising space, tools and materials: an example from RE

CLASSROOM STORY

Fiona's Year 2 class were studying the Christian ceremony of baptism and Fiona had made contact with the local Anglican church. The minister had kindly lent various Christian artefacts associated with baptism, including a scallop shell, a baptismal candle and a baptism certificate. Fiona also borrowed her own christening gown from her mum. Fiona constructed a baptism display using the artefacts and books and posters she had found. She left space on the boards for the children's work and reminded the children that the objects were special and therefore needed to de handled carefully.

Within a few days of the display being set up, Fiona noticed that the children appeared to lose interest in it. She was also unsure as to how far the children had understood what the items were and the role they played in the ceremony. After consulting the Anglican minister, Fiona decided to stage a baptism ceremony with the children. A visit to the church was made and the minister re-enacted part of the baptism ceremony using a doll for the baby and some of the children as members of the baby's family. The artefacts that had been in the classroom display were taken along and used. The minister was used to talking to children and explained the ceremony well, highlighting those aspects that he thought the children would understand. The minister used phrases like, 'in a real baptism we would.,.' to make it clear to the children that they were only watching a re-enactment.

The children really enjoyed their visit and back at school were able to talk about the events and link in the artefacts in a much more detailed way.

Using religious artefacts in the classroom

- Emphasise respect in relation to talking about and handling objects.
- Some artefacts may need to be protected, for example a Qur'an would not just be left around. Check the detail of how items need to be treated.
- Keep artefacts in suitable containers and clearly labelled. This will help to emphasise respect.
- Make distinctions between clothing so that 'dressing up' clothes, such as a bridesmaid's outfits, are separate from more significant items such as a Sikh turban.
- If you do role-play, make sure the children are reminded that they are not taking part in the real ritual.
- Invite a member of the focus community in to 'share' their experience of particular rituals.
- When demonstrating yourself, use language which 'distances' the activity from the real thing, for example 'at this point in the ceremony, the minister might...'.
- Children should not be asked to take part in anything that may offend them or their parents. This should be considered if prayers, for example, are going to be recited.

Equal opportunities

RE offers particular opportunities to address issues of equality and inclusion relating to special educational needs, cultural diversity and issues of class and gender. The principal aims of RE include helping children to reflect on their own values and experiences and developing positive attitudes towards others. RE should present children with opportunities to share their individual perspectives and learn from the perspectives of others.

In relation to special educational needs, we should be aware of the range of activities that we can use to explore religious understanding and concepts. Too often there is a heavy reliance on reading and writing skills in RE which can inhibit those with difficulties. In order to provide for all children, wide use can be made in RE of discussion, music, artefacts and visual aids specifically chosen to match the particular needs of the children. For example, children with visual impairment might benefit from exploring artefacts which can be handled, or from taking part in discussion. Children with hearing difficulties might be offered posters and art work relating to religious traditions. Looking at particular foods which relate to festivals is an activity which would engage many children with learning difficulties. The main thing is to be creative and make the best use of the particular skills the children have.

RE for all: festivals

One of the most popular RE topics in the primary school is festivals. The QCA scheme of work for RE (QCA/DfEE, 2000) contains six units across the year groups which focus on festivals and celebrations. The popularity of this topic is understandable given that most children will have had experience of celebrating something – whether it is explicitly religious or not. Religious festivals are one of the main ways in which young children experience their religious tradition and whether or not they understand the full significance of the festival, they will know how their family celebrates it. The features of many festivals also make them particularly suitable for use with children of all ages and abilities. Many festivals include preparation in the home, decorations, special food and clothing, gathering of the community, special services and traditions and so on. All of this means that there is ample opportunity to provide active, engaging activities for children which draw on their own experiences and allow them to contribute according to their own skills and qualities.

CLASSROOM STORY
Divali

Claire was working with a group of children who had a range of learning difficulties including behavioural and physical. She was keen to provide RE which would appeal to the children's senses and encourage them to share their experiences. She was also aware that the children were entitled to a full RE curriculum which included exploration of a range of world religions. During the Autumn term Claire prepared a unit on Divali from Hindu tradition (Divali is also celebrated by Sikhs). She consulted the QCA unit of work 'How and why do Hindus celebrate Divali?' selecting from and adapting it to meet the needs of her group. Her plan was for the children to spend the week in which the Hindu community would be celebrating doing a range of activities relating to Divali. Because many of the children had difficulty with reading and writing, Claire decided to focus on practical activities which drew on a range of curriculum areas. The activities she prepared included the following.

- Making shadow puppets which were then used to tell the story of Rama and Sita.
- Making diva lamps using clay which were then decorated.
- Circle time in which children shared special times they had experienced.
- Circle time talking about 'good and evil' and other stories the children knew where good overcomes evil.
- Making rangoli patterns using coloured chalks in the playground.
- Making traditional Hindu sweets with a volunteer mum.
- Playing traditional Hindu music while the children were working.
- Switching off the lights and lighting candles to tell stories from Hindu tradition.
- Preparing a display table with divas, books about Divali, greetings cards.
- Showing a video of a family celebrating Divali.
- Creating a dance based on the theme 'good and evil' using Hindu music.

Claire felt that the range of activities offered all the children in her group a chance to participate in the study of Divali. At the end of the week her group put on an assembly for the other classes showing all the work they had done. This final activity Claire felt really boosted the children's self-esteem as they shared their expertise about Divali.

PRACTICAL TASK PRACTICAL TASK PRACTICAL TASK PRACTICAL TASK PRACTICAL TASK

Identify a child you have worked with who had some kind of special educational need. Having read the classroom story above, consider what kind of RE activities would be most suitable for that child.

A SUMMARY OF **KEY POINTS**

> Learning in the humanities is affected by many other factors. A personalised learning approach will help you address these factors.

> High expectations are needed to achieve high standards of work.

> Those unfamiliar with the subject will need to do some research into English as an additional language (EAL).

> It is important to find out about the requirements of children with different types of special educational need and consider strategies for meeting these needs.

> Multicultural classrooms provide a rich resource for teaching and learning.

> It is important to ensure equality of opportunity for boys and girls through equal access to the curriculum and to resources.

> You can devise positive strategies in the humanities to ensure the inclusion of children from disadvantaged backgrounds.

MOVING *ON* >> >> >> **>** **>** **>** MOVING *ON* >> >> >> **>** **>** **>** MOVING *ON*

Standard C18, Standard C19

Review your own knowledge and understanding of the special needs of each group identified in Standard C18. Identify one aspect of SEN which you consider to be your weakest area, or alternatively one which is most relevant to your school or setting and carry out some personal research into it. Next, consider ways in which you might develop and improve the personalised provision you make for this group of children with special needs within your area of responsibility.

FURTHER READING FURTHER READING FURTHER READING FURTHER READING

Brown, E. (1996) *Religious Education for All*. London: David Fulton. This book focuses on the place of RE within special educational needs. It offers guidance and advice and some examples of topics taught to different age groups.

Claire, H. (1996) *Reclaiming Our Pasts: Equality and Diversity in the Primary History Curriculum.* Stoke-on-Trent: Trentham Books. Claire's research into issues such as equality and inclusion in history shows how the curriculum need not marginalise women or minority groups. She suggests further reading and a wide range of resources to assist you in planning for an inclusive curriculum.

DfES (2002) *Access and Engagement in History*. London: DfES. Available at http://publications.tea-chernet.gov.uk, this publication is aimed at KS3 but the ideas and suggestions are useful for primary teaching.

Ekwall, B.O.E (1960) *The Concise Oxford Dictionary of English Place names*. Oxford: Clarendon Press. A useful starting point for the origins of place names, e.g. Celtic, Scandinavian and meanings, e.g. 'by' (village),'beck' (stream).

Gateshill, P. and Thompson, J. (1992) *Religious Artefacts in the Classroom*. London: Hodder & Stoughton. This book offers a variety of ways in which religious artefacts can be used to support learning. There are lists and explanations of artefacts from a range of religious traditions together with advice about how they should be used.

George, D. (1999) *Gifted Education: Identification and Provision*. London: David Fulton. This book provides teachers with some useful ideas and worksheets to help them identify and meet the needs of the gifted and very able children in their classes.

Hall, D. (1995) *Assessing the Needs of Bilingual Pupils: Living in Two Languages*. London. David Fulton. Hall provides support, strategies and ideas for planning and assessing the work of children with English as an additional language, an issue which is difficult but which needs to be addressed if we are to have an inclusive approach to teaching and learning.

Homan, R. (2000) 'Don't let the murti get dirty: The uses and abuses of "artefacts"', *British Journal of Religious Education,* 23: 1. This article considers the appropriate use of religious artefacts in the classroom and argues that some of the ways they are presented to children might trivialise their significance to believers.

Howard, C. (1995) *Investigating Artefacts in Religious Education.* Norwich: RMEP. Detailed advice and guidance on the use of artefacts in the classroom. Different approaches are offered with explanations of the use and significance of the different artefacts.

Lewis, L. (2001) 'What's in a name?', *Primary Geographer*, 23:10.This article reminds us of the history behind our surnames, and how as teachers we can help our classes explore cultural influences through investigating registers. These cultural influences extend to local dialects and place names. Lewis offers key questions for us to explore at Key Stages 1 and 2.

Ofsted (2004) *Managing the Ethnic Minority Achievement Grant: good practice in primary schools.* London: Ofsted. This Ofsted report gives a number of examples of good classroom practice and of case studies.

Rutter, J. (1995/2000) *Refugee Children in the Classroom: A Handbook for Teachers*. Stoke-on-Trent: Trentham. There is an increasing number of children entering British primary schools from refugee backgrounds. This book provides some valuable insights and suggestions for managing potential problems and meeting their needs.

Smith, C. (2005) *Teaching Gifted and Talented Pupils in the Primary School: A Practical Guide.* London: ChapmanEducational.

Wallace, B. (2000) *Teaching the Very Able Child: Developing a Policy and Adopting Strategies for Provision.* London: NACE/Fulton.

www.dcsf.gov.uk/curriculum
Useful advice on strategies for supporting children with dyslexia, dyspraxia and other learning difficulties.

Useful websites

www.bbcactive.com/schoolshop
The website of BBC Active, containing information about recent resources on Black History.

www.nagty.ac.uk/
Website of the National Academy for Gifted and Talented Youth.

www.nationalarchives.gov.uk/pathways/blackhistory/
This site has resources for black and multicultural history.

www.qca.org.uk/qca_12071.aspx
This web page gives details of a bibliography produced by the QCA on teaching about multi-ethnic histories suitable for KS2.

www.standards.dfes.gov.uk/primary/publications/inclusion/newarrivals/
www.schoolsweb.gov.uk/locate/pupilsupport/eal/
www.literacytrust.org.uk/Database/EALindex
www.literacytrust.org.uk/Database/EALres.html
www.teachers.tv/video/
These websites provide information on methods and resources for supporting children learning EAL.

www.schoolhistory.co.uk/forum/
This website is for teachers to share tips and advice teaching history to children with SEN.

9
Making the most of links with literacy and mathematics

By the end of this chapter you will have:

- developed your understanding of the requirements for the skills tests in literacy and numeracy;
- developed your understanding of the potential links between the Framework for Literacy and Mathematics and the humanities;
- considered the links between the humanities and language and the potential for developing skills in both subjects;
- considered the links between the humanities and mathematics and the potential for developing skills in both subjects.

Professional Standards for QTS

Q16: To have passed the skills test in literacy and numeracy.

Q15: Know and understand the relevant statutory and non-statutory curricula and frameworks, including those provided through the National Strategies, for their subjects/curriculum areas, and other relevant initiatives applicable to the age and ability range for which they are trained.

Q17: Know how to use skills in literacy and numeracy to support their teaching and wider professional activities.

Q23: Design opportunities for learners to develop their literacy and numeracy skills.

The QTS skills tests in literacy and numeracy

In order to achieve Qualified Teacher Status, it is important to know that you are required to have passed the skills test in literacy and numeracy. This can be done at any of the centres set up in your area for the purpose. For detailed guidance on the test, see the website of the Training and Development Agency for Schools (TDA), www.tda.gov.uk/skillstests.

PRACTICAL TASK PRACTICAL TASK PRACTICAL TASK PRACTICAL TASK PRACTICAL TASK

Access the website and try the benchmark test to see if your skills are 'up to speed'.

The links with literacy

Literacy across the humanities

The language skills of reading, writing, speaking and listening are embedded within the National Curriculum for geography, history and citizenship, and in the National Framework for RE, all of which require children to develop their skills in communication throughout the primary school. In using oral and written sources, artefacts, maps, globes, statistics and charts, children are extending their skills in the use of all forms of language. Also, in each of these subjects, and in cross-curricular thematic work, children need to be able to communicate effectively what they have learned through talking, reading and writing.

The humanities are, above all, thinking and problem-solving subjects, where language and thought both play a large part. Research has shown how language and thought are so closely related as to be inseparable (Vygotsky, 1962, Bruner, 1990). Theorists see the development of skills in language as part of learning to think, not simply a by-product of it. Indeed, Bruner argues that it is social interaction and the language associated with it that promotes the development of thinking skills. He sees learning as an active process in which learners use their knowledge and understanding to construct new ideas. These theories are very relevant to the humanities.

Geography and literacy

Geography in the National Curriculum places a heavy emphasis on literacy and language skills. Geographical enquiries make use of all aspects of communication, and this is reflected in both the curriculum content and in activities used to deliver it. Activities involve children asking geographical questions, recording observations, expressing their views, using geographical vocabulary and communicating in different ways, reading and making maps, using secondary sources of information, debating and describing where places are and how they change. The need to question and explain is embedded in geographical study throughout.

In KS1, story is seen as an integral part of geography (Hamel and Langley-Hamel, 2006). Story can help children develop and extend a sense of place and provides a rich context for geographical understanding. This is true both in relation to their own localities and localities further afield. When learning about contrasting locations, such as those in Africa, story has been found to enrich children's conceptualisation of a very different environment and society. It can also assist them in making comparisons of two different places in the world. At the same time, of course, geographical knowledge and understanding can contribute to children's grasp of the importance of setting in a story.

At KS2, Cooper (2006) points out the value of poetry as a dramatic and evocative means of capturing the spirit of a place. Cooper also highlights the importance of drama as a valuable strategy for teaching geography. Toye and Evans (2006) describe how drama provides a stimulus for geographical learning and how it can present geographical issues and dilemmas in an accessible way. Writing about a role play on the topic of Kenya, they point out how different kinds of learning can be brought together through drama:

> *Through interacting with TiR (Teacher in Role) as Kilesi, the class were confronted with a dilemma which engaged their developing knowledge of Kenya and utilised their universal understanding of what it is to be a child with a problem.*
>
> (Toye and Evans 2006, p71)

When combined with history, for example in the study of an ancient civilisation, geography makes use of labelling skills, as in the example for Year 2 below.

Figure 9.1 Map of Ancient Egypt: Year 2 work

Russell (2008) outlines interesting ideas and resources for developing geographical non-fiction writing in her article 'A to Z of China: An alphabet journey through China'.

The National Framework for Literacy and the geography curriculum

The Framework for Literacy contains many units where there are potential links with geography. In the 'narrative' text type, there is reference to story settings in Years 1, 2 and 3; stories from other cultures in Years 1, 4 and 5; and in Year 4, stories which raise issues or dilemmas, which might be of a geographical nature. The non-fiction texts include labels, lists and captions, recounts, reports, information texts and explanations and arguments, all of which could be linked with geographical activities. Poetry texts include using the senses and 'really looking' which are important aspects of work on different places and environments.

Developing literacy skills through geography

Skills in literacy also relate widely to geographical activities. For example, children are expected to use language in ways which could relate to geography, such as: to recreate experiences; listen to others and recall their main points; extend their vocabulary and begin to understand subject-specific words; know how information can be found in non-fiction texts; write using lists, recounts, stories and specific settings; ask and answer questions; explain their views to others and use persuasive language; present clearly sequenced accounts; and use role play to illustrate different points of view.

History and literacy

History is also a subject which makes much use of language in all its forms and so the links with language learning are many. Cooper (2000), Bage (1999) and Hoodless (1998) have all carried out research into different aspects of the links between literacy and history. Groupwork, teacher modelling, story and the teaching of specific vocabulary have all been identified as important strategies in developing skills in both English and history. Cooper (2000) has also carried out considerable research into children's thinking skills in history and has summarised her work in this book. Most history is studied through the use of texts and oral accounts. Children's skills in communication are therefore developed continually in history in the course of reading, listening, writing and speaking, all skills without which it would be very hard to study history (Nichol, 2000). All of the teaching strategies used in teaching primary history relate to communication skills.

By the end of primary school, children are expected to have extended their skills in literacy considerably in the course of their history studies. They should recall, select and organise historical information; use dates and historical vocabulary; communicate their knowledge and understanding of history in a variety of ways, such as through drawing, speaking, writing or by using ICT. Teacher expectation is important in setting increasingly challenging objectives to ensure children's continuing progress. Close links with the revised *Framework for Literacy* will assist teachers greatly in planning for this progression (DfES, 2006).

Many schools use history-based sources as texts for the literacy hour. For example, deciding whether statements are fact, fiction or opinion, relates to both subjects. By learning to read and understand history-based texts within the literacy lessons, children are then able to make better use of these same texts in their history lessons. Ofsted has made very positive comments (Ofsted, 2007) about history in schools where such links between the two subjects have been successfully established.

CLASSROOM STORY

Matt was a PGCE trainee, who had studied history for his first degree subject. Since he had begun working on the PGCE course, and after his first two teaching placements, he had become very interested in the close connections between the teaching of history and English. He had been studying the National Curriculum for English as well as the National Literacy Strategy, and had discovered a great many similarities with the work prescribed for using sources in history. He decided that, both to provide a more coherent learning experience for the children in his Year 5 class, and to make best use of teaching time, he would try to link reading, writing, speaking and listening objectives closely with his work on Ancient Greece, which was on the school's long-term curriculum plan. He became very excited about the possibilities as he began to look more carefully at how he could plan a linked unit of work, which involved both subjects. He decided that he would introduce work on texts and writing in the mornings to begin with, and then develop the children's historical skills through the use of the same texts during his one-hour history lesson on a Thursday. He began to draw up the following plan.

Table 9.1 Links between literacy and history

English/NLS objectives	History objectives	Activities	Key words	Resources	Assessment
To learn and use new vocabulary; to discuss fact and fiction	To use legends to find out about events in Ancient Greece	Literacy: Read and discuss the story of the battle of Marathon; History: read and study pictures of Ancient Greece	Ancient, colony, Marathon, athlete, rebel, tactics, mainland, bay	A version of the legend of the battle of Marathon	Observe how well children begin to use key vocabulary; note how well children recalled information about Ancient Greece
To write own version of the legend	To recall, select and organise historical information	Literacy: Shared writing – start a new version of the legend; History: children complete own ending	As above	As above	In marking note use of new vocabulary and ability to select and organise information

---

PRACTICAL TASK PRACTICAL TASK PRACTICAL TASK PRACTICAL TASK PRACTICAL TASK

This task will help you to increase your knowledge of the requirements for history, English and the National Literacy Strategy, as well as how to use and understand it more fully.

Continue the planning started by Matt. Make use of the National Curriculum for both English and history in setting your objectives, ensuring that you are covering a range of word, sentence and text level work in accordance with the requirements of the NLS. You will need to think about planning for a further two sets of lessons linking work in English with history. For example, you may want to plan time for children to think about what the real facts of the situation were, and how the story has grown into epic proportions over the centuries. Could Pheidippides really have run such a distance, or has the story perhaps become exaggerated over time?

What is a legend, and is this how legends start? You would then need to think about allowing time for the children to share their ideas and develop their speaking and listening skills further through 'communicating their knowledge and understanding of history in a variety of ways'. Perhaps you could conclude the topic with presentations, displays or some drama?

The National Framework for Literacy and the history curriculum

There are a number of similar requirements within the Literacy Framework and the history curriculum. For example, within the 'narrative' units in Year 1 of the Framework, there is reference to traditional stories and recount texts, both of which might easily relate to learning about the past. Information texts are mentioned every year up to Year 4. Later years also include content such as myths and legends (Year 3), stories with historical settings (Year 4), older literature and classic/narrative poems (Year 5) and in Year 6, biography and autobiography. All of these clearly have links with history, or offer the potential for historical content and context to be used for work in literacy. There are also many other links within the 'non-fiction' and 'poetry' units, which are outlined on the website for the Framework for Literacy and Mathematics (www.standards.dfes.gov.uk/primaryframeworks). The full Frameworks for literacy and mathematics can be downloaded from this site.

Developing literacy skills through history

Links with historical skills occur throughout the year group objectives in the Framework for Literacy. The overlap of skills is evident in aspects of reasoning, exploring interpretations, sequencing, using evidence and sources, inferring writers' perspectives, comparing different types of texts, understanding underlying causes and points of view, analysing why things happened in the past, comparing how writers from different times and places present experience and use language, communicating the results of historical enquiry. For example, this Year 5 child has used his skills in literacy to write about the sources he used in an enquiry into his local area in the past.

> How can are begin to find out about change 'since the second world war?
>
> If I was trying to find out about…
>
> The story of the place in which I live Since, 1948 I would use, Maps, people, news papers, photographs.
>
> What people thought about my town in the 1950's I would use, people, documents and newspapers.
>
> What people did to entertain themselves in their spare time I would use, Videos, tapes, the internet, and maps.
>
> What it was like to go to school in the 1950's and 1960's I would use, diary's, Videos and people.
>
> What people worried about, I would use, a newspapers, diarys and people.
>
> Where people went for their holidays I would use, photographs, autobiography and home videos.

Figure 9.2 Sources for a local study

There are many examples of these links in books and journal articles on primary history. Cooper, in her chapter on 'History, the curriculum and communication skills', gives a number of examples from practice and a detailed analysis of the links between literacy objectives and historical thinking Cooper (2007, pp 94–96). There are other practical examples in the form of plans and case studies, such as Issue 41 of *Primary History* (Historical Association, 2005), and in Hoodless (2008).

RE and literacy

The National Framework for RE recognises that RE has a vital role to play in contributing to children's literacy. RE offers opportunities for reading, speaking and listening and writing. Here we focus on one of the main contributions that RE can make – that of helping children to understand religious literature. In the primary school, the focus tends to be on religious stories.

There are three main reasons for sharing stories from religions with children. Firstly these stories may have intrinsic value for children's development because they deal with universal themes of being human, in relationships with the world and other humans. Secondly, although the value of the story for the child may not be immediate, it may come into its own at a later date when familiarity with the story allows the adult to engage with other images and stories dealing with religious themes. A third reason for telling stories from religions to children is to help them learn to interpret such stories with reference to the texts and to their own experience and knowledge of the world. We are teaching them to be interpreters.

In planning your use of religious stories in the classroom, you will need to consider how you help children to:

- become familiar with the story and engage with it;
- interpret the story;
- put the story in the context of its religion of origin.

The choice of story is also important. You need to consider 'why this story, at this time, for these children?' When selecting religious stories to share with children, we should always use the same criteria that we would use for any story.

- Is the language appropriate for the children?
- Are the concepts within the story appropriate for the children?
- Will I be able to assist their understanding of the story?

The start of your preparation for using the story is to become familiar with it yourself. You need to research around the story at your own level to ensure that you have a good understanding of what it is about and how it is seen by the community to whom it belongs.

PRACTICAL TASK PRACTICAL TASK PRACTICAL TASK PRACTICAL TASK PRACTICAL TASK

Look at the Local Agreed Syllabus for your school.

- Which religious stories are listed?
- Which ones do you know already?
- Which ones, if any, do you feel comfortable telling?

Non-narrative texts

Much of religious scripture is not narrative. It is important that some of this material is made accessible to children, so that they begin to know what is inside the scriptures rather than simply treating them as artefacts. The Sikh scriptures, for example, are a collection of hymns, many of them about the wonders of nature and verses could be examined as poetry.

One consequence of Goldman's work in the 1970s and 80s (Goldman, 1964) was the promotion of children's literature, which implicitly explored religious ideas. Reading and discussing such stories was seen as central to RE. It was recognised that children's literature was of value at the current stage of children's development, but could also prepare them for comprehending central Biblical themes. Stories such as *Badger's Parting Gifts* by Sue Varley, and *Dogger* by Shirley Hughes, can help children understand some of the major themes of religious literature such as death, loss and reconciliation.

Religious literacy

Any domain of enquiry has its own vocabulary and own way of using vocabulary. Both religious and secular stories help develop concepts such as sacrifice, mystery and redemption, though at primary school stage the specific vocabulary may not be used. Children will also need support in beginning to understand terminology that is peculiar to specific religions.

PRACTICAL TASK PRACTICAL TASK PRACTICAL TASK PRACTICAL TASK PRACTICAL TASK

Find out what the following terms mean within Judaism:

Shabbat; Teffillin; Pesach; Torah; Ner tamid; Mezuzah; Phylacteries; Hannukiah.

Citizenship and literacy

Different aspects of communication and literacy appear throughout the citizenship curriculum in the *Handbook for Primary Teachers* (DfEE/QCA, 1999). At KS1, children are expected to share their opinions, talk about their feelings and listen to others, take part in discussions and debates. At KS2, the requirements are the same, but also include a focus on writing about their opinions and explaining their views. They are expected to carry out research into problems as well as to discuss and debate them. Children are also required to produce recorded evidence of their achievements, for example, in the form of diaries or records of achievement. The requirement to talk and listen to others extends to communicating with children in other countries by satellite, email or letters. They are also expected to know how to find useful information and advice for assistance with welfare issues. As you can see, the citizenship curriculum depends to a significant degree on effective skills in literacy just as good communication clearly underpins the role of the citizen in society.

The National Framework for Literacy and the citizenship curriculum

The narrative units in the Framework for Literacy include some potentially useful themes for making links with the citizenship curriculum. For example, the units on traditional stories and fairy tales occur in Years 1, 2 and 5, and may also be drawn upon from the unit on 'fiction genres' in Year 6. There is also an interesting unit of 'stories which raise issues/dilemmas' in Year 4. Traditional stories and tales often have a moral theme and may be selected to introduce, highlight or reinforce the objective of a citizenship lesson in a number of ways. For example, Aesop's Fables, the stories of Brer Rabbit or those of Anansi the spider all raise moral dilemmas on which to base discussion about people's feelings and the consequences of bad behaviour. In the non-fiction texts, there are units on instructions, which may be used to illustrate and develop children's understanding of the reasons for rules and regulations in society, and on the use of persuasion, a key interpersonal skill.

Developing literacy skills through citizenship

Opportunities for developing literacy skills abound in the citizenship curriculum. For example, there is a focus throughout on discussion, debate and listening to others, taking account of their opinions – all part of developing good relationships and respect for others. The exploration of complex issues and examination of dilemmas in citizenship can contribute to children's literacy skills within dramatic activities. Attitudes and assumptions in text might be raised in citizenship lessons and then further explored as part of their work in literacy, particularly the drama strand. Understandings derived from cross-curricular work linking citizenship and history may also be expressed effectively using written notes, as in this example of independent Year 6 research. This child has also summarized their understanding of some very important ideas.

Figure 9.3 Year 6 work on Ancient Greece

REFLECTIVE TASK

Consider the issues touched upon in this piece of work. How might you develop or consolidate them in a lesson plenary?

The links with mathematics

Many schools are making connections between literacy and the humanities, particularly with history. However, there are also many valuable potential links with mathematics. While schools often make links between mathematics and geography, there are equally important links with the other humanities subjects. In the study of people and their societies, many kinds of mathematics come into play, for example in the recording and interpretation of statistics and other data. Much of this is seen as more 'technical' or 'scientific', or too complex for primary children, but there are some types of mathematical data and skills that can be used effectively at this level.

In geography, data on rainfall, temperatures, population and occupation figures, heights, distances and scale all require mathematical skills. Charts, graphs, traffic surveys, factors in climate change, co-ordinates and maps also require numerical and data handling skills. In the Foundation Stage, there are numerous opportunities for geographical experiences which relate to mathematics. As Scoffham points out, children can measure short distances in footsteps or sort pebbles by size. They can also learn *to use positional vocabulary, such as on, under, next to, near. They can learn directions such as left, right, forwards, backwards while using control technology.* (Scoffham, 2004, p67). In chapter 8 of his work, Scoffham gives detailed guidance on the resources, necessary personal knowledge and suitable organisation of teaching mapwork skills. There are numerous ideas for work on distance, scale and direction which will enhance children's skills in mathematics at the same time as developing valuable skills in geography. Importantly, however, as Scoffham points out, remember not to take mapwork skills for granted or to expect too much all at once. Mapwork rests, as do so many other skills, on a sound understanding of mathematics, which may not be strongly developed in all primary children.

In history, many sources involve numerical data, such as census returns, statistics on all aspects to do with populations, trade and industrial production, and so on. Concepts of time and duration, shape in the environment, and sources involving money, charts, tables and graphs all depend upon mathematical skills in their interpretation and use. Time and chronology in the history curriculum require the ability to use numbers in their thousands and also an understanding of negative numbers. Children learn about time and chronology in many different ways and in many different contexts, gradually making mental links between their experiences to develop their concepts (see Hodkinson, 2002, 2006a, 2006b; Historical Association, 2006). Time is an extremely complex phenomenon. It can be considered a physical entity in its own right, dependent on the movement of the planets; it can be considered as a system of measurement; it can be seen as a cultural construct, differing in the way it is recorded and expressed, depending on the part of the world where it is being recorded, for example 'in the melting of a snowflake' for an Eskimo, or 'in the frying of a locust' for an African (Jahoda, 1963). Time can also be a psychological experience, expanding or shrinking depending on the type of activity you are engaged in, such as the Year 2 child who once told me that 'time seemed longer' when you were in assembly! Nevertheless, the ability to work with chronology and measure time rests on mathematical skills. The language that surrounds the concepts of time and chronology is rich and varied, and often depends for its accuracy on an understanding of number. Because of this, many children find it difficult to use temporal vocabulary appropriately and they will make wildly inaccurate statements in their early years, when trying out these new words. By the ages of eight or nine, however, some of the more able children have developed a fairly sophisticated understanding of the vocabulary and grasp of number to describe their understanding.

Religious education and citizenship make use of similar sources to these and equally depend upon the use of mathematics. For example, using religious calendars and interpreting statistics related to world religions require mathematical understanding and skills. This next section of the chapter, therefore, will consider mathematics across the whole of the humanities, using the Framework for Mathematics as the starting point.

Using and applying mathematics

The geography unit, 'Geography and numbers' in the QCA Schemes of Work, (www.standards.dfes.gov.uk/schemes2/geography) is a very useful starting point in assisting you to make use of the best links between mathematics and geography. In the Foundation Stage and at KS1, there are geographical activities which can be carried out around the classroom or the school which involve measuring distances and routes. Here children can begin to use mathematical language, such as words associated with counting, measuring and comparing distances. For example, in measuring out distances from one part of the school to another, they might use a metre stick and then decide whether the distance is longer, shorter, further or nearer than another. By the end of KS1, in each of the humanities subjects, children begin to understand how information can be represented in lists, tables or simple diagrams, such as timelines, timetables, temperatures, or lists of reasons for an event. They begin to understand the relationship of pattern to number. In history, number systems from the past are a constant source of interest for children in the early years of Key Stage 2. The number systems used by the Romans for example, are useful in consolidating children's understanding of place value (Hoodless, 2008).

Counting and understanding number

The development of number skills in the Foundation Stage and KS1 contribute to children's work with time charts, timetables, calendars and timelines, which are useful particularly in history and religious education. By Year 3 children are expected to be able to read, write and order whole numbers to at least 1000 and position them on a number line (DfES, 2006). These skills all relate to the use of dates and conventional timelines, and a growing understanding of chronology. In the later years of KS2, children learn about negative numbers, a difficult concept to grasp, but one which is crucial in an understanding of the BC/AD divide in historical chronology. Negative numbers are also important, of course, in geographical study of the weather and temperatures which fall below zero. Children's understanding of number can only be enriched by putting these somewhat abstract notions into a practical context such as that of the measurement of passing of time or understanding temperature readings.

REFLECTIVE TASK

Review the history study units and reflect on the opportunities for making links with number work within the history curriculum at KS1 and KS2. Consider opportunities for making these links with activities on citizenship.

Knowing and using number facts

There are also very close links between understanding and using number facts and the use of timelines. For example, number patterns help children understand how historical timelines are divided into decades and centuries. In fact, the use of a timeline based on decades could help children in Key Stage 1 with their learning in mathematics. Knowledge of addition and subtraction facts and skill in the use of place value will also support children in their ability to calculate and estimate spans of time.

(Hoodless 1996, p38)

Figure 9.4 Timeline of Ancient Greece

Geography makes wide use, of course, of the application of number facts, as in the following classroom story.

CLASSROOM STORY

Elena was inspired to enhance both numeracy and thinking skills within her geography lessons. Her class carried out a traffic count outside the school gates, counting how many vehicles went past in a 10-minute period every hour. Elena divided the class into seven groups – each group taking responsibility for collecting the data for their 10 minutes. The children stood at the school gates with a teacher/adult helper and timed 10 minutes, counting the traffic moving both ways. They recorded their observations on a chart like this:

Time	Amount of traffic
9.00 – 9.10	IIIII III (use tallying)
10.00 – 10.10	
11.00 – 11.10	
12.00 – 12.10	
1.00 – 1.10	
2.00 – 2.10	
3.00 – 3.10	

Elena recorded the 8.00 – 8.10 amount and 4.00 – 4.10. After school, Elena created a wall display outline living graph ready for the following day. In the next lesson the results were drawn on as a bar graph.

The children then decided on where to place the following statements onto the graph:

● Mrs. Stott, the lollipop lady, starts to walk home after the last child has crossed the road.

The children could have decided to put this statement around 9 a.m. as lessons/ assembly started, or after school shut in the late afternoon. The aim was for children to think and justify their choice, rather than there being one correct answer.

● Parcel Force delivers two parcels into school.
● A bus drives past full of people going to work.
● Mr. Jones the Year 6 teacher cycles into work.
● PC Duncan arrives to give a talk in assembly.
● Mrs Peters, the librarian, remembers to walk to the local newsagent to buy a birthday card for her mum.
● A road sweeper goes past picking up leaves and litter.
● The head teacher leaves for a meeting at the local secondary school.

Elena had attempted to make the graph appropriate for her children. The aim of the exercise was to make children really think about the graph's axes, and to justify their thinking.

PRACTICAL TASK PRACTICAL TASK PRACTICAL TASK PRACTICAL TASK PRACTICAL TASK

Consider the above activity and analyse the children's application of number in the course of completing their tasks.

Calculating

Children's knowledge of number facts might be put to good use in work on local history. For example, in learning about the complex style of windows in Elizabethan and Georgian buildings, they might want to know how many panes were used to make up the large windows that became fashionable in those times. They could be taught to use multiplication facts in their calculations in preference to extended addition to reinforce their learning in mathematics. Number facts and an understanding of percentages would also help considerably in the later years of KS2 when looking at statistics about populations in the past and the present, or immigration and emigration.

Understanding shape and space

Shape, and an understanding of how it is used in architecture, plays an important part in identifying buildings from different historical periods, where recognition of triangles, pyramids and symmetrical designs are often seen in Georgian buildings. The use of grid-references and co-ordinates are important skills in archaeology, which can be used in the classroom, as in the following story.

CLASSROOM STORY

Pat worked in an old-established primary school, which, she had discovered, stood on an ancient Roman site. The land had been, many hundreds of years earlier, the site of a Roman army camp. A visiting archaeologist had talked to her class about how the camp had been here and how Roman remains had been found during a dig at the site some years earlier. The spots where camp fires had burned could be pinpointed by discoveries of smelted metal remains in the soil, not too far beneath the surface.

Pat decided to try to re-create an archaeological 'find' for her Year 3 class. She collected as many old Roman 'remains' as she could. Luckily, the visiting archaeologist had left her a few things: an old Roman nail, several inches long, with a large, flat square head; some pieces of tiling from Roman buildings; and some scraps of broken pottery. She asked the caretaker to carefully remove a small patch of grass in the corner of the school grounds and there she carefully placed the artefacts. She and the caretaker replaced the soil and grass, but left one piece of pottery protruding from the surface.

After some introductory work on Roman Britain, Pat organised an opportunity for her class to work outside to do some 'archaeology'. The children surveyed the whole of the school grounds, searching for any kind of clues that they could find. At first they found litter, pieces of metal and modern pottery, until at last two children noticed the Roman piece in the soil. Using a ready-prepared outline plan of the grounds, the children were shown how to draw a grid with co-ordinates. The class was then asked to show on their plan where the piece of pottery had first been seen and to write below a note of the grid reference. This, of course, involved a great deal of very careful measuring in both directions to ensure accuracy.

The next lesson was the most exciting for the children. They went out in small groups, while a classroom assistant worked in the classroom with the others, and began carefully to dig into a small area around their first 'find'. Of course, in very little time, all the other objects were found and recorded with drawings carefully made on the grid in exactly the correct places to show where they were lying when they were discovered. Again, careful measuring was required. Some children found that their drawings at this stage were too big to fit into the grid, and so Pat suggested that they made a new grid on a larger scale, showing only the squares in the immediate area where the objects were found.

PRACTICAL TASK PRACTICAL TASK PRACTICAL TASK PRACTICAL TASK PRACTICAL TASK

Devise a list of potential questions designed to ensure the children use the co-ordinates on their grids. Think about how you might set up an activity like this in the classroom, or alternatively, develop it further through a visit to an archeological site or use of internet materials. (See *Primary History*, Issue 51, 2009 for further ideas and examples.)

The ability to locate places on a map or buildings on a plan are, of course, central to geographical studies. The unit on Tócuaro, in Mexico, requires considerable skill in understanding and using the globe and maps of the world, and of Mexico, to locate Tócuaro, and here, work on co-ordinates can link the development of skills in both geography and mathematics. In the Framework for Mathematics in Year 5, compass points and the ability to identify position on a grid of squares is required. The map below shows Tócuaro in its position, within the State of Michoacán, on the shore of Lake Pátzcuaro. Many questions could be set based on this map, to test children's skill in using co-ordinates, as well as other, more general questions.

Figure 9.5 Where is Tócuaro?

Measuring

In Years 5 and 6, children can begin to make detailed enquiries into the size of different places using maps. For example, the Standards website gives good examples of ways of challenging the more able children in work which links geography and mathematics, such as the following example:

> Ask the children to refer to a 1:25,000 Ordnance Survey map (or even, for some children, a 1:50,000 map) and work out how many centimetre squares on the map represent one kilometre square in real life. Children could then explore the areas of different-sized settlements.

> (www.standards.dfes.gov.uk/schemes2/geography)

Dollman (2005) makes an interesting link with maths in her article on food, where she describes how her Year 4/5 measured the distances our food travels across the globe.

The measurement of time is an aspect of mathematics which has close links across the humanities. In geography, the notion of different time zones around the world is a difficult one to grasp and depends heavily on mathematical understanding. In history, RE and citizenship, an understanding of the measurement of human experience over time is fundamental, since this understanding is important in interpreting timelines and calendars. The Framework for Mathematics requires that in the Early Years Foundation Stage, children learn *to use everyday language related to time; order and sequence events and measure short periods of time*. 'Knowledge and understanding of the world' in the Curriculum guidance for the Foundation Stage includes the development of a sense of time as one of its Early Learning Goals for history.

At Key Stage 1, the National Curriculum for History requires that children *place events and objects in chronological order* and *use common words and phrases relating to the passing of time*. By Year 5, children are expected in mathematics to interpret readings that lie between unnumbered divisions on a scale, a useful skill in reading historical timelines, which are often numbered in little detail. Quite clearly, mathematics and history merge in this area, and mutually support learning by contributing different dimensions and emphases. While mathematical understanding is essential for working with time and chronology in the humanities, the use of these concepts and skills strengthens and deepens children's under-standing of mathematics by providing a real life context for their learning.

Handling data

All subjects in the humanities make wide use of data handling. In the Early Years children sort objects, such as old toys and new toys, or objects from different places. They learn appropriate vocabulary and also learn to explain why they grouped them in particular ways. Throughout Key Stages 1 and 2, children learn to interpret and create lists, charts, tables and graphs to record the results of their humanities enquiries. Data handling and organising information in charts and diagrams, specified for Year 2, has many links with the handling of historical and geographical data, and the skills learned in mathematics could be transferred for application to a humanities topic.

In Years 5 or 6, children might use some census data by converting the numbers of people engaged in different occupations into a bar chart for ease of comparison. Spreadsheets enable them to create charts to illustrate which occupations were most widespread (Noall, 2000). Having used their mathematical skills to handle their data, they might then begin to use their historical skills to interpret the data to decide whether the area where the census was taken was working class or middle class. They might use geographical skills in finding where workers' home towns were and then create bar charts or scattergrams to illustrate this, along with working out the distances they travelled to their new places of work. In Year 5, the language of probability, the skill of constructing line graphs, timetables and calendars, and the use of maps have clear links with historical study. Similarly, in Year 6, collecting, processing and interpreting data to solve problems, the language of probability, and using scales have links with history and geography which could enhance learning in both subjects while also extending and applying mathematical skills to a real-life situation.

REFLECTIVE TASK

Consider one aspect of mathematics from the Framework for Mathematics, such as 'Using and applying mathematics', for a chosen age group. Think about how the skills learned in mathematics might be transferred to a humanities lesson.

A SUMMARY OF **KEY POINTS**

> The humanities provide useful material and real-life content for developing skills in literacy and mathematics.

> Most aspects of the Framework for Literacy and Mathematics can be related to humanities subjects and themes.

> The requirements of the Framework for Literacy and Mathematics need to be referred to in conjunction with the content of each humanities subject at the planning stage.

> There are many potential links between history and literacy, which schools are using.

> There are also many significant links between mathematics and geography, which schools are developing.

MOVING *ON* >> >> >> **>** **>** **>** MOVING *ON* >> >> >> **>** **>** **>** MOVING *ON*

Standard C17, Standard C27

Consider your own skills in literacy and numeracy and decide which is your weakest area, for example, data handling. Focus on developing your own skills in this area and consider ways in which you might introduce these into your teaching at an appropriate level.

FURTHER READING FURTHER READING **FURTHER READING** FURTHER READING

Cooper, H. (2007) *History 3–11: A Guide for Teachers*. London: Fulton. Cooper provides a list of the links between mathematics and history from the Foundation Stage to Year 6 on page 101.

Dollman, R. (2005) 'How the world comes to us', *Primary Geographer*, No. 58: 14–16. This article on food makes an interesting link with mathematics.

Goldman, R. (1964) *Religion in Childhood and Adolescence*. London: Routledge Kegan & Paul.

Hamel, K. and Langley-Hamel, K. (2006) 'How can geography make a significant contribution to a coherent and meaningful Key Stage 1 curriculum?' Chapter 9 in Cooper (2006) op. cit. This chapter looks at the importance of story in primary geography.

Historical Association (2009) 'Doing archaeology with children.' *Primary History*, Issue 51. London: Historical Association. This whole edition is devoted to archaeology.

Hodkinson, A. (2002) 'A coordinator answers: The development of chronological understanding in Primary History'. *Primary History*. Issue 31: 8–9.

Hodkinson, A. (2006) *Chronology Workshop*. London: Teachers' TV.

Hodkinson, A. (2006) *Developing Chronology at Key Stage 2*. London: Teachers' TV.

Hoodless, P. (1996) *Time and Timelines in the Primary School*. Teaching of History Pamphlet, no 69: 38. London: Historical Association.

The above four resources give a useful overview of children's developing sense of chronology.

Russell, K. (2008) 'A to Z of China: An alphabet journey through China', *Primary Geographer*, No. 66: 26–27. This article presents a novel way for children to present their work in geography.

Toye, N. and Evans, D. (2006) 'How can children connect to a distant place through drama?' Chapter 5 in Cooper (2006) op. cit. This chapter describes how drama can be used to support children's understanding of different places.

Useful websites

www.ordnancesurvey.co.uk

Ordnance survey website.

www.standards.dfes.gov.uk/primaryframeworks

The full Frameworks for literacy and mathematics can be downloaded from this site.

www.standards.dfes.gov.uk/schemes2/geography

Website for the QCA scheme of work for geography.

www.tda.gov.uk/skillstests.

The website on the skills tests. The site is user-friendly and provides information about the content and format of the tests, where to book one at a local centre, information about identity and about the rules governing procedures at the test centre. There are practice materials available on the site so that you can prepare in advance of taking the test.

10
E-learning and ICT through humanities teaching

By the end of this chapter you will have:

- developed your understanding of the requirements for the ICT skills test;
- developed your awareness of how to support your humanities teaching and wider professional activities with ICT;
- considered ways in which children can develop their ICT skills and use ICT to extend their learning in geography, history, RE and citizenship;
- developed your awareness of the resources available for both teachers and children;
- become aware of the need to safeguard children when they are using ICT.

Professional Standards for QTS

Q16: To have passed the skills test in ICT.

Q17: Know how to use skills in ICT to support their teaching and wider professional activities.

Q23: Design opportunities for learners to develop their ICT skills.

Q25 (a): Use a range of teaching strategies and resources, including e-learning.

The QTS skills tests in ICT

ICT is a vitally important subject across the humanities and in order to achieve Qualified Teacher Status, you are required to have passed the skills test in ICT. This can be done in any of the local centres set up for the purpose. In the test, you will have to demonstrate skills in word processing, using spreadsheets and databases, creating presentations, using e-mail and browsers. For detailed guidance on the ICT test, see the website of the Training and Development Agency for Schools (TDA), www.tda.gov.uk/skillstests.

PRACTICAL TASK   PRACTICAL TASK   PRACTICAL TASK   PRACTICAL TASK   PRACTICAL TASK

Access the website and try the benchmark test to test your ICT skills.

Supporting your teaching with ICT

The use of ICT in teaching all humanities subjects is a requirement of the National Curriculum (DfEE/QCA, 1999). While it is a statutory requirement at KS2, in KS1 it is left to the teacher to find appropriate opportunities for its use. It is important to stress here that the use of ICT needs to be a feature that adds to children's understanding of the humanities in some way, rather than being an ineffective addition to your lessons simply so that you can meet requirements. The choice of ICT to enable children to work more quickly, for example in sorting data on a spreadsheet, can further and deepen their learning in that area. As Jarvis points out, *You should be able to justify the choices you make and evaluate how the use of ICT has impacted on your teaching and children's learning* (Jarvis, 2003, p 5). However, to use ICT simply for its own sake in a lesson on history, geography, RE or citizenship is to misinterpret the meaning of the National Curriculum requirements.

Guidance on the requirements for humanities subjects and ICT, showing where there are links between them, is available on official government websites, such as BECTa, www.becta.org.uk and www.ictadvice.org.uk. Presentation software such as PowerPoint, and similar school software, can be a very effective and motivating presentation tool in the classroom. Sharing information with partner schools can be carried out using school websites, such as www.coxhoe.durham.sch.uk/Curriculum/Curriculum. A comprehensive list of resources, publishers of books and materials in hard copy and also on-line materials is available at www.CurriculumOnline.gov.uk. This is a very useful website, since you can enter the topic you are working on and go straight to the relevant materials.

PRACTICAL TASK PRACTICAL TASK PRACTICAL TASK PRACTICAL TASK PRACTICAL TASK

Using the internet, research the life of a significant person in recent history, such as Martin Luther King. Prepare a short Powerpoint presentation, including images and sound. When deciding on what text to include, ensure that it would be suitable for a range of reading abilities within your chosen age group.

Supporting your wider professional activities using ICT

Your own personal skills and confidence in using ICT are an important aspect of your teaching. Research at BECTa suggests that children's attainment can be improved through the use of ICT when used as part of a range of sound teaching strategies (BECTa, 2001). There is a wide range of software available to support primary teaching. Electronic resources for teachers include sites such as www.homeworkelephant.co.uk/teachers, which provides information and resources. While the site covers all Key Stages, you will find material here relevant to primary topics. The site is useful for quickly updating your own subject knowledge before teaching a topic. Chat rooms and forums for teachers are also developing and include sites such as www.teacherstalk.co.uk. This useful site enables you to write in with your queries as well as to see previous communications. Ictopus, www.ictopus.org.uk/, is a free website for primary education, and has information, news and a resource file for all humanities subjects.

Examples of the enormous range of ICT resources available for the humanities will be given below for each subject area. However, it is useful to know that there are websites for each subject's professional association. The website for geography is http://www.geography.org.uk/, and for history, you need to go to the website of the Historical Association www.history.org.uk. For Religious Education, you need to go to the website of the National Association of Teachers of Religious Education, www.natre.org.uk/, or the Professional Council for Religious Education www.pcfre.org.uk) and for citizenship education, the Professional Association for Citizenship Teaching, (ACT), www.teaching citizenship.org.uk/. The primary sections of these sites provide information about conferences, organising visits, the curriculum and resources, and on how to join the associations. They also provide additional information and links to articles on teaching the humanities topics from the associations' journals. Overarching organisations are the Humanities Association, found at www.hums.org.uk/ and the more recent Council for Subject

Associations (www.subjectassociation.org.uk/), where information across the humanities is available.

PRACTICAL TASK

Log on to one of the Professional Association websites mentioned above. Familiarise yourself with the site so that you will be able to refer to it easily if and when you find you need information and resources in the future.

REFLECTIVE TASK

Select some of the websites listed at the end of this chapter and review the information they provide. Consider their potential usefulness as a resource for teaching. For example, do they add to your subject knowledge; are they relevant to studies in the humanities?

ICT hardware to support humanities teaching

Useful information on the use of the whiteboard can be found on the website of the National Whiteboard Network (www.nwnet.org.uk). A helpful article in the Historical Association journal, *Primary History* (Fewster, 2005) outlines ways of getting started with the use of the whiteboard. For example, children can make decisions collaboratively by voting using 'voting pods', the results of which are shown in graphical form on the whiteboard for the children to see. The pods can be useful in situations where children have been asked to express their opinion on an issue in any of the humanities subjects. They can also be useful for assessment, in checking whether the class have learned something, for example, 'vote on which you think is the correct answer, a, b, or c'.

Personal Digital Assistants (PDAs) are small hand-held screens which can be used individually by children in conjunction with the whiteboard. Children can add their own data to a map, a piece of text, or a timeline, or they might annotate an image, and their work will appear on the class whiteboard. These types of activity increase motivation and add to the child's experience of personalised and collaborative learning, as well as providing additional opportunities for you to assess their understanding and knowledge. Digital cameras and video recorders are used to record visits, interviews and special events. When used with the computer for incorporating new material into presentations, they can be a very creative and motivating tool.

CLASSROOM STORY

Paula was nearing the end of a topic on Mexico and the Aztecs with her Year 6 class, which had involved a considerable amount of individual enquiry from books, information packs and the internet. She wanted to help the children collaborate in assembling both geographical and historical information they had found. Before the lesson, she placed a concept map covering key aspects of the topic on the class whiteboard. In turn the children placed brief pieces of information on the whiteboard from their PDAs to build up a complete picture of all their work. At the end of the lesson, Paula was able to review all of this information with the class and give children effective feedback on their work.

PRACTICAL TASK PRACTICAL TASK PRACTICAL TASK PRACTICAL TASK PRACTICAL TASK

Think about effective ways of using downloaded photographs from a digital camera in humanities lessons.

Developing ICT skills through the humanities

Work in the humanities enables children to develop skills in all aspects of ICT. Basic skills, such as becoming familiar with the keyboard and word processing, can be developed in each humanities subject. The use of desktop features is another initial skill which children absorb and put into practice as they work on their enquiry tasks. The use of ICT to produce, edit and enhance their work can make a great contribution to children's skill in organising and communicating their work in the humanities. Through the use of text-based web resources such as the on-line encyclopedia, *Encarta* (www.encarta.msn.com/), children can make simple notes, extending their skills in literacy. For example, Walsh (2003) describes how children read the notes accompanying each of the artefacts they were studying on the British Museum Compass website and then made their own simple notes for their 'museum display'. He explains that children can be encouraged to summarise by being asked to produce a list of points under headings such as, 'Five Things That Every Person Should Know About Henry VIII' (Walsh, 2003).

In writing and editing work, children use word-processing software and in finding and sorting data they can use databases and spreadsheets, along with using browsers for searching for information on the internet. Presentations involve the use of ICT, in organising and preparing information, making posters, or creating displays. The incorporation of images and text, including the use of digital images, sound and video footage, all develop useful ICT skills when using software such as PowerPoint. Examples of children's own presentations and web pages can be found on the internet at sites such as www.coxhoe.durham.sch.uk, where there are excellent examples of work produced for both teaching and learning. Cooper outlines the creation of a website by Year 3 children when visiting an Art Gallery (www.theherbert.org/learning/).They can use presentation and multi-media packages for sharing the results of their work with the rest of their class or a class in another part of the country.

E-mail is also widely used; many primary schools have links with other countries usually via email, to chat about aspects of their work and interests. Clearly there is great scope for the exchange of understanding about humanities subjects and issues, both between teachers and children. Video conferencing is another potentially exciting medium for exchanging ideas with schools in other countries.

As has been pointed out above, however, the use of ICT can only be justified if it is of benefit to children's learning. Jarvis indicates a number of benefits, which he considers do justify its use (Jarvis, 2003). He argues that ICT can support collaborative learning and enhance independent learning if tasks are planned in detail. *Every Child Matters* (DfES, 2004) points out that personalised learning is one of the most positive ways forward in ensuring that every child achieves their full potential, and the use of the internet is a major aid to differentiated enquiry work. Learning outcomes can be presented in many different ways using ICT and children can produce work of a very professional standard through the use of desk top publishing and presentation software. This part of the chapter will look at how ICT can support learning in the humanities, while at the same time, children are developing their skills in ICT through their application to other areas of the curriculum.

How ICT can support children's learning in geography

It is important to bear in mind that the National Curriculum requirement is for ICT to support learning in geography, therefore it is most important to have a clear idea of your geography objectives for each unit of work and for each lesson. Enquiry skills in geography are well supported by ICT. For example, QCA Unit 10, 'A Village in India', is one which is likely to prove challenging for most children who have no experience of life there. A starting point would be the Standards website (www.standards.dfes.gov.uk/schemes2/geography), where you will find an outline scheme of work and a set of key questions, around which children can organise their enquiries and generate further questions of their own. In asking the question, 'What are homes like in Chembakolli?' you could use websites, such as www.chembakolli.com, an award-winning website of ActionAid, where you can sign up to use interactive materials and purchase a TVROM and a video. Children could then be asked to complete a writing frame either on or away from the computer, comparing homes in their own town or village with the homes they have researched. In addition to developing children's skills in geography and building up their knowledge and understanding of places, children will have had the opportunity to utilise a wide range of skills in ICT such as extracting and interpreting key points from sources of information. In order to further develop links with citizenship and RE, you could set up a link, or twinning arrangement with a school in India, so that the children could exchange e-mails and find out about life in two very different places (see, for example, Halocha, 2007).

The requirement to study patterns and processes might be addressed effectively through using ICT in a study of rivers. General patterns in the behaviour of rivers and the processes involved in the changes they make to the landscape can all be recorded using ICT. In fact, this unit relies heavily in the use of ICT, for example, in finding out specific information about selected rivers, using CD-ROM or the internet; in using ICT to combine graphical, textual and numerical information; in using ICT to produce a project folder; and in showing awareness of audiences in their published materials or presentations.

The geography study unit on investigating coasts provides opportunities to raise the important issues of environmental change and sustainable development with children in Years 5 or 6. Key features of this unit include the opportunity to discuss with children the effect on the environment of major changes in land use, such as the building of an hotel. They can also begin to appreciate the need for careful management of environments such as the coastal regions and rivers in order to ensure sustainability. Searching for data on coastal erosion and pollution will help extend the children's skills in data collection and analysis. There is a wide network of webcams which provide excellent up-to-date information on coasts around the world, where children can see something of the environment and the weather conditions in different places.

The range of ICT resources for geography is immense, particularly the material available on the internet. However, this needs to be used with caution and you need to be sure that your sources of information are reliable, since some websites are quite open for people to enter any information that they wish! For geography, new and even more impressive websites become available each year. Google Earth, a useful resource for the more able upper KS2 children, points out how 'Google Earth lets you fly anywhere on Earth ' (www.earth.google.com/), and Google UK schools, www.google.co.uk/intl/en/schools/index, provides a number of lesson plans and enquiry activities, such as 'exploring your area'. These are activities which help to develop skills and understanding in geography, while making use of children's skills in using a range of ICT facilities in the course of an enquiry. A variety of resources in different formats can be found on www.primaryresources.co.uk/geography, while the BBC schools website, www.bbc.co.uk/schools, provides materials related to the QCA schemes of work, such as 'Where in the world is Barnaby Bear?' On the Geographical Association website you will find all the very useful weblinks included in the *Primary Geography Handbook* (Scoffham, 2005).

The computer is an excellent source of maps and sites which contain geographical information linked to history. For example, the site www.roman-britain.org/maps.htm has a detailed set of maps of Roman Britain, which show the locations of villas, forts, potteries, mines, etc, so that a good picture can be built up of Roman settlement patterns. The maps are also an excellent stimulus for encouraging children to make inferences about why there were so many small forts in particular places, such as on the borders and near Hadrian's Wall.

PRACTICAL TASK PRACTICAL TASK PRACTICAL TASK PRACTICAL TASK PRACTICAL TASK

Access the maps on the Roman Britain website and consider why the Romans chose particular places to build their towns and forts. Can the children begin to identify patterns and suggest reasons for these? Consider how you might be able to make use of this resource in a cross-curricular topic linking history and geography.

Digital images can be downloaded from a camera, scanned from existing slides or prints, saved from the internet, or obtained from CD-ROMS. In using such images, North (2006) argues that there is a potentially good link between visual literacy, geography and ICT, and that we should focus on developing children's skills in reading and interpreting pictures in the same way as we teach the reading of text. She points out *how photographs bring the real world into the classroom and can bring the subject alive.*

REFLECTIVE TASK

Consider this photograph, which shows part of the Rochdale Canal in central Manchester. This part of Manchester has been undergoing successive waves of development for over three centuries. Identify the different stages and types of development that have taken place and think about the environmental impact of each. Which has perhaps had the most/least impact?

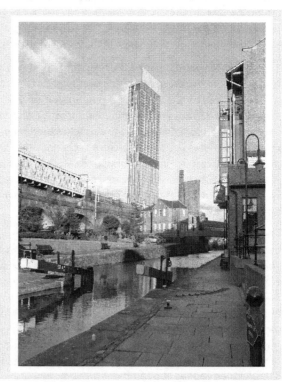

Figure 10.1 The Rochdale Canal, Manchester

How ICT can support children's learning in history

Walsh (2003) argues that there needs to be a good reason for using ICT in history instead of a book or other source. ICT should only be used if it can add something to a lesson. Cooper (2007) and Hoodless (2008) contain useful chapters on ICT in history, which outline a range of ideas, sources and useful websites and also provide examples of work in history.

Chronological understanding can be enhanced through the use of ICT. At Key Stage 1, simple programmes allow children to move images around the screen to produce a logical sequence. The increased level of interest and motivation produced by asking a child to rearrange a sequence of pictures into the correct time order, using the computer instead of paper, is considerable. At Key Stage 2, there is software for using and creating timelines, which provide an additional dimension to the learning of an important concept because of their motivational power and speed of operation. The BBC has produced an interactive timeline, useful for very able children in Years 5 and 6, www.bbc.co.uk/history/interactive/ timelines. A very child-friendly interactive timeline programme can be purchased from 'Soft Teach' www.curriculumonline.gov.uk. This programme provides some sample timelines ready-made, but also permits children to create their own, importing images, and inserting text and dates.

A major area where ICT can play a part in history teaching is in its vast supply of sources. Collecting and organising data, such as the artefacts found on historical websites, can provide opportunities for children to use spreadsheets and generate bar charts and graphs. The Learning Curve website, part of the National Archives, has one of the largest collections of history resources, with interactive materials for children (www.learningcurve.-gov.uk/howto/teacherict.htm). Walsh (2003) recommends starting with websites such as the BBC (www.bbc.co.uk/history), the QCA (www.qca.org.uk), the TDA (www.tda.gov.uk), Curriculum Online (curriculumonline.gov.uk) or BECTa (www.becta.org.uk). The British Museum has a large collection of artefacts available on its *Compass* website (http://www.thebritishmuseum.ac.uk/compass), along with a specific page for children (www.bri-tishmuseum.org/explore/families and children.aspx). The York Archaeological Trust has an excellent site for collections of finds from Roman, Anglo-Saxon, Viking and Medieval times in York (www.yorkarchaeology.co.uk/). Historic sites usually have their own websites and are increasingly developing interactive materials. The need to search these sites on specific topics to find particular information, or answer specific questions set in class, can further develop their skills in searching the internet and using search engines. Historical texts and numerical statistics often lend themselves ideally to database work. In particular, census and similar data is best used on the computer. Calculations and results can be displayed with such accuracy and speed that learning can be considerably enhanced, particularly when using detailed data such as in census returns.

There is a vast quantity of visual material for history, including video and film, from BBC and ITV history broadcasts, to TV dramas and films. Many books for teachers and resource packs of teaching materials, such as *Ready Resources*, (Hoodless, 2003) include CD-ROMS with collections of primary sources, such as portraits, sketches, photographs, sound recordings and video clips. English Heritage (www.english-heritage.org.uk) has a large website with an educational section on history. You will find educational games for children, publications, projects, educational resources and an excellent photograph collection, called Viewfinder.

You can search Viewfinder under themes, such as 'seaside' and find images from different periods, showing how a particular resort or seaside town has changed (see Mills, 2004).

There are, in addition, other organisations which specialise in particular historical themes, such as Mexicolore (www.mexicolore.co.uk).

Figure 10.2 Aztecs on a swing

(www.mexicolore.co.uk)

Children can write in to this website with questions, which are answered by a team of specialist consultants. The Mexicolore website also provides resources for the geographical theme on the village of Tócuaro. Many well known companies, such as Cadbury (www. cadbury.co.uk/cadburyandchocolate/Pages/cadburyandchocolate.aspx), among numerous others, provide a variety of educational resources. Historical sites and museums usually all have their own website, and very often these include a range of resources for teaching.

PRACTICAL TASK PRACTICAL TASK PRACTICAL TASK PRACTICAL TASK PRACTICAL TASK

Look up how to create a 'web trail' and create a simple one for a Year 4 class studying a topic on the Second World War. (See Jarvis, 2003, p26.) You will need to focus on one specific aspect of the war for your web trail to be effective, in the form of a question such as 'What was it like during the Blitz?'

How ICT can support children's learning in RE

A valuable use of ICT in RE is to enable children to access resources that may not be within easy reach of them. Many websites offer 'virtual tours' of places of worship or places of pilgrimage. Others give valuable information about specific religious traditions, both at the children's level and for teachers' own subject knowledge development.

The internet can also be used to establish links with children of different religious traditions and cultures. These need not necessarily be children living far away from the school. Many children live only a bus journey away from children whose lives may be very different to their own. Establishing a relationship with a school whose intake is very different from yours, via e-mail, for example, can give children the opportunity to learn what it is like to live in Britain as a Muslim, a Jew or a Christian.

CLASSROOM STORY

Julia was aware that the children in her Year 5 class had been discussing recent terrorist attacks, which had been reported on the news. She was concerned that, despite a great deal of work being done in the school about respect for others, many of the children in her class had a very stereotypical image of Muslims. Indeed, some of the children seemed to believe that the words 'terrorist' and 'Muslim' were interchangeable. The children had very little contact with the Muslim community, the intake of the school was primarily white British and Christian.

Julia considered bringing forward her RE topic on an introduction to Islam, but she felt uncomfortable presenting to children general information. She wanted the class to get to know Islam through real people. She decided to contact her old university friend whom she knew was working in a school across town that had a high intake of Muslim children. She and her friend set up a link with each other's schools in which, once a week, the Year 5 classes would e-mail each other as pen-friends.

The fact that the other children were mainly Muslim was not highlighted. Instead, their e-mail sessions focused on finding out about each other – what were their hobbies, football team, favourite TV programme. Of course the children in both schools noticed that their names were different and the cultural origins of names became a topic for study.

As the term passed, the classes began to ask questions related to lifestyle and beliefs. Festivals came up and they shared what they would be doing. The climax of the term was an invitation to Julia's class to come to a special assembly that the other class was presenting on the celebration of Eid.

How ICT can support children's learning in citizenship

Many of the points made above apply to citizenship education, where ICT is of major importance in gathering, interpreting and presenting information and ideas. Citizenship and global citizenship are areas of learning where there is a need for discussion, debate and thought, and here ICT has a useful role. King (2002) gives examples and case studies illustrating how global citizenship can be incorporated into curriculum planning. Once this stage has been considered, there are numerous strategies you can adopt to develop ICT as part of citizenship activities. You can video or tape-record children's discussions and views, interviews they have created or their dramatisations of issues or events that have previously been discussed. The interactive whiteboard can be used to record key points raised, perhaps in the form of a concept map, which can be saved for further use when ideas are developed in a subsequent lesson, or for re-capping ideas from a previous one. For topics which require interviews and questionnaires, you, or the children themselves, can use word-processing software to produce interview schedules and questionnaires.

To support children's writing and display work you can draw on wide-ranging sources on CD-ROM, the internet, or photocopiable materials from information packs, and create word banks on issues which have been raised in circle time or class discussions. These banks have many uses, one of which is the facility to enable more detailed differentiation for children of differing abilities. The creation of a structured learning environment might include differentiated web trails, writing frames, or alternatively a series of tasks on CD for children to use independently. You might use ICT to create your own illustrated stories, information pages and questions. Children could then make use of these materials in their own work.

Software which allows children to combine text and images can help children produce the results of their work on citizenship issues in an effective way, such as in the form of a poster, an enhanced display, a class newspaper or a web page. In decision-making activities, the use of 'voting pods' enables you to show the results on the whiteboard in various formats, such as lists or graphs. Children's work can be saved, perhaps for subsequent use in lessons, or for assessment purposes. For children with special needs, video, tape recorders, cameras and computers can all greatly aid their work, while at the same time enhancing their learning experiences and enabling them to produce a pleasing outcome.

ICT can be most effective when it is used to illustrate and inform complex ideas in citizenship, which might be beyond children's experience. For example, the debate on climate change could be illustrated by the creation of two newspaper clips, as in the following classroom story.

CLASSROOM STORY

Ross teaches a Year 6 class and feels that they need to make more effective use of their skills in ICT. He decides to link some of this work with a QCA topic he is doing in citizenship on 'In the media – what's the news'. He is very interested in climate change, having just read an article in *Primary Geographer* on sustainability, and has put together some materials on this issue using his own research. He has created two 'newspaper clips' which give opposing points of view, and also a web trail, which has the potential to provide detailed information on what is currently known and thought about it by different groups. He initiates the topic by presenting the following 'clips' on the interactive whiteboard:

The Daily

'The human effect'

Researchers have recently added more worrying evidence on what we know about the way humans are affecting climate on the earth. Detailed studies carried out over the last ten years and published today show that the emissions of harmful gases are having a more rapidly damaging effect than was previously thought. It is believed that the polar ice caps could melt within the next few years causing rapidly rising sea levels, flooding in many parts of the globe and an even more rapid rise in temperatures. Scientists urge world leaders to agree on measures to slow down the rate of these worrying changes.

The Weekly

'Climate change? It has always happened.'

Our science editor has been looking into these alarmist claims about global warming. He has taken the long view of this issue and has found that over the millennia, the earth's climate has frequently warmed up and then cooled down again. Look at the Middle Ages, when grapes were grown in England, and then the Victorian era, when rivers and lakes frequently froze solid. These new findings are just showing us yet another part of the cycle of warming and cooling that has always happened on the earth. Climate change? Yes, but human activity is not the cause of it.

Ross asks the children to read through the clips and then to identify the different points they make to support their views. He then sets the children the task of working through a web trail which he has made, which provides detailed evidence and gives access to both points of view. This research involves the use of the internet and also of other materials that Ross has put together on a CD. The children's researches take two further lessons and also include some homework time which has been allocated to this work.

In his final lesson, Ross calls the class together for a debate and a vote. Children give their own opinions based on what they have found out both at school and at home and a very heated debate ensues. Ross records the debate for his own use later on, and makes notes in a shared writing activity with the class. The lesson ends with a vote taken on the issue. The children use their voting pods, and Ross shows the results on the interactive whiteboard.

PRACTICAL TASK PRACTICAL TASK PRACTICAL TASK PRACTICAL TASK PRACTICAL TASK

Create your own 'newspaper clips' and web trails on a citizenship issue that you consider important. Make sure that the reading level is appropriate in both of these resources, or produce the web trail at two or three different levels to meet the different needs within a Year 6 class.

Safeguarding children

Ensuring that children are safe when using internet sources is essential. Teachers need to research into what is available and then find ways of incorporating these resources into their teaching. There are also issues concerning the use of visual sources and the taking of digital photographs of children. There is valuable advice on the BECTa website (www.becta.org.uk) and also at www.bgfl.bridgend.gov.uk.

REFLECTIVE TASK

Consider teaching strategies and resources that you could use or create to ensure children's safety while using digital sources.

A SUMMARY OF **KEY POINTS**

> It is necessary to have passed the QTS skills tests in ICT to gain Qualified Teacher Status.

> One of the most useful ways of supporting your teaching is to use ICT for information on planning, finding information and communicating with other teachers.

> You can support your wider professional activities through the use of websites with information for teachers on issues such as marking, planning, job hunting. You can also improve your own subject knowledge through the use of good internet websites, such as the website of the various Professional Associations for the humanities subjects.

> There are opportunities for children to develop their ICT skills when learning geography, history, RE and citizenship in areas such as word processing, the use of databases and spreadsheets, presentation software, the use of internet browsers and e-mail.

> E-learning can support children's learning in humanities topics through providing access to a wide range of resources and data, first hand and secondary sources, virtual tours, sites, art galleries, museums, places, peoples and religions around the world.

> It is important to safeguard children when they are using internet resources.

MOVING *ON* > > > > > > MOVING *ON* > > > > > > MOVING *ON*

Standard C17, Standard 27

Refer to the 'Learning across the National Curriculum' section of the NC Handbook for Primary Teachers, and note the thinking skills which are outlined there. Devise ways in which you might link thinking skills development in the humanities with activities which would benefit from the use of ICT. For example, consider some of the key issues that you explore during sessions on citizenship and identify activities that could be supported by ICT.

FURTHER READING FURTHER READING **FURTHER READING** FURTHER READING

Allen, J., Potter, J., Sharp, J. and Turvey, K. (2007) *Primary ICT: Knowledge, Understanding and Practice.* (3rd edn.) Exeter: Learning Matters. A recent book on ICT across the curriculum.

BECTa (2001) *Primary Schools of the Future – Achieving Today.* Coventry: BECTa. A BECTa conference paper.

Cooper, H. (2007) *History 3–11: A Guide for Teachers.* London: Fulton. (Chapter 6 gives a useful overview of some of the key issues and uses of ICT, with additional recommendations for useful websites and software.)

Fewster, S. (2005) 'Using a whiteboard'. *Primary History*, Issue 39, 8–20.

Halocha, J. (2007) 'Citizenship through school twinning'. *Primary Geographer,* Number 62: 36–38.

Hoodless, P. (2003) *History: Ready Resources, Books 1–8.* Leamington Spa: Scholastic. Photocopiable resources are available in the books, and images and video clips on the CD-ROM. There are also Ready Resources for geography and RE, which make cross-curricular links with citizenship and global citizenship.

Hoodless, P. (2008) *Teaching History in Primary Schools.* Exeter: Learning Matters. See Chapter 9 for e-learning and ICT in history.

Jarvis, G. (2003) *Using ICT in Primary Humanities Teaching.* Exeter: Learning Matters. A detailed book on ICT in the humanities.

King, H. (2002) 'Global citizenship in practice'. *Primary Geographer,* Number 46: 18–20.

Mills, M. (2004) 'Using the English Heritage Viewfinder website'. *Primary History*, 37: 32–36.

Morris, G. and Willy, T. (2007) 'Eight doorways to sustainability'. *Primary Geographer,* Number 64: 34–35.

North, W. (2006) 'Visual literacy, ICT and geography.' *Primary Geographer*, Number 60: 32–34.

Norton, M. (1999) 'Making the most of ICT at Key Stage 2', *Primary History,* 21: 7–9.

Smart, L. (1999) 'ICT – high profile in 1999-2000: but will you use it in your history teaching?' *Primary History,* 22: 6–7.

Walsh, B., (2003) 'Is there a place for the computer in primary history?' *Primary History*, 34: 26–29.

The above articles link the humanities with ICT in a variety of ways.

Scoffham, S. (2005) *Primary Geography Handbook*. London: Geographical Association. There are references to ICT throughout the book.

Useful websites

www.bbc.co.uk

A very useful and reliable website for ideas and resources.

www.bbc.co.uk/history/interactive/timelines.

An interactive timeline produced by the BBC, however, this would be useful mainly for very able children in Year 5 and 6.

www.becta.org.uk

www.bgfl.bridgend.gov.uk

www.ictadvice.org.uk

These sites give advice on safeguarding children when using the internet and digital sources.

www.thebritishmuseum.org/explore/families_and_children.aspx

A specific webpage for children.

www.cadbury.co.uk/cadburyandchocolate/Pages/cadburyandchocolate.aspx

Website for Cadbury's.

www.chembakolli.com

Website for information on the village of Chembakolli in India.

http://www.coxhoe.durham.sch.uk/Curriculum/Curriculum.htm

www.greatrissington.ik.org

www.theherbert.org/learning/

Examples of good schools websites.

www.curriculumonline.gov.uk

Website of Curriculum Online set up to support the education sector.

http://earth.google.com

The website for Google Earth.

www.encarta.msn.com/

The website for Encarta, an on-line encyclopedia.

www.english-heritage.org.uk

Website for English Heritage.

www.geography.org.uk

The website of the Geographical Association.

www.google.co.uk/intl/en/schools/index

Website which has useful lesson plans and links to Google to search for related resources.

www.history.org.uk

Website of the Historical Association.

http://www.homeworkelephant.co.uk/teachers

Useful for developing your own background subject knowledge.

www.hums.org.uk

The website of the Humanities Association.

www.learningcurve.gov.uk/howto/teacherict.htm

The Learning Curve website, part of the National Archives, has some useful ideas for teaching history using ICT.

www.mexicolore.co.uk

A useful website for the Aztecs study unit.

www.natre.org.uk

Website of the National Association of Teachers of Religious Education.

www.nwnet.org.uk

Website of the National Whiteboard Network.

www.primaryresources.co.uk/geography

Useful for resources on geography.

http://www.roman-britain.org/maps.htm

Website with interactive maps useful for work linking history and geography.

www.subjectassociation.org.uk/

Website of the Primary Subjects Association, useful for information across the curriculum.

www.tda.gov.uk/skillstests.

The website on the skills tests. The site is user-friendly and provides information about the content and format of the tests, where to book one at a local centre, information about identity and about the rules governing procedures at the test centre. There are practice materials available on the site so that you can prepare in advance of taking the test.

www.teacherstalk.co.uk

Chatroom for teachers.

www.teachingcitizenship.org.uk

Website of the Citizenship Association.

www.yorkarchaeology.co.uk/

The website of the York Archaeological Trust. This website contains pictures of artefacts from Roman, Anglo-Saxon, Viking and Medieval times found in York.

11

Out-of-school learning; multi-professional learning

By the end of this chapter you will have:

- been introduced to a rationale for out-of-school learning;
- considered the wide range of contexts and opportunities for out-of-school learning;
- thought about catering for children with SEN and EAL on field trips and visits;
- read some examples of out-of-school learning in the humanities;
- considered the variety of incidental experiences from which children learn about humanities subjects;
- considered the organisation of out-of-school learning, including safety, risk assessment and liaising with other professionals to provide effective multi-professional learning contexts.

Professional Standards for QTS

Q24: Plan . . . out-of-class work to sustain learners' progress and to extend and consolidate their learning.

Q30: Establish a purposeful and safe learning environment conducive to learning and identify opportunities for learners to learn in out-of-school contexts.

Q32: Work as a team member and identify opportunities for working with colleagues.

Q33: Ensure that colleagues working with them are appropriately involved in supporting learning and understand the roles they are expected to fulfil.

Introduction

All humanities subjects use fieldwork as a teaching strategy. Children learn from their experiences out in the environment and the resources it offers are essential learning tools in geography, history, RE, and citizenship alike. The value of learning outside the classroom lies partly on its motivational power and partly on the opportunities it provides for learning in real life contexts. Young children are active learners who readily absorb information and learn from their surroundings and experiences. Out-of-school learning therefore builds on this prior learning. It is meaningful and helps them relate their school work to real life experience. Another great benefit of learning outside the classroom is the opportunity it creates for building closer relationships among children and between children and their teachers. All these factors contribute to a valuable, and often more memorable and enjoyable learning experience taking place.

There are several basic concerns identified in the above Standards, however, which need to be addressed before taking children outside the classroom. Obviously, parental permission must first be obtained in writing, both to inform the parents and to meet insurance requirements. Secondly, the safety of the children is paramount. Adequate support from parents/carers and classroom assistants or nursery nurses is important to ensure a low child-to-teacher ratio. Better quality learning is also likely to take place if the children can work in small groups supported by an adult. Team work and ensuring that all adults are familiar with the aims and objectives of the visit are all necessary parts of the work involved in setting up a visit. Risk assessment and pre-visits by the teacher are both important aspects of the planning of fieldwork and these will be discussed in more detail below.

A wide range of learning contexts are used in out-of-school learning, such as art galleries, museums, theatres, historical and geographical sites, places of worship, shopping streets and local centres within communities, to name just a few. Each of these contexts has much to offer each individual subject within the humanities, but very often, they can offer valuable learning in relation to cross-curricular topic work in the humanities. It is also important that teachers recognise and value the contribution that support staff and other professionals can make to out-of-school learning and that they plan and prepare to include this in their visits. This important aspect of fieldwork is also discussed in greater detail below.

Effective use of other adults

Most museums have an education officer, sometimes trained as a teacher, who has detailed knowledge of the collections your class is visiting. These professionals can greatly enhance children's learning while at a museum with their extensive specialist knowledge and also with their enthusiasm for the subject. Additionally, they have access to a wide range of resources, such as artefacts, which will further enhance the children's experience. It is always worthwhile, therefore, to contact the education officer before visiting a museum to find out what resources and services may be available to you.

The same is true of historical or geographical sites. There is often a field officer or ranger who will have specialist knowledge of the site and who will be prepared to talk to your class during the visit. Experts in many fields will also be able to offer involvement and training in their own specialist skills, such as theatre skills, music or art. The important point here is to be sure to include making contact with these professionals and sharing your aims for the visit with them. They will be able to make a good contribution to your work in most cases.

Why plan out-of-school experiences?

Learning is not limited to classroom experiences and as child development theorists, such as Piaget have shown, children are active learners from birth, making sense of their multi-sensory environment. Travelling to school children are experiencing the sights, sounds and smells of their local environment. As teachers we can plan activities to help pupils question and understand their surroundings and use these to develop and extend classroom-based work. It is a child's entitlement, as part of the National Curriculum, to experience learning outside the classroom. To illustrate this, study the quotes below:

> *It [geography] develops knowledge of places and environments throughout the world, an understanding of maps, and a range of investigative and problem-solving skills both inside and outside the classroom.*
>
> (DfEE/QCA, 1999, Geography, p14)

> *In their study of localities (and themes), children should: carry out fieldwork investigations outside the classroom.*
>
> (DfEE/QCA, 1999, Geography, p20)

Pupils should be taught how to find out about the past from a range of sources of information, historic buildings and visits to museums, galleries and sites.

(DfEE/QCA, 1999, History, pp104, 105)

Meet and talk with people [for example, people who contribute to society through environmental pressure groups or international aid organisations; people who work in the school and the neighbourhood, such as religious leaders, community police officers]

Develop relationships [for example, taking part in activities with groups that have particular needs, such as children with special needs and the elderly]

(DfEE/QCA 1999, Citizenship, p141)

Taking children out of the classroom helps to develop a range of skills including group work and decision-making. The fresh air and the sensory experiences help all kinds of learner to remember and learn from the locality and its inhabitants. In the section on inclusion in the National Curriculum there is a reminder that some children may require activities to be adapted to enable them to be included and participate actively and safely in geography fieldwork.

REFLECTIVE TASK

Think back to any out-of-school learning that you experienced as a child and consider the following questions: How much of it do you remember? What did you learn from the experience? In what ways was it more or less effective than learning in the classroom?

What do we mean by outside experiences?

Outside experiences extend from the playground to distant localities. The school grounds offer a wealth of opportunities from weather recording and orienteering to field sketching and surveys (see Figure 11.1). The buildings can be studied for types of materials and design elements that help us to date the building approximately. The car park can provide opportunities for mapping cars by the town registered on the tax disc. The delivery of goods to the school can be analysed by questioning What? Why? When? How?

Outside the school grounds provides a wealth of people, buildings and landscapes to be studied. In a short walking distance from many schools, children can learn about traffic, houses, shops, work places, parks and religious and historic buildings and visit useful places such as the local library.

Figure 11.1 Opportunities to teach in the school grounds

Visits beyond the school catchment area require extra travel arrangements and more detailed planning for health and safety. Coaches can be booked to transport classes to a range of learning environments including: a farm, the seaside, a castle, an archaeological site, a river or canal or an extensive museum site such as the Ironbridge Gorge Museum (www.ironbridge.org.uk). Additional adult support will be required, and you will need to make a pre-visit to check on facilities at the site.

Organising a geography field trip

The preparation stage

A geography subject co-ordinator has included details of planning a trip in their school handbook to help other teachers carry out the exercise. The advice starts with planning a walking trip within the school's catchment area (see also Table 11.1). Here are ten stages in planning an out-of-school experience which is within walking distance of the classroom:

1. The idea for a trip.
2. Reconnaissance of site.
3. Plan activities for children.
4. Risk assessment of site/activities.
5. Letter to parents.
6. Design resources, prompt sheet for other adults with stopping points and key features to show children.
7. Collect replies from parents.
8. Reconnaissance of site with class teacher/other adults to familiarise them.
9. Prepare children in class – look at route maps, name roads, consider directions, etc.
10. The trip!

Table 11.1 differences between planning a local trip (walking) and planning a trip further afield using a coach

Think about	Local trip – walking	Coach trip
Time needed to plan	2 to 4 weeks	4 weeks to 12 months. Phone venue to check availability. Phone coach companies approved by LEA – July very popular time for school visits. Check coach has seat belts and toilet. Visit the site to meet the education officer and confirm facilities for children, including facilities for children who might be ill on the day, have an accident, or who need special support.
Cost	Free	Need to pay for coach, venue and insurance. Work out cost per pupil and method for collecting money.
Insurance	Check with LEA and headteacher. Write to parents/carers for permission, to provide information and seek helpers.	Check with LEA and headteacher. Write to parents/carers for permission, to provide information and seek helpers.

Risk assessment

For any trip, whatever the distance, it is good practice to consider the possible risks, and to plan strategies for a risk-free trip. Lots of advice on risk assessment and planning trips can be obtained from your local education authority, teaching unions and the DfES. However, you will need to visit the site yourself in advance, to assess its suitability. Make a note of all hazards and how you can minimize risks to children's safety. Consider what resources you will need to bring to the site and what facilities are already available, including those for children with SEN. You will need to complete a risk assessment form back in school.

While at the site, you will need to plan in some detail how the children will need to be organized and what features will be a focus for learning. The practicalities of working on that particular site must be considered. For example, if there are particularly hazardous spots, you could ensure your 'trail' or site activities take place well away from them. If visiting a river or canal, note the condition of the banks and whether they are safe, so that you can ensure children do not venture too close to the edge if they are unsafe or unprotected. Think about background noise; will a whole class be able to hear your instructions or warnings? If you feel this could be a problem, plan to work in small groups. Try to ensure that you will be able to keep an overview if children are going to work in groups. If the weather may be poor on the day, make some contingency plans. It is also important to establish a code of conduct for children's behaviour outside the classroom, both for reasons of safety and future reputation of your school.

A very important consideration is the use you make of other adult helpers, such as parents, carers or other untrained people who may be working with the children. You will need to be clear about your objectives for the trip and ensure that you share these with all adults who will be accompanying the class. Once you have planned the activities for the children and prepared any necessary resources or materials, share these with helpers. You could either send them a leaflet outlining your plans in simple terms, or you could ask helpers to come into school at the end of a day and talk through the plans with them. You will also need to advise helpers on the potential risks of the site and advise them on ways of dealing with these. Give advice on managing behaviour and also about helping the children with their learning, such as talking to them, asking questions, scribing for them, making suggestions and encouraging them to look carefully with a focus on the learning objectives. Lastly, ensure that all helpers know the planned route and that they know about safety arrangements and contingency plans.

REFLECTIVE TASK

Imagine you are a teacher at a meeting with helpers. Try to anticipate the questions they might ask and consider how you could respond to them.

Interview with a geography co-ordinator
How do you train up the adults going on your trip?
Ask helpers to call in the day before – written instructions will be ready for them with where to go and what to point out – actual 'talk' ready for them to dictate to children. This is important for follow-up in the classroom to ensure all children have seen and learnt the same information.

Details on toilets, time for activities, where and when to meet for lunch, and time for meeting back at the coach.

Any tips on not losing any children?
Ideally maximum of 6 children per adult – each adult responsible for constantly counting their 6 children. A list of all children and the adults responsible for that child on trip provided to all adults. This helps in case a lost pupil is found so they can be returned to their designated adult. School badges worn by all children.

Why do they not wear name badges?
Security.

How do you get helpers?
Parents, mum helpers, classroom assistants.

Do you need to do police checks on helpers?
Check with your head, LEA guidelines.

Risk assessment of site

Trainee teachers visited Lathkill Dale in Derbyshire June 2002 to consider the risk assessment of a countryside location. While walking through the valley many primary school parties passed by. We could observe some of the techniques teachers employed to minimise the risks.

The major risks noted were:

- crossing country road to start of footpath;
- walking over slippery limestone boulders;
- walking through an area of stinging nettles;
- potential for scree falling from exposed rocks;
- walking past animals, such as sheep.

Some risks can be minimised in the advice contained in the letter sent to parents, e.g. wearing long trousers and long-sleeved tops help when walking through nettles. Wearing trainers or shoes with good grip helps when walking over slippery boulders. Some risks can be minimised in the discussion with adult helpers. For example, discuss what is said to the children before leaving the coach about lining up and 'best behaviour'. Explain the need to choose suitable points and the best method of crossing the road, such as ways of stopping the traffic and organising the children to walk quickly across in pairs. It is always a good idea for adults to wear bright clothing, which helps children to locate you and allows traffic to see you in advance. During the field trip, when coming up to areas of nettles, suggest that helpers give advice to children to put their hands in the air to avoid being stung. When walking past sheep, advise adult helpers to keep their group of children close to them, to avoid the sheep becoming alarmed. When walking over slippery boulders, advise adults to guide children across, keeping their hands out to help them. If there is a danger of scree falling, care needs to be taken in choosing a route to avoid the scree. If it is considered likely, then hard hats need to be worn.

Table 11.2 provides a summary.

Table 11.2 Minimising risk

Risk	Methods to minimise	
Crossing country road to start of footpath	Guidance given to children	Guidance given to adult helpers/clothes visible
Walking over slippery limestone boulders	Letter to parents – suitable shoes	Guidance to adult helpers
Walking through area of stinging nettles	Letter to parents – long trousers and tops	Guidance to adult helpers/ plan route to minimise
Scree falling from hillside	Plan route to minimise	Use hard hats
Walking past animals – sheep	Guidance to children	Guidance to adult helpers

PRACTICAL TASK PRACTICAL TASK PRACTICAL TASK PRACTICAL TASK PRACTICAL TASK

Walk from your home for 15 minutes. On your return journey make a note of possible risks. For each one plan how you would minimise the risk.

Remember walking with children takes three to four times longer than walking on your own!

Schools have become used to carrying out risk assessments, and many have devised their own checklist for all staff. The advantage of a school-agreed form is it reminds the trip organiser of a variety of issues to consider. Figure 11.2 shows a copy of one school's risk assessment form.

HEALTH AND SAFETY – RISK ASSESSMENT

Visit to:
Carried out by:
Date of assessment: **Signed:**
Copy of assessment and required actions to Headteacher

Potential hazards	Control measures	Arrangements/action to be taken by
1. ENVIRONMENTAL ISSUES e.g. weather, geographical		
2. TRANSPORT e.g. vehicles, drivers, etc.		
3. EQUIPMENT, CLOTHING, SUBSTANCES		
4. ACTIVITIES AND PROCEDURES e.g. programme of activities, free time		
5. SUPERVISION. COMPETENCE, DISCIPLINE		
6. OVERALL PLANNING, MONITORING AND CONTROL e.g. Accommodation Emergency contacts and communication Insurance LEA notification Medical arrangements Parental Information Research Special needs Visits abroad		

Hazard identified	Action required	To be carried out by	Date reported	Date completed

Figure 11.2 Example of a school's risk-assessment form

Letter to parents

Figure 11.3 shows an example of a letter to parents of children in Year 6. Notice that the letter does not specify which day out because it depends on the weather and the availability of extra classroom assistants.

Headteacher Mrs Jones
ABC Primary School
Road, Town
City DE1 2FG
Tel: 01234 567890

9th April 2002

Dear Parents

During the next few weeks (up until May 10th) Y6 will be studying a Geography based topic about Wonford. We would like to take the children out into the local area, to do some fieldwork. When we go out will depend very much on the weather. Further information will be sent home nearer the time. Please sign the slip below if you agree to your child taking part in the fieldwork.

Yours sincerely

Mrs Smith
Geography Co-ordinator

I agree to my child .... taking part in fieldwork in the local area, during the next few weeks (up until May 10th).

Signed........................... (Parent/Guardian)

Figure 11.3 Example of a letter to parents regarding out-of-school activity

Planning the learning experience

Having made all the necessary practical preparations for a successful out-of-classroom experience, you will need to think carefully about the activities that will make up the children's learning experience on the visit. There are some well-known examples of activities, such as 'treasure hunts' or 'treasure trails'. Either you or staff at the site will need to have hidden a series of clues of 'finds' around the site and the children then have to follow the trail, marked on a map or plan in order to find them. Alternatively, you might plan a 'nature trail', making use of 'journey cards' to collect leaves and so on. These activities all help children to develop their mapwork skills. A link with mathematics could provide more challenging work for the more able children, if you asked them to list the grid references for their finds when back in school. Orienteering activities enable children to make use of directions, distances and symbols. At a more local site, walks to shops or parks help children to observe geographical features and express their opinions.

CLASSROOM STORY

Anna was in her final teaching placement, planning activities for her Year 2 class to help them learn key mapwork skills. The school playground had an eight-point compass drawn on it. Anna planned an enjoyable lesson whereby groups of six to eight children with an adult followed directions and paced out their steps to locate hidden laminated cards. On finding the card, the children turned it over to draw the symbol on their worksheets.

The worksheet had simple instructions and a recording table like the one below.

Direction	Distance	Symbol
North	18 paces	△
South West	30 paces	□

CLASSROOM STORY

Jenny was studying rivers with her Year 5 class. She liked to compare the local stream with a contrasting stream of similar size in Wales, which was studied as part of a residential visit to Wales. This year the children stayed in a Field Study Centre in central Wales. The staff at the centre were very helpful and suggested a suitable nearby stream. Jenny undertook a risk assessment and decided the location was ideal – a small stream with a bridge across it where the children could study the width, depth and speed of the river in safety. A member of staff from the Field Centre accompanied the class and assisted with taking measurements. As he wore waders, he was able to enter the stream and measure the depth at several different points so the children were able to see evidence of both erosion and deposition.

Jenny's school was within a five-minute walk of a local stream. It ran through a small park with paths on either side and several bridges across it. Every year Jenny took children to study the stream and although she was very familiar with the site she always undertook a separate risk assessment prior to the visit to check that there were no new hazards along the route and by the stream.

Prior to the visit Jenny discussed the field trip with her class. Using a range of maps the children traced the route of the stream from the local area to the sea. They also made a list of enquiry questions, for example:

Describing:

- What is the stream like?
- Is it clean or dirty?
- How wide is it?
- How deep is it?
- How fast does it flow?
- Are there any meanders?

Explaining:

● How did it come to be like this?

Responding:

● What do we like/dislike about the stream?
● What can we do to improve the area of the stream?

Predicting:

● What might the stream be like in the future?

The children then decided how they might find answers to their questions and devised a table to record their data.

The visit

The children were divided into groups of six, each with a responsible adult. They walked along the side of the stream and recorded what features they had observed including evidence of erosion and deposition. They were able to stand on the bridge and measure the width of the stream at this point. They also measured the flow by having a 'dog biscuit' race. This involved three children at a time dropping dog biscuits (biodegradable) from the bridge and timing how long they took over a 10-metre stretch. Usually the stream was also shallow enough for Jenny to don her wellington boots and measure the depth.

As the school had collected data for a period of time the children were able to compare their findings with the records of previous years.

After the visit

Back in the classroom, the children analysed their results. The visit often inspired fierce debate about how the area could be improved. In the past groups of children had written letters to the local paper and helped the local Community Association by clearing litter and planting bulbs and wild flowers.

In order to reinforce what the children had learnt, Jenny created a model landscape with a heap of sand and a garden hose. Within minutes the water running off the sand had created a landscape of meandering river valleys and the children could easily recognise the features water creates as it erodes, transports and deposits material.

Points to be aware of when planning a river study

● Remember that rivers can be very dangerous and a careful risk assessment is essential.
● Rivers can change dramatically according to weather conditions – always check that it is safe.
● You need to find a safe place where children can stand, e.g. a bridge.
● Don't allow children to go too near – riverbanks can give way without warning.
● Adequate supervision is essential, e.g. one adult to six children.

Out-of-school learning in history

Field trips and site visits in history can, of course, be equally as hazardous as those in geography. Castles and archaeological sites in particular can pose serious dangers to young children, such as falling from heights, down into wells or pits, cuts and grazes from rough or broken masonry, and the danger of falling into deep water in wells or moats. Therefore the advice given above, particularly in relation to risk assessment, also needs to be heeded on history fieldwork. Practical arrangements also need to be made in advance, as in the following classroom story.

CLASSROOM STORY
Key Stage 2 history

A Year 5 class in a semi-rural primary school was engaged in a local history study unit investigating how their area had changed since the nineteenth century. As part of the project a fieldwork activity was planned to the nearby Victorian church where the children were to study the gravestones to try and find out something about the local area in the nineteenth century. Before the visit, permission had been arranged through the vicar and churchwarden. Children were carefully briefed about the visit including safety and appropriate behaviour in the churchyard. In the previous lesson, fieldwork tasks were discussed including:

* recording written information about people who used to live in the area;
* identifying and addressing key issues such as where people lived, what jobs they had and family size.

Several parents had agreed to help with the visit allowing children to be divided into small groups and a short briefing sheet was prepared for the adult helpers. For the visit the children were equipped with notebooks, a brief task sheet and a digital camera was available to share.

On arrival at the churchyard the objectives of the activity were reinforced but quickly the children were enthusiastically exploring the gravestones and making both written and visual records. The groups were supported by the adults but children worked surprisingly independently and much perceptive discussion was in evidence.

After about 30 minutes the teacher brought the class together to discuss initial findings and to address any difficulties before the class resumed their investigations.

In the follow-up lesson groups summarised their findings on flipchart paper and briefly explained to the rest of the class what they had found out about the local people in the Victorian period, highlighting areas such as occupations, popular names and status.

This scenario highlights key aspects of good historical fieldwork including careful planning and preparation. Fortunately there is much useful published material to support this and for the graveyard study Purkis (1995) proved invaluable. Safety was prioritised and the availability of adult helpers was an asset here as well as enhancing the children's learning experience. The emphasis in this fieldwork was on children recording, analysing, making deductions and posing questions. Children were being given responsibility to undertake genuine research not constrained by detailed worksheets. Follow-up work to this fieldwork activity was again based on careful preparation, the teacher assembling a range of relevant sources of evidence including old maps, photographs, census materials, trade directories and church records which the children could use to make links to their own churchyard data.

PRACTICAL TASK PRACTICAL TASK PRACTICAL TASK PRACTICAL TASK PRACTICAL TASK

Re-read the classroom story above and make a note of all the practical considerations and arrangements that had to be made before and during the visit to the graveyard.

Out-of-school learning in RE

Out-of-school learning is equally important in RE and citizenship as in the other humanities subjects. There are always interesting religious sites, centres and places of worship to visit in or near your locality. The following classroom story makes links between RE and citizenship, showing how it is possible to raise children's awareness and understanding of the different communities that live nearby and throughout Britain and their ways of life.

CLASSROOM STORY

Rachel's Year 1 class had been studying the theme 'Our neighbourhood' and had been visiting buildings and shops in the area immediately surrounding the school. Rachel was aware that not two miles down the road there was a locality very different from the one the children were used to. She decided to take her class on a tour of Rusholme, which had a large Asian community of predominantly Muslim background. She visited the area herself and made contact with some shopkeepers and the Imam of the mosque which was located behind the main shopping area. She asked if she could bring her class along and whether there was anyone who would be able to have a chat with the children and answer their questions.

Back at school Rachel went through the school's usual procedures for arranging a trip. In her letter to parents she explained the nature of the trip and the value she felt it had for the children. Several parents volunteered to join the party, including two Asian parents who were familiar with Rusholme.

To prepare the children for the trip, Rachel introduced them to the mosque and its role in Muslim people's lives. The children saw pictures and video material of Muslim children. The children were made aware that when they entered the mosque they would be removing their shoes and covering their heads. All the children were asked to bring a head covering appropriate for the visit and they discussed what might be suitable. The two Asian parents came in to tell the children about Rusholme and what they would see there.

On the day of the visit the party travelled to Rusholme by bus and began their tour by walking along the main road looking at the shops and their contents. They made notes and drew pictures of the shop names and what they were selling. One of the children suddenly recognised where they were and exclaimed, 'Oh we came here for a curry on my mum's birthday.' Rachel had arranged for stops at three shops. One sold general hardware but also stocked religious artefacts; another was a grocer's and the children were fascinated by the wide range of foods, many of which they had never seen before. The owner of the shop offered all the children some traditional sweets, and though a few children were initially hesitant, most tried them out. The final shop they visited was one which provided for the Muslim community particularly, stocking books, clothes, artefacts and audio-visual material. The owner of the shop showed the group round, explaining what things were and answering the children's questions. Some of the children bought greetings cards and Rachel took the opportunity to stock up on items to add to the 'Islam box' back at school.

The final visit was to the mosque where the Imam talked about how Muslim children used it. He told them about prayer times and the after-school classes that children attended. He also told them of the social events and children's clubs that were held in adjacent buildings. Rachel was delighted with the success of the visit, which she felt had showed the children a very different area but one which was so local to their school. The children's eager responses, appropriate questions and excellent follow-up work back at school all indicated that the trip had been very worthwhile.

PRACTICAL TASK PRACTICAL TASK PRACTICAL TASK PRACTICAL TASK PRACTICAL TASK

PRACTICAL TASK

Take some time to visit a local place of interest, a place of worship or a museum. Study the features of the building and its interior, including the materials on display. Consider how long and tiring it would be for young children if they had to look around every detail in this way. They would be complaining and needing the toilet and their lunch before long! Bearing this in mind, devise a simple tour or 'treasure hunt' for a Year 3 class, based around the points of interest you have noted. Keep the activities short and interesting. The children will not necessarily be able to do a lot of recording at the time, but it is useful if they have some information to take back to the classroom. This will then serve as stimulus material for further follow-up work, such as art and creative and descriptive writing.

REFLECTIVE TASK

Review the non-statutory guidance for PSHE and citizenship (DfEE/QCA, 1999, p136–141). Consider how you might address some of the features of this curriculum within your own humanities teaching.

The role of other professionals and experts

There is a great deal of expert help available for out-of-school learning. A large group of professionals who can provide valuable support in out-of-school learning, are of course, the classroom assistants and special needs support staff who might accompany the class. The 'Senco', or Special Needs Coordinator may not accompany the class on the visit, but it is useful to refer to them if children with SEN are among those going on the visit. They can give valuable advice on how to include such children in out-of-class activities safely and profitably. Other support staff include learning mentors and specialist support staff who work with children with English as an Additional Language (EAL) or learning difficulties such as autism. EAL support colleagues understand the factors involved in planning and during the visit to enable bilingual learners to understand and participate, whilst developing their knowledge of English. You can assist them greatly by sharing your planning for the visit with them, particularly the specific vocabulary that you will be using during the planned learning activities. Any other specialist support staff accompanying children on the visit also need to be included in the planning of activities and practical arrangements. The teaching assistant (TA) is another very valuable source of knowledge and support in out-of-school learning. TAs often have considerable experience and knowledge of the locality, and can therefore make a very valuable contribution to planning, preparation and the provision of resources and ideas for a visit.

A second important group of professionals includes those available to provide support at field centres or parks, such as park rangers, and education officers based in, or responsible for, most museums and historic sites. While not strictly 'professionals', local priests and vicars, rabbis and imams have a great deal of expert knowledge and insight that they can share on a visit. Local communities often have their own centres or sites in large towns and cities, such as the Irish centre and the Jewish Museum in Manchester, staffed by people with detailed and extensive knowledge of the history and traditions of their respective communities. These professionals and experts can greatly enhance children's learning at a museum with their specialist knowledge and also with their enthusiasm for the subject. They will have the skills to introduce children to a wide range of resources, such as artefacts, and will know of strategies for motivating the children and provide a good learning experience for you too.

However, it is necessary to confirm your visit and planned activities well in advance. Other professionals at the site who will be working with you during your visit will need to know what your aims and objectives are and what kind of activities you have planned or would wish your class to do. They will also need to know the ages and general abilities of the children as well as important information on any children with SEN or with disabilities, for which special arrangements may need to be made. Some discussion in advance about the focus of their contribution and its suitability for your class will be helpful in ensuring a successful visit.

A SUMMARY OF KEY POINTS

> Safety is a crucially important consideration in humanities fieldwork. Risk assessment must be undertaken prior to any out-of-school learning.

> Professionals on site with specialist knowledge and skills should be consulted prior to a visit.

> Preparation and planning need to be detailed for all out-of-school learning. This needs to include a previsit.

> All adults helpers need to be fully briefed and informed, prior to the visit, about safety issues and the planned learning experience, so that they can make effective contribution.

> Survey any locality where you are teaching for places of interest and potential educational value.

> Remember to take account of, and plan for, the role of other professionals in out-of-school learning.

MOVING ON > > > > > > MOVING ON > > > > > > MOVING ON

Standard C37, Standard 40, Standard 41

Carry out a survey of potentially useful contexts for out-of-school learning in your area which you might be able to use, bearing in mind the cost implications. Review your humanities curriculum and consider what opportunities there are for incorporating visits to these sites into your teaching.

FURTHER READING FURTHER READING FURTHER READING FURTHER READING

Bowles, R. (1999) *Resources for Key Stage 1 and 2*. London: Geographical Association. A directory of useful resources.

Catling, S. et al. (2006) 'Access denied?' *Primary Geographer*, Number 59: 35–37. Raises issues of access to local facilities for the disabled, making a link with citizenship.

Chambers, B. and Featherstone, J. (1995) *Awareness into Action – Environmental Education*. London: Geographical Association. A good starting point for developing children's awareness of local and global issues.

DfEE/QCA (1999b) *The National Curriculum: Handbook for Primary Teachers in England: Key Stages 1 and 2*. London. DfEE. See pages 136–141 for the Framework for personal, social and health education and citizenship at Key Stages 1 and 2.

Historical Association (2003). *Learning through museums and galleries*. Primary History, Issue 35. This whole issue is on the use of museums.

Historical Association (2009). *History and environmental education*. Primary History, Issue 52. This whole issue in on history and environmental education.

Harrison, S. (2004) 'Using museums and artefacts'. *Primary History,* Issue 37: 18–21. Valuable insight into the use of museums is provided by a history inspector.

McHale, S. (2006) 'Valuing the outdoors'. *Primary Geographer*, Number 61: 14–15. This article explains how valuing the outdoors can help children develop a sense of place.

Scoffham, S. (2004) *Primary Geography Handbook*. London: Geographical Association. See particularly Chapters 10 and 13 on fieldwork and using the school locality.

Morgan, J. (2001) 'Teaching multicultural geographies'. *Primary Geographer*, Number 45: 4–5.

Owens, P. (2007) 'Why fieldwork matters to every child'. *Primary Geographer*, Number 63: 12–14.

Richardson, P. (2006) 'The importance of speaking and listening in enquiry fieldwork'. *Primary Geographer*, Number 59: 9–10.

Whitworth, K. (2006) 'Discovery visits: What's new at English Heritage for schools?' *Primary History*, Issue 43: 14–17. Useful articles on geography and history, some of which make cross-curricular links.

Useful websites

www.hrp.org.uk/

Website for the Historic Royal Palaces in London, which has some good interactive graphics.

www.teachernet.gov.uk/teachingandlearning/library

Provides information on the value of out-of-school activities related to citizenship.

12
Children's spiritual, moral, social and cultural development and citizenship education

By the end of this chapter you should:

- understand how children's learning can be affected by their physical, intellectual, linguistic, social, cultural and emotional development;
- understand the role that the humanitites play in children's spiritual, moral, social and cultural development and citizenship;
- be able to plan links between the humanities and spiritual, moral, social and cultural development and citizenship.

Professional Standards for QTS

Q1: Have high expectations of children and young people including a commitment to ensuring that they can achieve their full educational potential and to establishing fair, respectful, trusting, supportive and constructive relationships with them.

Q2: Demonstrate the positive values, attitudes and behaviour they expect from children and young people.

Q5: Recognise and respect the contribution that colleagues, parents and carers can make to the development and well-being of children and young people, and to raising their levels of attainment.

Q18: Understand how children and young people develop and that the progress and well-being of learners are affected by a range of developmental, social, religious, ethnic, cultural and linguistic influences.

Q19: Know how to make effective personalised provision for those they teach, including those for whom English is an additional language or who have special educational needs or disabilities, and how to take practical account of diversity and promote equality and inclusion in their teaching.

Introduction

The 1988 Education Reform Act requires schools to provide a curriculum which *promotes the spiritual, moral, cultural, mental and physical development of pupils*. This requirement is built into the National Curriculum, and the second of the two aims of the school curriculum states that:

> *The school curriculum should aim to promote pupils' spiritual, moral, social and cultural development and prepare all pupils for the opportunities, responsibilities and experiences of life.*

> (DfEE/QCA, 1999, pp11–12)

Government guidelines are clear that spiritual, moral, social and cultural development (SMSC) are not subjects which just appear in timetabled sessions. They permeate the whole of school life, which includes curriculum subjects, school ethos and collective worship. SMSC is about the relationships between all the people who work in a school, and the relationships children are encouraged to develop in the wider world.

In recent years there has been a great deal of interest in children's understanding of the world they live in. The Children and Worldviews Project led by Clive and Jane Erricker (2001), involving different groups of children over several years, has attempted to investigate how children interpret and find meaning in the world around them. For many children these meanings are linked to their religious backgrounds, but not for all. Another avenue of study has been the ethnographic research at Warwick University (Nesbit, 2001) in which researchers have sought to investigate how children from different religious backgrounds develop and understand their sense of identity. This work has highlighted the dangers of 'pigeon-holing' children into specific religious traditions, when they themselves demonstrate a much more 'fluid' perception of who they are.

There is also a requirement for schools to address citizenship. The school curriculum should pass on enduring values, develop pupils' integrity and autonomy and help them to be responsible and caring citizens capable of contributing to the development of a just society (DFID/DfEE/QCA, 2000). An interesting discussion on the concept 'citizenship' and its changing role in education over the last few decades is provided by Mary Thornton, writing in *Education 3–13* (2002). Its changing fortunes are linked closely to the political climate. A detailed comparison is given between the role of citizenship in the 1990 National Curriculum and the present-day curriculum. The author discusses how BEd courses have adapted to these changes.

Every Child Matters, SMSC and citizenship

Every Child Matters: Change for Children (DfES, 2004) emphasises the needs of the individual child, making children's well-being and their personal development key concerns in relation to their future success. The Children Act, passed in 2004, made the agenda of *Every Child Matters* a legal requirement. Since then, a series of documents has been published which provide guidance under the act to support local authorities and their partners in implementing this agenda, such as the *Children's Plan* (www.dfes.gov.uk/publications/childrensplan).

Every Child Matters (ECM) focuses on the principle of personalisation in learning and requires that every child should succeed, regardless of their background. The humanities are key areas of learning in which children's personal aptitudes and interests can be taken into account, and therefore teachers need to weave the objectives and key features of ECM into their humanities teaching. For example, the recent Ofsted report *History in the balance* (2007) recommends that the principles of *Every Child Matters* are reflected in the history curriculum, particularly in providing children with the knowledge and skills to understand the modern world, using links with other subjects (Hoodless, 2008b).

The government's aim is for children's services, including education, to be carefully coordinated to ensure that every child, whatever their background or their circumstances, has the support they need in order to:

- be healthy;
- stay safe;
- enjoy and achieve;
- make a positive contribution;
- achieve economic well-being.

SMSC and citizenship are aspects of humanities teaching which relate closely to these aims. As McCreery et al. point out,

> The Every Child Matters *agenda requires us not only to contribute to children's ability to enjoy and achieve, but also draws our attention to children's wider lives and experiences ...*
>
> (McCreery et al. 2008, p69)

The humanities subjects make extensive use of children's own lives and experiences of place, time, faiths and societies, as well as building upon them, for example through out-of-school learning. They are therefore very well placed to meet the agenda of ECM. The sections below explore what we mean by spiritual, moral, social, and cultural development and citizenship education. Clearly there is much overlap and we should not worry unduly about whether something has to 'fit' within one category or another.

Spiritual development

The school curriculum should:

- pass on enduring values;
- promote children's self esteem and emotional well-being;
- help them form and maintain worthwhile and satisfying relationships based on respect for themselves and for others, at home, school, work and in the community;
- develop their ability to relate to others and work for the common good;
- enable children to respond positively to opportunities, challenges and responsibilities, to manage risk and to cope with change and adversity;
- enable them to appreciate the relevance of their achievements in life and society outside school.

> (DfEE/QCA, 1999, pp11–12)

The notion of spiritual development is perhaps the most difficult term to deal with in this context. There may endless definitions of the term but it is necessary to have some working definition upon which to base our approach. Traditionally, RE has seemed to be the natural 'home' of spiritual development, but it is required of all curriculum subjects. OFSTED has described spiritual development as relating to:

> *That aspect of inner life through which pupils acquire insights into their personal existence which are of enduring worth. It is characterised by reflection, the attribution of meaning to experience, valuing a non-material dimension to life and intimations of an enduring reality. 'Spiritual' is not synonymous with 'religious'; all areas of the curriculum may contribute to pupils' spiritual development.*
>
> (OFSTED, 1994, p21)

Moral development

The school curriculum should:

- *develop principles for distinguishing between right and wrong;*
- *develop pupils' integrity and autonomy;*
- *equip them to make informed choices at school and throughout their lives;*
- *equip pupils, as consumers, to make informed judgments and independent decisions and to understand their responsibilities and rights.*

(DfEE/QCA, 1999, pp11–12)

Moral development is not just about teaching children what is 'right' or 'wrong'. Rather, it is about helping children to recognise that decisions have to be made in life and that they, as individuals, need to develop their own sense of what it means to behave in a moral way. The school's role is to offer children a framework for dealing with moral issues and to develop skills and qualities in the children in order that they become independent in their moral thinking. OFSTED has put it this way:

Schools can do much to encourage young people in their early years by providing them with a moral framework within which to operate and, as they mature, by helping them to decide what they hold as right and wrong, why they do so, and how they should act - that is, that they should behave well, in accordance with a moral code.

(OFSTED, 1994, p11)

Social development

The school curriculum should:

- *help them to be responsible and caring citizens capable of contributing to the development of a just society;*
- *promote equal opportunities and enable pupils to challenge discrimination and stereotyping;*
- *develop their awareness and understanding of, and respect for, the environments in which they live;*
- *secure their commitment to sustainable development at a personal, local, national and global level;*
- *prepare pupils for the next step in their education, training and employment.*

(DfEE/QCA, 1999, pp11–12)

Children's social development relates to the way in which they operate as individuals within the wider society. It involves developing an understanding of the way in which society works. The first social structure that children encounter is usually the family circle. When they begin school they are faced with a much larger group of people, among which they are only one, and they have to develop skills to enable them to operate within this wider group. Many of the skills learned in this setting prepare children well for the even wider society beyond the school gates. OFSTED describes social development as *concerned with the skills and personal qualities necessary for individuals to live and function effectively in society* (OFSTED 1994, 15).

Cultural development

The school curriculum should:

> ...*develop knowledge, understanding and appreciation of their own and different beliefs and cultures and how these influence individuals and societies.*
>
> (DfEE/QCA, 1999, pp11–12)

Cultural development refers to children's increasing understanding and command of those beliefs, values, customs, knowledge and skills which, taken together, form the basis of identity and cohesion in societies and groups. (OFSTED, 1994, p16)

Cultural development in our schools involves the recognition that the children we teach represent many different traditions. Their cultural background is diverse and the patterns and traditions of life need to be recognised. Even children from similar racial backgrounds will identify primarily with the cultural norms experienced through living with their family and we, as teachers, need to be careful that we do not make assumptions about children's cultural backgrounds. Cultural development will involve making children aware of this diversity.

Citizenship

The National Curriculum describes the knowledge, skills and understanding involved in citizenship education under four headings. These suggest that citizenship will help pupils in:

- developing confidence and responsibility and making the most of their abilities;
- preparing to play an active role as citizens;
- developing a healthy, safer lifestyle;
- developing good relationships and respecting the differences between people.

Citizenship education involves *gaining the knowledge, skills and understanding necessary to become informed, active, responsible global citizens* (DFID/DfEE/QCA, 2000).

Approaching SMSC and citizenship through the humanities

It seems clear that when we think of SMSC and citizenship, we are not thinking of separate subjects on the timetable or the provision of particular topics. SMSC and citizenship are not so much about content but about approach – it is about how we do something rather than what we do. Whenever we are planning units of work in any of the humanities subjects, we should be thinking about how this work contributes to the children's spiritual, moral, social or cultural development.

Geography and SMSC and citizenship

With careful planning, geographical units of work can be enhanced by emphasising spiritual, moral and cultural approaches. Table 12.1 demonstrates the links between geography and SMSC.

Table 12.1 Geography and SMSC

Key Stage 2 themes	Spiritual	Moral/ethical	Social	Cultural
Water	The *wonder* of nature. The *beauty* of landscapes, e.g. tumbling waterfalls. The *power* of floods.	Conflicting views and attitudes on dealing with floods and protecting coastal areas.	Different perceptions to flood hazards and solutions.	Different cultural views about nature and natural forces.
Settlements	The *wonder* and *beauty* of buildings, e.g. size of skyscrapers, interesting architecture such as the new Urbis and Lowry buildings in Manchester/ Salford.	Conflicting views and attitudes over how to use land on the edge of cities, and redeveloping inner city areas.	Social segregation in cities in less economically developed countries (LEDCs) and more economically developed countries (MEDCs). Different attitudes to solving urban problems, e.g. traffic congestion.	Different cultures within cities, different lifestyles. Impact of globalisation.
Environmental issues	The *wonder* of creation and biodiversity. *Appreciating* the wealth of resources on our planet. *Threats* to our planet, e.g. pollution.	The impact of development on indigenous people. Conflicting views and attitudes over resource use/ conservation.	Different attitudes about recycling, using renewable energy sources, e.g. wind farms.	Different cultural values for individuals, groups, pressure groups, governments, e.g. government views at earth summits.

CLASSROOM STORY

Dean was looking for inspiration for the Year 5 class he would be teaching in his next placement after the summer holidays. He had been asked to develop a unit of work on sustainable development. He flicked through his growing pile of newspaper cuttings and stopped at one about the famine in Zambia, southern Africa. The accompanying photograph of children standing on cracked land was thought-provoking. He put this article to one side. Continuing his search he came across a letter to the editor complaining about aid to Africa, and hadn't we given too much over the years? What's the point – they still have famine – where did the money go?

Dean had a video from Breakfast TV of a report highlighting flood warnings in the UK as 84mm of rain had fallen in three days, the highest for 30 years.

There was definitely too much water in some places, too little in others. Looking through the National Curriculum, Dean made a note of:

- water and its effects on landscapes and people;
- water as an environmental issue, caused by change in an environment;
- a study at a range of scales - local, regional, national;
- places and environments in the news;
- how places fit within a wider geographical context and are interdependent.

He also had information about the Earth Summit (Rio+10) held in Johannesburg (South Africa) where one of the key topics discussed was water. Representatives from over 100 countries met to discuss water. Dean was thinking that his class could prepare for a mini summit representing Zambia and the UK and their views on water. He realised that in a topic like this, there would be good opportunities to draw the children's attention to the moral and cultural considerations involved. Table 12.2 shows the unit of work that Dean began to create.

REFLECTIVE TASK

Discuss with your peers what you think the SMSC issues involved in the above story might be. Consider how you might begin to address them with a Year 6 class.

Geography can contribute to children's understanding of citizenship and address the aims of ECM by building on their confidence and sense of well-being. At Key Stage 1 children are helped to play an active role as citizens by taking part in simple debates about topical issues. Geographers love studying the news events both local and further afield. A local issue could include one such as building houses on a local playing field. Children can develop an understanding of what can improve or harm their local environment. They can gain an awareness of the views of different people and learn about some of the ways people look after their local environment. Children could study the issue of litter and rubbish in our local area and some solutions such as recycling bins. Transport and the noise and air pollution it creates could also be studied. They learn to recognise how their behaviour affects other people, and to make real choices.

Geographers study how people use natural resources taken from the environment and the impact this has on the environment and people's lives. This can be linked into the children's use of resources, highlighting their role as responsible citizens. Actions the children can take include switching off lights as they go out to play, turning off taps or placing their waste in recycling bins. At Key Stage 2 there are many opportunities to enhance the delivery of both geography and citizenship. Children need to be given activities to help them:

- talk and write about their opinions, explaining their views;
- research, discuss and debate topical issues, problems and events;
- understand that resources can be allocated in different ways and that these economic choices affect individuals, communities and the sustainability of the environment;
- think about the lives of people living in other places and times, and people with different values and customs;
- recognise and challenge stereotypes;
- meet and talk with people;
- take responsibility.

Table 12.2 The unit of work that Dean created

Enquiry questions	Learning objectives Children should learn:	Possible teaching strategies	Learning outcomes Children are able to:	Notes
Do we need water?	Vital for survival Personal use of water Water for farming Water for industries, etc.		Say how much water per day we need to drink Say how much of their bodies are made of water Say how long you can survive with no water List uses of water	
Where do we get our water from?	How does it get to our taps? Water cycle		Label a water cycle diagram Describe how water gets to our taps in the UK Describe how villages in Zambia get their water from boreholes and lakes to their houses Describe the journey of a water droplet	
What causes rain?	Relief rain Convectional rain		Place labels onto a wall display of relief rain Describe how hot water/ steam turns to droplets when reaching cold air/ surface	
Does too much or not enough rain matter?	Damage caused by floods Damage caused by droughts	Stimulus – read story 'Bringing the rain to Kapiti plain' by Verna Aardema	Sort newspaper headlines into too much rain, not enough rain Describe the damage to homes and fields in the UK Describe the damage to crops and animals and people in Zambia	
How can people manage water?	Build reservoirs Transport by pipes or lorries Buy from another country Desalination of sea water Cloud seeding Dig drainage ditches Use sand bags Build up banks of rivers Use weather forecasts to plan		Sort strategies into flood control/drought Describe one strategy with a picture and words	

Useful ideas: http://www.education.ed.ac.uk/esf/resources/figs/5-3-4.html (MMU & University of Edinburgh website - Educating for a sustainable future).

A unit of work based on waste and recycling can help children develop both their geographical understanding of environmental issues and sustainable development and their role as responsible citizens. The children can carry out surveys on household waste and the school's waste. They can consider the types of waste, e.g. paper, glass, plastics, food, etc. and where the waste goes (recycling/landfill sites). The journey from home/school to a landfill site can be mapped. The process of decomposition of waste from weeks for food products to hundreds of years for plastics can be researched. Landfill sites are the UK's main method of waste disposal – this could be compared to countries such as Egypt where most products are recycled or re-used, and families specialise in collecting waste to recycle. In Brazil, the city of Curitiba has won awards for its environmental policies encouraging recycling. As an example, Oldham in Greater Manchester has approximately 400 landfill sites, most of which have been filled and built upon, e.g. with schools and housing estates.

The children can invite in to interview experts such as the recycling officer for the local council or a spokesperson from an environmental group such as Greenpeace or the Groundwork Trust. Having researched and discussed this topic the children could design solutions, e.g. a radio jingle to encourage recycling, a new road sign to show people where to recycle, a new wheelie bin design to help families sort their waste. They could consider why recycling is thought necessary, for example, to reduce the amount of waste going to landfill sites.

CLASSROOM STORY
Citizenship through geography

Marlborough Road Primary School is situated near the centre of a small town. As part of the 'Citizenship' programme the pupils have been encouraged to take an active role in improving the local environment. The head teacher runs an 'Eco Club' that meets regularly to discuss environmental issues and looks at ways the children can be involved. Some years ago, the children undertook an environmental audit of the area and decided that the local stream, which ran through a park near the school, was much in need of attention. They contacted a local group of conservation volunteers and with their help and encouragement the children planned a 'cleanup' of the stream. They invited parents and other members of the local community to help and this proved so successful that it has now become an annual event. In addition, each class in the school has been involved in the planting of trees, bulbs and wild flowers along the banks of the stream. The children have also written letters to the local paper to ask people to take care of the area.

Another successful campaign by the school's 'Eco Club' targeted energy consumption, especially electricity. The children designed posters which were placed by every light switch and plug socket round the school reminding everyone to switch off lights and equipment. There was even a poster by the kettle in the staff room which politely reminded the teachers not to boil more water than was necessary! At the end of the year everyone was amazed at how much electricity had been saved.

PRACTICAL TASK PRACTICAL TASK PRACTICAL TASK PRACTICAL TASK PRACTICAL TASK

Carry out some personal research to develop your own understanding of global warming and the need for sustainable development.

History and SMSC and citizenship

There are many examples of how the history curriculum contributes to the spiritual, moral, social, and cultural development of children and citizenship education. Bage (1999) discusses how stories about the past can be used to expose, for example, issues of morality in an understandable way for young children. Claire (1996) believes such stories can also be used to promote positive attitudes towards equality and diversity.

Almost every topic in history involves sensitive issues. For example, in Victorian history and the history of the early twentieth century in Europe and the USA, racism proliferated and was accepted as the norm. In studying very recent family history, there are inevitable problems and issues which need to be either avoided or treated with extreme caution. In earlier times, there was slavery, execution and even human sacrifice. The handling of these issues and the way in which they are approached is critically important.

There is also the issue of bias in historical sources. Every source is written or produced by a person with their own set of beliefs, values and prejudices, and often these appear within the source that they produce. Again, dealing with bias and prejudice is an aspect of teaching history which can be challenging for the teacher who has the task of exposing these different viewpoints without unduly favouring one point of view over another. Indeed, the question of how you deal with your own perspectives and opinions without influencing your class is a difficult one to resolve. Nevertheless, it needs careful consideration and, if handled effectively, can contribute greatly to children's personal and social development.

Both of these dilemmas are illustrated in the story below, where Jane had to deal with difficult content and with her own opinions about it, as well as those of other teachers in her school.

CLASSROOM STORY
Moral development through a unit on the Aztecs

Jane was beginning to plan in detail for a topic on the Aztecs. She knew that this was in some ways a controversial topic, particularly when it came to teaching about the religious beliefs and practices of the Aztecs. This topic had not previously been included in the school's long-term planning, but Jane had seen several excellent sources relating to Aztec times. She had also been to Mexico for a long holiday and had become very enthusiastic to include a new and different part of the world in the history curriculum for her class.

The major problem that Jane struggled with was Aztec religious belief and practices. They had carried out what seem to us today extremely barbaric religious rites, which involved the sacrifice to their gods of thousands of people in a single day. These were special feast days for the Aztecs and occurred regularly throughout the year. On very important religious festivals, as many as 20,000 people would be sacrificed in one day.

However, this was not the end of the problem for Jane. Many of the children's books she obtained for teaching the topic emphasised the method of sacrifice (removing the heart from living victims and offering it to the gods) and made it a focal point of studying the civilisation. This rather insensitive treatment of the subject matter only highlighted the problem and also began to draw her plans to the attention of other staff in the school.

The teachers all had different views. These ranged from the opinion that the topic was unsuitable and should not be taught at all. At the other extreme, some thought it should be taught from the perspective of the Aztecs themselves. Presumably, it was argued, they did not see their actions as wrong, because they believed what they were doing was the will of the gods and also necessary to keep the sun rising every day. What concerned Jane was how she could reconcile this view with the SMSC principles she needed to be fostering among the children in her class.

REFLECTIVE TASK

Discuss Jane's dilemma with your peers and decide how best she should deal with it. Read some of the background to the history of the Aztecs to assist you in your decision-making (for example, see Townsend, 1992).

Look at the National Curriculum requirements for teaching about the Romans. Consider the issue of tackling the theme of slavery. While this is an unacceptable practice to us now, it was an accepted part of the running of the Roman Empire.

Because history is a study of human behaviour in the past, it automatically includes the study of citizenship and the key issues involved in this. The dilemmas, conflicts and eventual consensus arrived at in the past provide a context for present-day notions of citizenship. In the British Isles, there have been long-established systems in place in the form of moots, councils, common law, courts and Parliament to maintain established ideas of what makes a responsible citizen. Past events also provide exemplars of the ways in which society has gradually established a value system which supports citizenship today.

Of course, another facet of citizenship is that of human rights. History provides us with endless examples of societies where there has traditionally been a lack of such rights. It also furnishes the curriculum with the story of how human rights and rights of all people to be treated as equal citizens have slowly been won, more so in some parts of the world than in others. An interesting view of citizenship is discussed by Brown and Harrison (1998), who have researched the experiences of children in different times and places in relation to their rights as citizens. Children's stories about experiences that illustrate abuses or recognition of their rights throw a valuable light on the close relationship between history and the study of citizenship.

All historical studies impinge in some way on issues related to citizenship, and the school history curriculum offers many varied opportunities to incorporate some citizenship work within a history theme or study unit. Cooper (2007) gives examples of how local, national and global history can provide opportunities for developing practical links with the citizenship curriculum. Below, the classroom story looks at notions of democracy in the ancient past and in the present. By using role play activities children can internalise and identify to some extent with the experiences of people living at a different time and in different circumstances. This is a challenging task for you to undertake, but consider the classroom story below and how the activity really does the teaching for you.

CLASSROOM STORY

Sandra was in the middle of teaching a topic to her Year 5 class about Ancient Greece. She had begun to work with the class on discussion about the nature of Greek society, how it was organised and how the earliest notions of 'democracy' began to arise. It dawned on her, as she looked further into the subject of democracy, that past and present notions of this idea are very different. Sandra decided to begin to discuss democracy as we understand it today, so that the children might be clear about the focus of the work.

At the beginning of the lesson on Greek democracy, therefore, Sandra asked the children if anyone could explain what this means. Of course, several hands went up, and the children explained that we believe in democracy and that it means all people are equal. The children were less clear about the political aspect of the concept, however, so Sandra explained that in a democratic system, everyone is entitled to vote for their rulers or government. The class briefly discussed what is meant by Parliament, MPs and elections, then Sandra moved on to the role play she had devised.

She told the class that they were to imagine they were all ancient Greeks, living in a Greek democracy. They had been told that today all citizens were to vote on the important issue of whether there should be a new parthenon building on the hill just outside the town. This had been a controversial issue, because many people felt that the grazing land for their sheep and goats would be lost. This was badly needed to feed the population, which had begun to get much larger in recent years. Sandra was to be the town governor, organising the voting, but first she organised two opposing groups to discuss the issues raised. Each group had their own point of view, which they discussed animatedly, using the information Sandra had provided. After some time, Sandra announced that it was now time to vote; she asked all voters to sit on the carpet.

When the class had sat down, Sandra looked surprised, and asked why all the slaves and servants were there. Children who had been assigned these roles had to return to their seats, and were not allowed to vote. Sandra then looked shocked and asked why the girls were there. She pointed out that surely everyone knew that women were not citizens and could not expect to vote. The girls then returned to their seats and were not allowed to vote either. The remaining ten boys then took a vote, and because Sandra had carefully ensured that these were those allocated upper class roles, such as politicians and town dignitaries, the parthenon won the vote.

Following the vote, Sandra finished the lesson with a discussion about the fairness of this voting system, and whether the class thought it was really a democracy. She concluded by explaining how notions of democracy can vary over time and place. The children then went on in their next history lesson to make comparisons between notions of democracy in Ancient Greece and the present day, beginning to realise that even ideas change over time.

REFLECTIVE TASK

In your own time, note down a dictionary definition of modern democracy. Look at the history units of work for Key Stage 2 and select an example of how life in the past was organised in a system which was not democratic in the sense that we use the term today. Make a note of the similarities and differences.

RE and SMSC and citizenship

The QCA RE Non-statutory Framework gives us a focus for exploring SMSC and citizenship within RE. The children will be involved in exploring the spiritual, moral, social and cultural aspects of the religious traditions to which they are introduced. At the same time they will be reflecting on this learning in the light of their own experiences and backgrounds. In this way children can explore world religions as 'models' for spiritual, moral, social and cultural development, and compare them to their own sets of beliefs and values. Such an approach will involve children in a variety of personalised learning activities which draw their attention to aspects of ultimate human concern. Several writers within RE have explored such activities which encourage children to reflect on their own values in the light of their RE learning (see the research and further reading section at the end of the chapter).

CLASSROOM STORY
Spiritual development
Anne was teaching her Year 1 class a unit of RE taken from the QCA scheme of work for RE. The unit was called 'What does it mean to belong?' and the children had been talking about the different groups to which they belong, focusing on families. Anne felt that the work that the children were doing was rather superficial and she was struggling to find ways of exploring the notion of how special it is to 'belong'. She felt that she wanted to bring a more 'spiritual' awareness to the children's reflections. Using ideas from the book *Values and Visions* (Burns and Lamont, 1995) she decided to alter the structure of her lessons.

She decided to begin each RE session with some 'stilling'. She set the atmosphere for the children entering the room by playing some music very quietly. The children were encouraged to sit in a circle and close their eyes to listen to the music. When the music stopped Anne asked the children to focus on their breathing – to be aware of each breath in and out. Then she would talk the class through some relaxation techniques.

The session would then continue with Anne talking the children through aspects of the notion of belonging. She would ask them to think about questions she offered them, each session taking a slightly different focus. For example, in the first session she asked them just to think of the word 'belong' and what they understood by it. The follow-up to the stilling exercises took a variety of forms. Sometimes it was followed by discussion, sometimes by sharing as in circle time, and sometimes through children producing art work or poetry.

Anne found that the children enjoyed the sessions and began to look forward to them. She realised that the techniques and approaches she was using could also be applied to other subject areas – anywhere where children were being asked to respond from a personal point of view.

Further work then included making links with children's own experiences and what it means to belong to a religious community. In similar stilling exercises the children were asked to put themselves into other children's shoes to imagine what belonging in their tradition might mean to them.

PRACTICAL TASK PRACTICAL TASK **PRACTICAL TASK** PRACTICAL TASK **PRACTICAL TASK**

Select an RE topic from any scheme/unit of work and identify the key concepts that it presents to children. Make a list of 'stilling' activities you might try to encourage children to reflect upon and respond to the concepts. Consider how you might evaluate children's learning through such activities.

Within RE, a focus on citizenship will involve children in recognising that the notion of 'the good life' varies from one community to another. What is valued and prized among one group may not be valued by another. Similarly, there may be some actions and ways of living that are acceptable to one community, but which are not tolerated by another. Through RE, children will be encouraged to identify, not only their role as citizens of this society, but to explore where this notion of citizenship comes from, what religious teachings might underpin it, and how religion affects notions of citizenship today.

A key understanding that children need to explore is that while many of them may live their lives outside of a religious context, there are many people in the world who do not draw a distinction between the religious and the secular. For many, their faith offers a framework on which to base their choices and decision-making. This has implications for the classroom, because teachers will need to take this into account as they explore citizenship issues with children from different faith backgrounds. A further concern for teachers will be for them to explore their own prejudices and stereotypical images, recognising that they too need to learn about others' faiths in order that they may offer children positive images of other people.

Many of the Attainment Target 2 type aims of RE have strong links with citizenship and it should not be difficult for teachers to identify the links for themselves (see Figure 12.1). Religious themes which might be studied in relation to particular traditions will often have clear links to citizenship, for example belonging, identity, change, rules to live by, family life.

Figure 12.1 Example of links between RE and citizenship

CLASSROOM STORY

David had been teaching a Year 3 class in a large suburban primary school which served a predominantly white working-class community. David had found that the relationships between the children were not as positive as they should be, with children suspicious of each other and often unwilling to work together or share activities. One of the phrases which the children often used was 'It's not fair' in response to requests from him or when comparing their own situation with another child's.

David decided to use the phrase as a theme for some RE/citizenship work. Recognising that the theme began to explore the concept of justice, he felt that he needed to encourage the children to think through issues relating to what is just and what is not on a wider scale than their own lives. He began with the children's own experiences and provided activities which encouraged the children to think about situations in which they felt they had been treated unfairly. He used circle time, independent writing and drawing as vehicles for this. He also gathered some children's books in which 'fairness' featured as a theme.

He then moved the children on to stories from religious traditions which explored the same kinds of theme. The children were familiar with some Christian stories so David began with these. He took two of Jesus' parables: the Prodigal son (Luke 75: 11-37) and the Rich man and Lazarus (Luke 16: 19-31). He used them to show the children Jesus' teaching about the nature of God and God's relationship with humankind. He encouraged discussion around the parables allowing children to recognise the tensions within the stories.

He then introduced them to concepts of fairness within Hinduism as part of their study of other world faiths. The children had done previous work on Hinduism, looking at festivals and family life. He introduced the terms dharma (as referring to duty) and karma (as referring to actions and their consequences). The children then made up stories which they acted out to show the notion of 'consequences'. David also introduced them to the life of Gandhi and his struggle to achieve what was 'fair'.

David hoped that by the end of the unit of work, the children would be able to recognise that 'fairness' is not always a straightforward thing and that understanding context, perspective and motivation is important.

REFLECTIVE TASK

Examine an RE syllabus (e.g. from a local education authority) and identify RE topics which you feel have links with citizenship. Consider ways to bring the two areas together in activities.

A SUMMARY OF **KEY POINTS**

> **SMSC and citizenship have been built into the primary curriculum by the Education Reform Act 1988 and by the revised National Curriculum. Government guidelines are clear that these subjects should permeate school life.**

> Guidelines for the development of each of spiritual, moral, social and cultural dimensions of children's education are laid down.

> SMSC and citizenship are not about the content of your teaching but about the approach you take. It is about your attitudes and how you teach.

> Citizenship is identified as an area to be taught in the primary National Curriculum. Key aspects of citizenship are described.

> Each of the humanities subjects contributes to citizenship education.

MOVING *ON* > > > > > > MOVING *ON* > > > > > > MOVING *ON*

Standard C18, Standard C19

Choose one of the humanities subjects discussed in this book and identify aspects which relate to spiritual, moral, social and cultural development and citizenship education. Plan teaching and learning activities which will make these links and consider their contribution to the *Every Child Matters* agenda.

FURTHER READING FURTHER READING **FURTHER READING** FURTHER READING

Burns, S. and Lamont, G. (1995) *Values and Visions. A Handbook for Spiritual Development and Global Awareness*. London: Hodder & Stoughton. This book provides many useful examples of how children's spiritual development can be a focus within a range of activities.

Claire, H. (2005) 'Learning and teaching about citizenship through history in the primary years', in Historical Association, *Leading Primary History*. London: Historical Association. A useful summary of key principles and ideas for linking the two subjects.

Clough, N. and Holden, C. (2002) *Education for Citizenship: Ideas into Action*. London and New York: Routledge Falmer.

Hicks, D. (2002) *Citizenship for the Future. A Practical Classroom Guide*. Godalming: WWF-UK. These are both very useful resources for the classroom, full of examples of children's work and ideas for activities.

DfEE/QCA (1999c) *The National Curriculum. Handbook for Primary Teachers in England Key Stages I and 2*. London: DfEE/QCA. Outlines of the guidance for all National Curriculum subjects – also includes guidance on citizenship.

Draycott, P. (ed.) (2002) *Primary RE. PSHE and Citizenship*. Birmingham: Christian Education Publications. A useful publication illustrating the links between these aspects of learning.

OFSTED (1994) *Spiritual, Moral, Social and Cultural Development. An Ofsted Discussion Paper*. London: OFSTED. A detailed consideration of the meaning of each of the terms and the ways in which they might be in evidence in schools.

Rowe, D. (2001) *Introducing Citizenship: A Practical Handbook for Primary Schools*. London: A. & C. Black. A useful introductory guide.

Townsend R. F. (1992) *The Aztecs*. London: Thames & Hudson. This is a comprehensive but readable account of Aztec culture and beliefs.

Useful websites

www.dfes.gov.uk/publications/childrensplan

www.education.ed.ac.uk/esf/sg/sec3/sec3-l.html. Website for primary school case studies teaching 'culture'. A joint MMU and University of Edinburgh website called 'Educating for a sustainable future'. This is a useful website on education for a sustainable future.

References

Alexander, R., Rose, A. J. and Woodhead, C. (1992) *Curriculum Organisation and Classroom Practice in Primary Schools: A Discussion Paper*. London: DES.

Allen, J., Potter, J., Sharp, J. and Turvey, K. (2007) *Primary ICT: Knowledge, Understanding and Practice*. (3rd edn.) Exeter: Learning Matters.

Ashton, E. (1999) *RE in the Early Years*. London: Routledge.

Bage, G. (1999) *Narrative Matters: Teaching and Learning History Through Story*. London: Falmer.

Bage, G. (2000) *Thinking History*. London: Routledge Falmer.

Baker, C. (1988) *Key Issues in Bilingualism and Bilingual Education*. Clevedon: Multilingual Matters.

Baker, C. (2000a) *A Parents' and Teachers' Guide to Bilingualism*. (2nd edn.) Clevedon: Multilingual Matters.

Baker, C. (2000b) *The Care and Education of Young Bilinguals: An Introduction for Professionals*. Clevedon: Multilingual Matters.

Baker, C. (ed.) (2001) *An Introductory Reader to the Writings of Jim Cummins*. Clevedon: Multilingual Matters.

Baker, J. (2002) *Window*. London: Walker Books.

Bastide, D. (1999) *Co-ordinating Religious Education across the Primary School*. London: Falmer Press.

Bastide, D (2004) *Religious Education 4–11*. (2nd edn) Abingdon: Routledge.

BECTa (2001) *Primary schools of the future – Achieving today*. Coventry: BECTa.

Bent, J. (1992) *The Green Banana Hunt*. Leamington Spa: Scholastic.

Blaylock, L. and Johnson C. (eds) (1997) *A Teacher's Handbook of Religious Education*. Derby: CEM.

Bloom, B.S. (1964) *Taxonomy of Educational Objectives: The Classification of Educational Goals*. London: Longman.

Blyth, W.A.L. et al. (1976) *Curriculum Planning in History, Geography and Social Science*. Bristol: Schools Council Publications.

Blyth, W.A.L. et al. (1990) *Making the Grade for Primary Humanities*. Milton Keynes: Open University Press.

Bowles, R. (1999) *Resources for Key Stages 1 and 2*. London: Geographical Association.

Boys, R and Spink, E. (Eds.) (2008) *Teaching the Foundation Subjects*. London: Continuum.

Breuilly, E. and Palmer, S. (2001) *Teaching with Text. Religious Education 5–7*. Leamington Spa: Scholastic.

Brown, E. (1996) *Religious Education for All*. London: David Fulton.

Brown, M. and Harrison, D. (1998) 'Children's voices from different times and places.' in C. Holden and N. Clough (eds), *Children as Citizens. Education for Participation*. London: Jessica Kingsley.

Bruner, J.S. (new edition, 1977) *The Process of Education*. Harvard: Harvard University Press.

Bruner (1990) *Making Sense: The Child's Construction of the World*. London and New York: Routledge.

Buck, M., Inman, S. and Moorse, K. (1994) *Educating the Whole Child: Cross-Curricular Themes within the History Curriculum*, Occasional Paper 10. London: Historical Association.

Burns, S. and Lamont, G. (1995) *Values and Visions – A Handbook for Spiritual Development and Global Awareness*. London: Hodder and Stoughton.

Carter, R. (ed.) (1998) *Handbook of Primary Geography*. London: Geographical Association.

Catling, S. et.al. (2006) 'Access denied?' *Primary Geographer*, No. 59: 35–37.

Chambers, B. and Featherstone, J. (1995) *Awareness into Action – Environmental Education*. London: Geographical Association.

Chambers, B and Donert, K. (1996) *Teaching Geography at Key Stage 2*. Cambridge: Chris Kington Publishing.

Claire, H. (1996) *Reclaiming Our Pasts: Equality and Diversity in the Primary History Curriculum*. Stoke-on-Trent: Trentham Books.

Claire, H. (2001) *Not Aliens: Primary School Children and Citizenship/PHSE Curriculum.* Stoke-on-Trent: Trentham Books.

Claire, H. (2004) *Teaching Citizenship in Primary Schools.* Exeter: Learning Matters.

Claire, H. (2005) 'Learning and teaching about citizenship through history in the primary years', in Historical Association, *Leading Primary History.* London: Historical Association.

Clough, N. and Holden, C. (2002) *Education for Citizenship: Ideas into Action.* London and New York: Routledge Falmer.

Cooper, H. (2000) *The Teaching of History in the Primary School.* (3rd edn.) London: David Fulton.

Cooper, H., Rowley, C. and Asquith, S. (2006) *Geography 3–11: A Guide for Teachers.* London: Fulton.

Cooper, H. (2007) *History 3–11: A guide for teachers.* London: Fulton.

Cox, K., Goddard, G. and Hughes, P. (2000) *Primary Curriculum Guide.* London: David Fulton.

Davies, G. (1999) 'Should world religions be taught to primary school children in predominantly white, traditionally Christian areas? A survey of headteacher attitudes in West Wales.' *Journal of Beliefs and Values*, Vol. 20, no. 1.

Davies, J. and Redmond, J. (1998) *Coordinating History across the Primary School.* London: Falmer Press.

DCSF (2008) *Statutory Framework for the Early Years Foundation Stage.* London: DCSF.

DCSF (2009) *Independent Review of the Primary Curriculum: Final Report (The Rose Review).* London: DCSF.

DES (1978) *Special Educational Needs. Report of the Committee of Enquiry into the Education of Handicapped Children and Young People.* (The Warnock Report) London: HMSO.

DES (1989) *The Education Reform Act 1988: Religious Education and Collective Worship.* (Circular 3/89). London: DES.

DES/HMI (1985) *Aspects of Primary Education. The Teaching and Learning of History and Geography.* London: HMSO.

DFE (1988) *Education Reform Act 1988.* London: HMSO.

DFE (1994) *Religious Education and Collective Worship.* (Circular 1/94). London: DFE.

DfEE/QCA (1998a) *Geography. A Scheme of Work for Key Stages 1 and 2.* London: DfEE/QCA.

DfEE/QCA (1998b) *History. A Scheme of Work for Key Stages 1 and 2.* London: DfEE/QCA.

DfEE/QCA (1998c) *RE. A Scheme of Work for Key Stages 1 and 2.* London: DfEE/QCA.

DfEE/QCA (1999a) *Geography: The National Curriculum for England.* London: HMSO.

DfEE/QCA (1999b) *History: the National Curriculum for England.* London: HMSO.

DfEE/QCA (1999c) *The National Curriculum: Handbook for Primary Teachers in England: Key Stages 1 and 2, including the National Curriculum Attainment Targets.* London: DfEE/QCA.

DfEE/QCA (2000) *Expectations in Religious Education at Key Stages 1 and 2.* London: QCA.

DfEE/QCA (2000) *Curriculum Guidance for the Foundation Stage.* London: DfEE/QCA.

DfES (2002) *Access and Engagement in History.* London: DfES.

DfES (2003) *National Standards for under 8s Daycare and Childminding.* London: DfES.

DfES (2003) *Excellence and Enjoyment: a strategy for primary schools.* London: DfES.

DfES (2004) *Every Child Matters: Change for Children.* London: DfES.

DfES/MMU (2002) *Birth to Three Matters.* London: DfES.

DfES/TTA (2002) *Qualifying to Teach: Professional Standards for Qualified Teacher Status and Requirements for Initial Teacher Training* (Circular 2/02). London: DfES/TTA.

DFID (Department for International Development)/ DfEE/QCA (2000) *Developing a Global Dimension in the School Curriculum.* London: DfEE.

Dollman, R. (2005) 'How the world comes to us.' *Primary Geographer*, No. 58: 14–16.

Draycott, P. (ed.) (2002) *Primary RE. PSHE and Citizenship.* Birmingham: Christian Education Publications.

Durbin, C. (2001) 'Urban myths', *Primary Geographer*, October 2001, pp. 14–16.

Ekwall, B.O.E (1960) *The Concise Oxford Dictionary of English Place names.* Oxford: Clarendon Press.

Equiano, O. (1789/1995) *The interesting narrative and other writings.* New York: Penguin.

Erricker, C. (ed.) (1993) *Teaching World Religions.* Oxford: Heinemann.

Erricker, C. (2001) 'From silence to narration: a report on the research methods of the Children and Wordviews Project.' *British Journal of Religious Education*, Vol. 23.3.

Eyre, D. et al. (2002) 'Effective teaching of able pupils in the primary school, the findings of the Oxfordshire Effective Teachers of Able Pupils Project.' *Gifted Education International*, Vol. 16:2.

Fewster, S., (2005) 'Using a whiteboard.' *Primary History*, Issue 39, 8–20.

Fines, J. and Nichol, J. (1997) *Teaching Primary History*. Oxford: Heinemann.

Foley, M. and Janikoun, J. (1996) *The Really Practical Guide to Primary Geography*. Cheltenham: Stanley Thornes.

Freeman, J. (2002) 'The education of the most able pupils: a creative future.' *Education Review*, Vol. 15:2.

Friedman, W J. (ed.) (1982) *The Developmental Psychology of Time*. New York and London: Academic Press.

Gagné, R. (1985). *The Conditions of Learning* (4th ed.). New York: Holt, Rinehart & Winston.

Galton, M., Simon, B. and Croll, P. (1980) *Inside the Primary Classroom*. London: Routledge & Kegan Paul.

Gardner, H (1993) *Multiple Intelligences: The Theory in Practice*. New York: Basic Books.

Gateshill, P. and Thompson, J. (1992) *Religious Artefacts in the Classroom*. London: Hodder & Stoughton.

Geographical Association (2001) *Primary Geographer Assessment Special*. Sheffield: Geographical Association.

George, D. (1999) *Gifted Education: Identification and Provision*. London: David Fulton.

Grimmitt, M. (1991) *A Gift to the Child*. London: Simon and Schuster

Grimmitt, M. (2000) *Pedagogies of Religious Education*. Great Wakering: McCrimmon.

Hall, D. (1995) *Assessing the Needs of Bilingual Pupils: Living in Two Languages*. London. David Fulton.

Halocha, J. (1998) *Co-ordinating Geography Across the Primary School*. London: Falmer Press.

Halocha, J. (2007) 'Citizenship through school twinning.' *Primary Geographer,* No. 62: 36–38.

Hamel, K. and Langley-Hamel, K. (2006) 'How can geography make a significant contribution to a coherent and meaningful Key Stage 1 curriculum?' Chapter 9 in Cooper (2006) op. cit.

Harrison, S. (2004) 'Using museums and artifacts.' *Primary History,* Issue 37: 18–21.

Harvey, A. (1991) *Stormy Weather*. London: Macmillan.

Hayes, D. (1999) *Foundations of Primary Teaching* (2nd edn). London: David Fulton.

Hicks, D. (2002) *Citizenship for the Future. A Practical Classroom Guide*. Godalming: WWF-UK.

Higgins, S., Baumfield, V. and Leat, D. (2001) *Thinking Through Primary Teaching*. Cambridge: Chris Kington Publishing.

Historical Association (2003) 'Learning through museums and galleries.' *Primary History*, Issue 35.

Historical Association (2007) 'History in the Foundation Stage and Early Years, 3–8.' *Primary History*, Issue 45.

Historical Association (2009) 'Doing archaeology with children.' *Primary History*, Issue 51. London: Historical Association.

Historical Association (2009) 'History and environmental education.' *Primary History*, Issue 52.

Hodkinson, A. (2002) 'A coordinator answers: The development of chronological understanding in Primary History.' *Primary History*. Issue 31: 8–9.

Hodkinson, A. (2006a) *Chronology Workshop*. London: Teachers' TV.

Hodkinson, A. (2006b) *Developing Chronology at Key Stage 2*. London: Teachers' TV.

Homan, R. (2000) 'Don't let the murti get dirty: The uses and abuses of "artefacts".' *British Journal of Religious Education,* Vol. 23:1.

Hoodless, P. (1996) *Time and Timelines in the Primary School.* Teaching of History Pamphlet, No 69:38. London: Historical Association.

Hoodless, P. (1997) 'Why Teach about Time in the Primary School?' *Primary History*, Issue 17, Nov: 11–12.

Hoodless, P. (ed.) (1998) *Teaching History and English in the Primary School: Exploiting the Links*. London: Routledge.

Hoodless, P. (2002) 'An investigation into primary school children's developing awareness of time and chronology in story and historical fiction.' *Journal of Curriculum Studies*. Vol. 34:2. 173–200.

Hoodless, P. (2003) *History: Ready Resources, Books 1–8*. Leamington Spa: Scholastic.

Hoodless, P. (2008a) *Teaching History in Primary Schools*. Exeter: Learning Matters.

Hoodless, P. (2008b) 'Every child matters: addressing the needs of the child in learning about the past.' *Primary History*, Issue 50: 14–17.

Horton, A. M. (1995) *Teaching about the Aztecs: A Cross-curricular Perspective*. London: Historical Association.

Howard, C. (1995) *Investigating Artefacts in Religious Education*. Norwich: RMEP.

Hughes, S. (1993) *Dogger*. London: Red Fox.

Inkpen, M. (1996) *Nothing*. London: Hodder Children's Books.

Jacques, K. and Hyland R. (eds) (2007) *Professional Studies: Primary and Early Years*. (3rd edn.) Exeter: Learning Matters.

Jarvis, G. (2003) *Using ICT in primary humanities teaching.* Exeter: Learning Matters.

Jarvis, P. and Parker, S. (2006) *Human Learning: An Holistic Approach*. London: Routledge.

Johnson, P. (1998) *A Book of One's Own*. London: Hodder & Stoughton.

King, H. (2002) 'Global citizenship in practice.' *Primary Geographer,* No. 46:18–20.

Kyriacou, C. (1995) *Effective Teaching in Schools*. (2nd edn.) London: Nelson Thornes.

Kyriacou, C. (2007) *Essential Teaching Skills*. (3rd edn.) London: Nelson Thornes.

Lewis, L. (2001) 'What's in a name?' *Primary Geographer*, No 23:10.

Lewis, L. et al. (2002) 'New methods for studying blind children's understanding of familiar space.' *British Journal of Visual Impairment*, Vol. 20: 1.

Linden, J. (1999) *Understanding World Religions in Early Years Practice*. London: Hodder and Stoughton.

Lomas, T., Burke, C., Cordingley, D. and Tyreman, L. (1996) *Planning Primary History for the Revised National Curriculum Key Stages 1 and 2*. London: John Murray.

Marsden, B. and Hughes, J. (eds) (1994) *Primary School Geography*. London: David Fulton.

Martin, F. and Owens, P. (2004) 'Young children making sense of their place in the world.' Chapter 5 in Scoffham (2004) op. cit.

McCreery, E., Palmer, S., and Voiels, V. (2008) *Teaching Religious Education: Primary and Early Years.* Exeter: Learning Matters.

McHale, S. (2006) 'Valuing the outdoors.' *Primary Geographer*, No. 61: 14–15.

Mills, M. (2004) 'Using the English Heritage Viewfinder website.' *Primary History*, Issue 37: 32–36.

Morgan, J. (2001) 'Teaching multicultural geographies.' *Primary Geographer*, No. 45: 4–5.

Morris, G. and Willy, T. (2007) 'Eight doorways to sustainability.' *Primary Geographer,* No. 64: 34–35.

National Advisory Committee on Creative and Cultural Education/DfEE (2001) *All Our Futures: Creativity, Culture and Education* (NACCCE Report). London: DfEE.

Nesbitt, E. (2001) 'Ethnographic research at Warwick: some methodological issues.' *British Journal of Religious Education*, No. 23,3.

Nesbitt, E. (2002) *Intercultural Education. Ethnographic and Religious Approaches.* London: Hodder and Stoughton.

Nichol, J. (2000) 'Literacy, text genres and history: reading and learning from difficult and challenging texts.' *Primary History*, Issue 24: 13–17.

Nichol, J. and Dean, J. (1997) *History 7–11: Developing Primary Teaching Skills*. London: Routledge.

North, W. (2006) 'Visual literacy, ICT and geography.' *Primary Geographer*, No. 60, 32–34.

Norton, M., (1999) 'Making the most of ICT at Key Stage 2.' *Primary History,* Issue 21: 7–9.

OFSTED (1994) *Spiritual, Moral, Social and Cultural Development. An Ofsted Discussion Paper*. London: OFSTED.

OFSTED (1999a) *Standards in Geography*. London: OFSTED.

OFSTED (1999b) *Standards in History*. London: OFSTED.

OFSTED (2000) *Primary Subject Report: Religious Education 1999–2000*. London: OFSTED.

OFSTED (2001) *Primary Subject Report: History 2000–2001*. London: OFSTED.

OFSTED (2004) *Managing the Ethnic Minority Achievement Grant: good practice in primary schools*. London: OFSTED.

OFSTED (2007) *History in the balance. History in English schools 2003-2007*. London: OFSTED.

Ota, C. (2000) 'Stories told and lessons learned: meeting beliefs, values and community through narrative and dialogue.' *Journal of Beliefs and Values*, Vol. 21, no. 2.

Owen, D. and Ryan, A. (2001) *Teaching Geography 3–11: The Essential Guide*. London: Continuum.

Owens, P. (2007) 'Why fieldwork matters to every child.' *Primary Geographer*, No. 63: 12–14.

Peters, R. S. (1966) *Ethics and Education*, (1st edn.) London: Allen & Unwin.

Petty, G. (1993) *Teaching Today: A Practical Guide*. Cheltenham: Stanley Thornes.

Phillips, M. and Phillips, T. (1998) *Windrush: The Irresistible Rise of Multi-racial Britain*. London: HarperCollins.

Pollard, A. (2008) *Reflective Teaching: Evidence-informed Professional Practice*. (3rd edn.) London: Continuum.

QCA (1998) *Model Syllabuses for Religious Education (Model 1: Living Faiths Today and Model 2: Questions and Teachings)*. London: QCA.

QCA (2000) *Schemes of Work for Geography, History and Religious Education at Key Stages 1 and 2*. London: QCA (also available at www.standards.dfee.gov.uk/schemes).

QCA (2004) *Religious Education: The non-statutory national framework.* London: QCA.

Richards, C. (1999) *Primary Education – At a Hinge of History*. London: Falmer Press.

Richardson, P. (2006) 'The importance of speaking and listening in enquiry fieldwork.' *Primary Geographer*, No. 59: 9–10.

Rosen, M. (2001) *We're Going on a Bear Hunt*. London: Walker Books.

Rowe, D. (2001) *Introducing Citizenship: a practical handbook for primary schools*. London: A. & C. Black.

Russell, K. (2008) 'A to Z of China: An alphabet journey through China.' *Primary Geographer*, No. 66: 26–27.

Rutter, J. (1995/2000) *Refugee Children in the Classroom: A Handbook for Teachers*. Stoke-on-Trent: Trentham.

Safran, J. (2002) 'Supporting students with Asperger's Syndrome in general education.' *Teaching Exceptional Children*, May/June, 34:5.

SCAA (1997a) *Expectations in Geography at Key Stages 1 and 2*. London: SCAA.

SCAA (1997b) *Expectations in History at Key Stages 1 and 2*. London: SCAA.

Scoffham, S. (2004) *Primary Geography Handbook*. Sheffield: Geographical Association.

Smart, L., (1999) 'ICT – high profile in 1999–2000: but will you use it in your history teaching?' *Primary History*. Issue 22: 6–7.

Smith, C. (2005) *Teaching Gifted and Talented Pupils in the Primary School: A Practical Guide*. London: Chapman Educational.

Snowdon, C. (2001) 'Fire! Tan!', *Primary Geographer*, No. 18: 10.

Taba, H. (1962) *Curriculum Development*. Harcourt, Brace & World.

TDA (2007) *Professional Standards for Teachers*. London: TDA.

Thornton, L. and Brunton, P. (2004) *The Little Book of Time and Place*: edited by Featherstone, S: Featherstone.

Thornton, M. (2002) 'A rose by any other name: teaching primary teachers citizenship, or PSE, or social studies or....' *Education 3–13*, Vol. 30. Glasgow: Collins.

Thornton, S. J. and Vukelich, R. (1988) 'The effects of children's understanding of time concepts on historical understanding.' *Theory and research in social education*, Vol. 16 (1), 69–82.

Townsend, R. F. (1992) *The Aztecs*. London: Thames & Hudson.

Toye, N. and Evans, D. (2006) 'How can children connect to a distant place through drama?' Chapter 5 in Cooper, et al. (2006) op. cit.

Turner-Bisset, R. (2005) *Creative Teaching: History in the Primary Classroom*. London: David Fulton.

Vygotsky, L.S. (1962) *Thought and language*. New York: MIT Press.

Walford, R. (2001) *Geography in British Schools, 1850–2000: Making a World of Difference*. London: Woburn Press.

Wallace, B. (2000) *Teaching the Very Able Child: Developing a Policy and Adopting Strategies for Provision*. London: NACE/Fulton.

Wallace, B. (ed.) (2002) *Teaching Thinking Skills across the Primary Curriculum*. London: David Fulton.

Wallace, B. and Bentley, R. (eds) (2002) *Teaching Thinking Skills across the Middle Years*. London: David Fulton.

Wallace, B. (2003) *Using History to develop Thinking Skills at Key Stage 2*. London: NACE/Fulton.

Wallace, G. (2008) 'Refugee Boy: Geography, inclusion and inequality.' *Primary Geographer*, No.65: 27–29.

Walsh, B., (2003) 'Is there a place for the computer in primary history?' *Primary History*, Issue 34: 26–29.

Wambu, O. (1999) *Empire Windrush: Fifty Years of Writing about Black Britain*. London: Phoenix Press.

Whitworth, K. (2006) 'Discovery visits: What's new at English Heritage for schools?' *Primary History*, Issue 43: 14–17.